The Transition Towards Revolution and Reform

The Arab Spring Realised?

Sonia L. Alianak

EDINBURGH
University Press

Dedicated to
Thomas M. West IV, Ani Alianak, Thomas A. Alianak

Special thanks to
Janis Alianak, Nellie Davila, Larry Mansker

Edinburgh University Press Ltd
The Tun – Holyrood Road
12 (2f) Jackson's Entry
Edinburgh EH8 8PJ
www.euppublishing.com

Typeset in 11/13pt Monotype Baskerville by
Servis Filmsetting Ltd, Stockport, Cheshire
and printed and bound in Great Britain by
CPI Group (UK) Ltd, Croydon CR0 4YY

A CIP record for this book is available from the British Library

ISBN 978 0 7486 9271 2 (hardback)
ISBN 978 0 7486 9272 9 (webready PDF)

Contents

CHAPTER 1

Introduction

Calls for 'social justice', 'dignity' and 'freedom' resonated in the Arab Middle East in 2011. The winds of change that blew and swept over the region led to attempts at revolution in some countries, as in Tunisia (Chapter 2) and Egypt (Chapter 3), and reform in others, such as in Morocco (Chapter 4) and Jordan (Chapter 5), events collectively known as the 'Arab Spring'. This book attempts to arrive at a theory of revolution, that of a Hierarchical Dissonance (HD) in Values between rulers and ruled, a term which I coined in my 1987 study of the Iranian Revolution (Alianak 1987) and which I have modified for this study. The present book also addresses the question of why some countries underwent reforms and others attempted revolutions through the Pendulum Model which I devised in my 2007 book *Middle Eastern Leaders and Islam: A Precarious Equilibrium*, which depicts a dynamic, interactive relationship between rulers and ruled at times of crisis when leaders used religion to stabilise their rule. I posit here that the two monarchs I study, Muhammad VI of Morocco and Abdullah II of Jordan, used religion and survived whereas the secular leaders of Tunisia and Egypt, Ben Ali and Hosni Mubarak, tended, among other errors, not to resort to the palliative of religion to equilibrate the stability of their rule, and hence did not survive.

This study hopes to contribute towards the development of a 'fourth generation' theory of revolution, which Jack A. Goldstone (2001) urges us to develop in the twenty-first century in order to explain the phenomenon. It also attempts to contribute to theories of reform as they apply to the Middle East.

It further theorises about the outcomes of the revolutions in Tunisia and Egypt and reforms in Morocco and Jordan, by asking whether the Arab Spring has been realised so far (up to summer 2013), and whether movements towards restoration are taking place where 'stability' is re-emphasised. Here the study introduces the concept of a 'threshold' beyond which the palliative of religion is not as effective as in the past in dealing with the hierarchical dissonance in values or priorities.

The Pendulum Model

The Pendulum Model is a dynamic, interactive model that analyses the relationship between rulers and the ruled at a time of crisis brought about by a hierarchical dissonance in values or priorities (whether security-related, political, economic, social, or involving foreign affairs). It therefore goes beyond merely state-centred or society-centred theories in the literature of Middle Eastern studies, which emphasise either leaders or society exclusively.

In an ideal situation, the pendulum is in an imaginary equilibrium, hanging vertically as the leader's rule reaches the point of stability in power. When the pendulum swings to the left of the equilibrium point into the area of the society, this signifies the increasing stability of the leader's rule. However, when the hierarchies of values or priorities of the ruler and the ruled, which coincided sufficiently at the time of equilibrium, experience further dissonance causing a crisis to arise, this tends to push the pendulum past the equilibrium point into the right, into the area of the leader, which signifies a threat to the stability of the leader's rule. The leader then tries to push back the pendulum towards equilibrium as much as possible to re-establish stability using co-optation, and/or repression, democratic experiments, and religion.

This ideal of equilibrium of stability is, according to Goldstone, 'problematic' and is never fully achievable or normal (2001: 171–2). According to my findings, the hierarchies of values or priorities of rulers and ruled do not usually coincide and are constantly fluctuating in situations of negotiation and renegotiation in scales between and within each value as rulers and ruled interact. Where they are sufficiently close there is an increase in the stability of the ruler. But when an intolerable gap develops between these hierarchies, the resulting dissonance leads to attempts at revolution.

Hierarchical Dissonance in Values or Priorities hypothesis

My Hierarchical Dissonance (HD) in Values or Priorities hypothesis posits that the process of attempting revolution occurred in the Middle East where rulers and ruled experienced an intolerable dissonance in their respective perceived values or priorities (with the rulers increasingly emphasising stability and security and the ruled increasingly emphasising equality of economic opportunities), where the ruled perceived no hope of redress given the existing governmental structures and processes (with the ruled demanding the taking of matters into their own hands through democracy to bring about prosperity and dignity and to correct perceived injustices) and saw a favourable balance in forces (with mass participation mobilised through social media supported by external media and foreign governments), and where the rulers (ageing, corrupted, with divided elites, losing military backing) had deteriorated and did not or could not undertake effective diversionary tactics and methods.

My HD hypothesis also posits that the hierarchical dissonance between the values of the ruler and the ruled decreases where the ruler is perceived to be just and where he resorts to religion, with which he imbues the diversionary

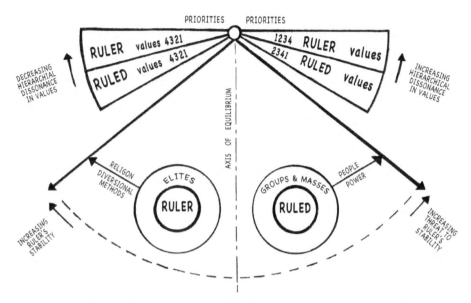

PRIORITIES   PRIORITIES

RULER   values 4321   1234   RULER   values
RULED   values 4321   2341   RULED   values

DECREASING HIERARCHIAL DISSONANCE IN VALUES

INCREASING HIERARCHICAL DISSONANCE IN VALUES

AXIS OF EQUILIBRIUM

RELIGION DIVERSIONAL METHODS   PEOPLE POWER

ELITES   GROUPS & MASSES

RULER   RULED

INCREASING RULER'S STABILITY   INCREASING THREAT TO RULER'S STABILITY

THE PENDULUM MODEL AND HIERARCHICAL DISSONANCE IN VALUES

methods he undertakes, and this results in the process of transitioning towards reform.

The following is an explanation of the above diagram, which depicts the dynamic interaction between ruler and ruled in terms of the Pendulum Model and the Hierarchical Dissonance in Values hypothesis. The ruler is surrounded by supporting elites which could, or which tend to, include crony capitalists, ruling family members, prestigious religious institutions such as al-Azhar (in Egypt), ruling party leaders, intelligence and security officials, and the military (when it sides with the ruler). The ruled, on the other hand, are composed of middle- and working-class members, university-educated young people, members of professional associations, labour union workers, other civil society organisation members, opposition parties, and the masses (the street), who are mobilised by new media (the Internet, social media, YouTube, satellite TV, mobile phones). Faced with HD, the ruled resort to people power and hence pose a threat to the leader's stability by attempting to push towards reform or revolution. Faced with HD, the ruler resorts to religion (transitioning towards reform) and/or to diversionary methods, such as co-optation, repression and illiberal democracy, which, if they are not imbued with religion or are ineffective, result in attempts by the ruled to transition towards revolution. The hierarchies of values or priorities are summarised thus in the diagram: 1 stands for stability, 2 for economic values, 3 for political values and 4 for social values. Where they tend to coincide for the ruler and the ruled, there is an increase in the stability of the ruler (1, 2, 3, 4); where there is a dissonance, the ruler's priorities are again depicted as 1 (stability), 2 (macro-economy), 3 (illiberal democracy), 4 (social dimension), whereas the priorities of the ruled which change are depicted as, first, economic justice (2), second democracy (3), third social values (4), and last stability (1). The greater the gap between the priorities of the ruler and the ruled, the greater the threat to the ruler's stability.

Definition of reform

The concept of reform employed in this study can be defined as follows:

> A reform is a process of change in political, and/or economic, social or religious, rules and institutions arrived at through constitutional means.

Definition of revolution

The concept of revolution employed in this study can be defined as follows:

> A revolution is a process of change in government rulers, and in the fundamental political, and/or economic, social or religious, rules or institutions of a political system, by unconstitutional means, which may include the use or threat of violence.

It is necessary here to clarify the terms employed in the above definition and to distinguish revolutions from other forms of change and violence.

First, revolution is a process of change, and an unconstitutional process at that. Moreover, this process need not necessarily be sudden, abrupt or of short duration, but may extend over many years (Leiden and Schmitt 1968: 4). However, it is different from reform, since while the end products of both processes may be the same type of politico-social and/or politico-economic change, and while they both may run their course over many years, they differ in that revolution is an unconstitutional process while reform is a constitutional one (Schrecker 1966: 37 and 49).

Secondly, revolution involves the unconstitutional change of government rulers, that is, the official holders of political power. However, not all unconstitutional changes of government personnel are revolutions. Some such changes may be termed purges and *coups d'état*. According to Edward Luttwak, 'A coup consists of the infiltration of a small but critical segment of the state apparatus, which is then used to displace the government from its control of the remainder' (1969: 12).

Therefore, thirdly, revolution involves not only unconstitutional change of government rulers, but also one or more fundamental changes (Johnson 1966: 138–40) in the political, social, economic, and/or religious principles (rules of the game) and organisations of the state. Thus, unlike coups, which involve just unconstitutional changes of personnel, revolutions involve changes in principles and organisations of government as well.

Theorists, however, disagree about the nature of these changes. Hannah Arendt emphasises political freedom in her book *On Revolution*, where she writes: 'Only where change occurs in the sense of a new beginning . . . where the liberation from oppression aims at least at the constitution of freedom can we speak of revolution' (Arendt 1963: 28). Samuel Huntington, in *Political Order in Changing Societies* (1968: 264), and Ted Gurr in *Why Men Rebel*, emphasise socio-political change. In the words of Gurr, revolution is a 'fundamental socio-political change accomplished through violence' (1970: 4). Karl Marx emphasised economic changes, which themselves lead to socio-political change. This study considers the nature of the change involved in the principles and institutions of a political system to be at least political, but also possibly social, economic and/ or religious. Further, in any of these sectors changes may occur in one or several fundamental aspects, as Chalmers Johnson in *Revolutionary Change* aptly points out in his typology of simple and total revolutions (1966: 139).

Fourth, although the literature on revolution posits that revolution involves violence or the threat of violence, revolutions may be non-violent, as seen in some of the Arab Spring countries. Violence may be defined as the threat or use of force. It provides us with a second characteristic by which to distinguish revolution from reform and also from demonstrations, strikes, or social change, although these may be precursors of revolution. Revolution is different from war as well, for whereas both involve violence, the latter is inter-systemic while the former is intra-systemic (Johnson 1966: 13). Moreover, violence that does not result in change of personnel and in fundamental political, social and/or economic change is not termed revolution here. By the same token, as soon as such changes occur, the violent movement is termed revolution even if it lasts for a short period of time. Further, revolutionaries may resort to non-violent mass gatherings and demonstrations, as seen in the Middle Eastern countries studied.

The above definition points to a continuum (ranging from simple to total) of revolutionary change. It also includes conservative counter-revolutions which result in a change of personnel and fundamental policies and/or institutions. In this context, the Middle Eastern countries I study, Tunisia and Egypt, are transitioning towards revolution and are vulnerable to counter-revolutions – for example, the ousting of the democratically elected Egyptian President, Mohamed Morsi, on 3 July 2013.

This leads to the need to analyse the outcome of revolutions. Has the Arab Spring been realised so far? Have the promises of the 2011 revolutionaries, based on their hierarchy of reducing inequality, of promoting democracy and economic prosperity, been realised so far, especially in Tunisia and Egypt? These may be the eventual goals of most revolutions, but in actuality their record is usually poor, according to E. Weede and E. N. Muller, who studied the phenomenon worldwide (1997). The more immediate goals of the revolutionary leadership are more realizable, such as the expanding of its state authority, changing the rules of the game of access to power, and the restructuring of institutions and beliefs (Goldstone 2001: 169). However, even in this regard Tunisia and Egypt are still transitioning, as will be seen in the case studies in this book. Why, then, do revolutions happen?

Some pertinent theories of revolution and reform

The many explanations in the theoretical literature that this study sifts through, analyses and uses as referents in the HD hypothesis in order to understand specifically the transition towards revolution and reform in the Arab Spring countries covered, Tunisia, Egypt, Morocco and Jordan, may be grouped under 'ruled-oriented' and 'ruler-oriented' theories.

'Ruled-oriented' theories

Which revolutionary actors, constituting the ruled, are to be studied? Why do they revolt?

Who revolts? These theories place an emphasis on the actors who revolt. They study changes in the ruled which lead them to revolt. Some authors write in terms of masses' and individuals' participation in a revolution; others in terms of groups and their collective action; others in terms of classes and their leadership; and still others in terms of informal organisations.

Many of the advocates of the theory of mass society approach revolutions from the angle of atomisation of individuals owing to the breakdown of group life and their subsequent arousal and mobilisation by revolutionary leaders or ideologues, as expounded by Eric Hoffer and José Ortega y Gasset. Pertinent to this study is Eric Hoffer's idea of the atomisation of the unemployed, put forward in his book *The True Believer: Thoughts on the Nature of Mass Movements* (Hoffer 1951). For these individuals, the social ties to groups provided by employment are severed, which causes them to experience anxieties, barrenness and meaninglessness regarding their individual existence and makes them readily believe intellectuals and doctrinaire voices (Hoffer 1951: 33, 46, 51, 72). Thus, revolutionary mass movements are created when atomised individuals are discontented, and acquire a sense of power and faith in the future (Hoffer 1951: 7–10, 89, 99, 115, 121). José Ortega y Gasset, in his book *The Revolt of the Masses*, elaborates on the role of ideologies and intellectuals in creating a 'new state of mind', which is individualistic and rationalistic, among the masses (1932: 111–12, 131).

Also emphasising mass mobilisations is the new literature on 'contentious politics', as presented by Charles Tilly and Sidney Tarrow (2007) and Jack Goldstone (2001). Indeed, in their definition of revolution they include formal and informal mass mobilisation and efforts to force change through non-institutionalised actions (Goldstone 2001: 142). The writings of all the mass theorists apply to my explanation of Middle Eastern mass demonstrations preceding the oustings of Ben Ali in Tunisia and Hosni Mubarak in Egypt in 2011.

The role of individuals in joining revolutions is also applicable in my case studies, as it has been analysed by rational choice theorists. Here the work of T. Ireland and G. Tullock should be mentioned. According to Ireland, a revolutionary situation would exist where the individual calculated that the utilities of joining the revolutionaries exceeded the costs and saw himself as a 'tipping point'– perceived, that is, that his actions would make a difference. The situation would end when the individual perceives the cost of participation to exceed the utilities he derived from further participation (Ireland 1967: 49–66). Tullock added to these cost–benefit calculations of individuals in joining the revolution the fun value of participating in the revolution, the probabilities of revolutionary success or failure, and the chances of various types of injuries (Tullock 1971: 87–100; 1974: 4–60).

However, rational choice models faced the problem of collective goods and their effect on discouraging the participation of individuals. More recent studies of rational choice have overcome the collective action problem by introducing the element of group identification, and hence have concentrated on what kinds of group structures favour protest action while concentrating on the identity, network ties and leadership of groups, which historical comparative case studies, like my present book, have dwelt upon (Goldstone 2001: 164–5). These ties are reminiscent of the role of individuals at Tahrir Square in Egypt, for example.

The role of groups and alliances between them is analysed by Samuel Huntington in his book *Political Order in Changing Societies* (1968). During modernization, political and social changes extend political consciousness to new groups. If this proceeds at such a rapid rate that it becomes impossible for the existing political institutions to assimilate them, the politically aspiring groups become inclined towards revolution. 'Revolution' is thus 'the extreme case of explosion of political participation' (Huntington 1968: 266). However, whether a revolution will be actualised depends on the alliances of these groups of intelligentsia, slum dwellers and peasants (Huntington 1968: 302–3). It is worth noting that in the Tunisian and Egyptian cases all these groups struck informal alliances through their virtual online and actual participations in the mass demonstrations that erupted. Also, the neoliberal economic policies created crony capitalists on the one hand and highly educated young individuals on the other, who aspired to increased participation and the sharing of economic benefits.

However, revolutions are not always the result of modernisation. Here, Charles Tilly, in his book *From Mobilization to Revolution* (1978), attempts to construct a theory independent of the rate of modernisation, by emphasising the collective action of groups which have been mobilised and which are involved in a conflict with other groups and the incumbent government over resources. His approach represents the political conflict approach, which this study also covers. For Tilly, it was the lack of political power of new associational groups that led directly to political violence (rather than leading to it indirectly through psychological processes, as argued by Ted Gurr and discussed below). According to Tilly, unlike communal localised traditional groups like the peasants, these associational groups can be organised and mobilised. Tilly's 'mobilisation model' posits a group as mobilised when it has broadened its control over one or more of the following resources: normative, coercive and utilitarian resources (Tilly 1978: 5). Once a group is mobilised it is ready for collective action. New associational groups usually engage in proactive collective action because they demand entry to the polity. A revolutionary situation begins when 'a government previously under the control of a single polity becomes the objective of competing mutually exclusive claims on the part of two or more distinct polities' (such as the pro- and anti-Morsi groups in Egypt during the summer of 2013). This ends 'when a single sovereign polity regains control over the government' (Tilly 1978: 191).

The role of classes (based on economic factors) in revolutions is stressed by Karl Marx. The oppressed class, which represents the new mode of production, develops a class consciousness and unity and realises that the only way to overcome this barrier is through an armed struggle (Marx and Engels 1959). However, classes are groups that are too big to unite their members sufficiently for action, a point which Vladimir Lenin recognised in his concept of the vanguard, the politically conscious element of the oppressed class, as the leader of the revolution (Lenin 1970).

In the Middle Eastern attempts at revolution in Tunisia and Egypt, both the middle and the working classes participated peacefully without any top leaders (no visible vanguard, in other words), but rather through mass mobilisation accelerated by modern media including the Internet, social media (Facebook, Twitter and YouTube), which fed satellite TV stations like Al Jazeera from Qatar. Here, informal ties prevailed.

On the basis of the 1989–91 revolutions in Eastern Europe, Goldstone, back in 2001, suggested the importance of studying informal groups in theorising about revolutions (Goldstone 2001: 153). However, he tended to overemphasise the role of leadership in the form of one or two individuals who combine the roles of the visionaries ('people oriented') and pragmatic organisers ('task oriented') (Goldstone 2001: 157); these, although important in the post-revolutionary phase, were not prominent in the leaderless pre-revolutionary phase, which was based on mass movements attempting to bring about revolutions in the Middle Eastern countries studied here.

Why do the ruled revolt? The role of the ruled in revolutions is emphasised by 'deprivation' theorists and 'injustice' theorists. Deprivation theorists concentrate on changes in the aspirations and expectations of the ruled which lead to cognitive dissonance, whereas injustice theorists concentrate on perceptions by the ruled of 'injustice', rather than on perceptions merely of deprivation, which lead them to revolt. Certainly, both theories are valid in the Middle Eastern countries covered, and hence both are incorporated in my HD hypothesis.

Deprivation theories approach revolutions from the angle of cognitive dissonance, which occurs as a result of certain directions of change, rates of change and particular factors causing this change, whether political, ideological, economic, social, military or religious. The resultant frustration people feel leads to their collective anger and hence to their revolt.

Some theorists emphasise that improvements in one or more conditions of society increase people's expectations of and desires for further improvements in the same conditions or other conditions. If the latter do not match, or if they depart from, these expectations, people get frustrated and revolt. According to Crane Brinton, in his *Anatomy of Revolution*, revolutions occur when the rate of improvement does not keep up with the rate of rise in aspirations. It is when a society is improving economically that it aspires to more economic gain (Brinton 1965: 32). When groups in such a society come to feel that, although their economic activity is improving, it is hindered from realising its full potential, they feel annoyance, restraint, and hindrance and revolt (Brinton 1965: 32, 34). Inasmuch as Brinton writes about macro-economic improvements, his study partially explains high GDP growth in pre-revolutionary Tunisia and Egypt. But this alone is not the whole picture.

Here, Alexis de Tocqueville hints at what later was regarded as 'relative deprivation' (RD) by James Davies and Ted Gurr. For Tocqueville, aspirations rise owing to improved conditions but conditions thereafter remain the same. He writes that economic improvements and the lessening of oppression by the government, which is intent upon reforming itself, lift some of the people's grievances or alleviate them. This has a spill-over effect on 'those left untouched' (Tocqueville 1856: 214). The untouched people now want redress too. And if the needs of the ruled are not met, they may consider the situation to be intolerable and revolt against the regime. This is more in line with the frustrations felt by Tunisian and Egyptian unemployed university graduates.

Instead of general economic conditions, W. Laqueur emphasised improvements in education (1968). As people become more highly educated, they tend to see more social and political problems and feel more discontented about them, and expect to change for the better to occur. If these latter expectations are not met by the social and political structures over the long run, people get frustrated and revolt (Laqueur 1968: 503). This certainly applies to Tunisia, with its high and growing rates of literacy and of university graduates.

Some writers have argued that it is not the improvement of conditions but their deterioration that brings about revolutions. Notable here is Karl Marx.

According to Marx, the worsening of the economic conditions of the working class intensifies their discontent, and makes them despair and revolt (Marx and Engels 1959).

Other authors, such as James Davies, have pointed out that what is important is the sequence of change – namely, a prolonged period of objective economic and social improvement followed by a sudden sharp decline which creates a dissatisfied state of mind in the population. This leads to the subjective fear that 'the great effort will be quite lost; their mood becomes revolutionary' (Davies 1962: 5). Davies, in his article 'Toward a theory of revolution' (1962), calls this process the 'J-Curve'. However, he becomes inconsistent when he compares the expectations of the people, a state of mind, to the actual rise and fall of 'objective economic and social development' rather than to the people's perceptions of these changes. Moreover, he does not take into account the people's perceptions of the governmental structures and processes. My HD hypothesis takes into account perceptions in the hierarchies of values or priorities of the ruled, and also their having lost hope of redress from existing governmental structures and processes, revealed through public opinion polls, the demands of protesters expressed at demonstrations, and the statements of the revolutionaries.

Ted Gurr, in *Why Men Rebel* (1970), considers perceptions. His major contribution lies in his 'aspirational deprivation' hypothesis, which includes 'relative deprivation', as an 'increase in men's value expectations without a concomitant change in value position or potential'. He considers deprivation not only in terms of welfare values (economic values, land, skills), but also interpersonal (social status, ideational coherence) and power values (political participation and security) (Gurr 1970: 26, 112–13). However, he fails to consider religious values, which have provided the motive force behind such Middle Eastern revolutions as the Iranian Revolution and the Mahdi uprising in the Sudan.

Gurr defines 'relative deprivation' (RD) as 'actors' perception of discrepancy between their value expectations and their value capabilities'. Here, the value expectations are 'the goods and conditions of life to which people believe they are rightfully entitled'; and value capabilities 'are the goods and conditions they think they are capable of getting and keeping' (Gurr 1970: 24). A person's point of reference here may be 'his own past condition, an abstract ideal, or the standards articulated by a leader as well as a "reference group"' (Gurr 1970: 25). RD played an important role in the attempts at revolution in Tunisia and Egypt.

But is RD that significant in explaining the start of revolutions? Some writers, for example Leonard Berkowitz (1968), Peter Lupsha (1969), Barrington Moore (1978) and Jack Goldstone (2001), have questioned the importance of using deprivation by itself. Berkowitz, a psychologist, in his *Roots of Aggression*, emphasises that for aggressive behaviour nearness to the desired goal may be more important than the extent of deprivation (Berkowitz 1968: 307–22). Certainly Egyptians viewed the success of Tunisians in ousting Ben Ali as making their removal of Mubarak a near-possibility, and this gave them more courage to revolt.

Although Gurr mentions, among other factors, that a revolution occurs when people believe they are unjustly deprived, Lupsha and Moore give 'injustice' a central place in their theory of revolution. According to Lupsha:

> One can get angry and aggressive because one's values or sense of justice (a learned phenomenon) have been affronted, without any blocking to the individual's goal directed activity or awareness of any personal 'want–get ratio' deprivation, or any personal feelings of anticipated frustration. (Lupsha 1969: 288)

Moore, in his book *Injustice: the Social Bases of Obedience and Revolt* (1978), seeks to answer the question of why some people can live and suffer in an oppressive environment and not revolt, whereas others exist in equal or less oppressive situations and do revolt. He sees no correlation between severity of suffering and rebellion. Therefore, he concludes that the moral order of society, rather than suffering, should be concentrated upon in studying revolutions. So long as the ruled accept the moral order of society and the inevitability of injustice, no revolution arises. The ruled, according to Moore, first perceive an unjust situation; secondly, they come to realise that this is not inevitable; thirdly, they decide to revolt and perceive that they can and ought to do so (Moore 1978: 462, 492). When the illusion of the inevitability of an unjust situation, such as inequality, is removed by the mockery of intellectuals and later by wide sections of the population, political revolution results and older forms of privilege are replaced by a new moral order (ibid.: 493–4). The people see the rulers as oppressors and plunderers who have not lived up to their obligation to take care of their subjects. The language of reciprocity, or of the mutual obligations of rulers and ruled for the benefit of the whole community, is seen as an ideological cover for exploitation. The result is a perception of injustice. Then, the ruled act on a sense of moral outrage by revolting (ibid.: 509–10). Goldstone uses perceptions of justice as one component in his study of revolutions. My study finds that it was this sense of injustice felt by the people, as depicted in their cries and calls for 'dignity', that was a significant factor leading to the attempts at revolution in Tunisia and Egypt.

'Ruler-oriented' theories

People's perception of injustice alone is not enough to trigger revolutions; there is also the need to consider people's perceptions of the ruler's ineffectiveness (Goldstone 2001: 148). Unjust rulers may be tolerated if they are perceived to be effective in delivering nationalistic or economic goals, or if they are perceived to be too effective, making it difficult to challenge the regime. Hence, it is important to study not only the ruled but also the rulers. My HD hypothesis considers them both along with their interactions.

Ruler-oriented theories of revolution analyse the ineffectiveness of the rulers, their deterioration, and their inability to conduct effective diversionary tactics and methods – all of which are included in my HD hypothesis. Different authors emphasise different aspects of the role of rulers: (1) their isolation, (2) their inability to adapt to new conditions, (3) their loss of power, (4) divisions within them and alienation of some parts of them, (5) their loss of faith, (6) their inefficiency and corruption; or some combination of these factors. Moreover, the writers see the rulers as ruling classes or elites or coalitions of groups instead of as a monolithic unit.

Leiden and Schmitt recognise that the rulers should have deteriorated, but suggest that unless the insurgents are aware that the rulers have weakened they will not revolt (1968: 53–4). Also, according to Arendt, revolutions can break out at a time of loss of authority, and succeed only 'if there exists a sufficient number of people who are prepared for its collapse, and at the same time, are willing to assume power, eager to organise and to act together for a common purpose' (1963: 112).

How is the theorist to operationalise the concept of 'elites'? Harold Lasswell centres his study around formal leadership. Although for him 'elite' is a classificatory and descriptive term covering both leadership and the strata of society from which leaders emerge, he concentrates his attention on cabinets, 'executive committees', which are directly involved in the decision-making process (Lasswell *et al.* 1952: 6, 22–6). In spite of the fact that this makes his material more manageable, it has its shortcomings, for it ignores informal leadership in the ruling class, which, as James Bill points out, is vital for an understanding of politics in developing nations (Bill 1972: 9). This is especially important in the Middle East. According to Steffen Erdle (2010), the elite in Tunisia shunned occupying formal governmental positions and preferred instead the informal behind-the-scenes power positions which prevailed in pre-revolutionary times, as will be seen in the Tunisia chapter of this book. But they suffered ultimately because these 'crony capitalists', who were mainly from the ruling family, did not admit individuals into their ranks except by marriage, blocking normal elite circulation of talented individuals, which resulted in a destabilising of the regime, as my case study illustrates.

How do theorists view the elite characteristics which make them vulnerable to revolutions from below? Vilfredo Pareto, in his book *The Mind and Society*, concentrates on the isolation of the elite and its degeneration in his explanation of revolutions. An elite's dominion would be 'perpetual' if it combined intelligence with fitness to use force (Pareto 1935: 1,531). This stability could be maintained if there is an adequate circulation of individuals, where the gifted people would rise into the elite and the degenerated elements of the elite would fall into the ranks of the masses (Pareto 1935: 1,431). However, this circulation is not maintained in real life. The 'governing class . . . brings its own ruin'

(Pareto 1935: 1,555n.). Having maintained itself in power over a long period of time by force and intelligence, it finds out that it may subsist on shrewdness and without the use of force for some time, and it gives more vent to its desires to amass wealth. Therefore it readily accepts and emphasises the entrance into its ranks of individuals with 'instinct residues', which promote wealth. Class circulation slows down; in time the number of individuals with group-persistence instinct residues dwindles; an imbalance between intelligence and force results (Pareto 1935: 1,432, 1,515–16, 1,555). The elite is unable to defend itself and very often resorts to humanitarian moves. Such conditions, where 'a humanitarian aristocracy . . . is closed or stiffly exclusive', represents 'the maximum of insecurity' (Pareto 1935: 1,516). Then revolutions occur. Pareto adds that an imbalance, where force is emphasised to the detriment of intelligence in the elite, would also result in revolution (Pareto 1935: 1,541, 1,564). My case studies show that the attempted revolutions in Tunisia and Egypt resulted from poor elite circulation, among other factors. Humanitarian measures undertaken at the last moment by the regimes were not considered to be serious, and excessive use of force backfired and resulted in the toppling of the leaders.

Gaetano Mosca's formulations, in his *Ruling Class*, are basically similar to Pareto's. He recognises the importance of intelligence and force for the elite, which for him is composed of the government and a second stratum of executives whose level of 'morality, intelligence and activity' determines the stability of the 'political organism' (Mosca 1939: 404). He recognises the need for elite circulation. Therefore, the elite undermines its political position by failing to accommodate new social types, which arise owing to changes in commerce, forced emigration, discoveries, wars or other social changes (Mosca 1939: 199, 221).

One such change, also pertinent to the Middle East, is its sustained population growth in recent times. According to Goldstone, when this is in excess of economic growth, it alters the relations between the elite of the state and the population, often leading to instability. Jobs become scarce and inflation rises. This results in the elites benefiting disproportionately *vis-à-vis* other groups, and when it upsets the 'normal process of elite recruitment and social mobility' it leads to severe damage to state effectiveness and justice as perceived by the protesters, which is a precursor to revolution (Goldstone 2001: 149). This situation was certainly true in Tunisia and Egypt, where the increasing number of highly educated university students could not find jobs much less be recruited to the ranks of the elite of 'crony capitalists'.

Elite theory also emphasises regime breakdown and revolutions due to deep elite divisions, defections and polarisations. According to J. C. Scott, where the elites are united and head fiscally and militarily sound states, they are largely invulnerable to revolutions from people below (Scott 1985, 1990). A. Groth also agrees that no revolutions will occur unless the elite is divided, no matter how strongly the masses support the insurgents. His explanation of revolutions is based on divisions within the elites, the struggle of groups within them, and/or the alienation of some of them. Both of his two types of revolutions, elite-affiliated and elite-isolated, require this precondition. The former occurs when parts of the status quo political elite give active support to or are at least benevolently neutral to the activities of the revolutionary movement. The latter happens when the elite is divided (Groth 1966: 7, 11, 16, 18). Under such conditions the elite is weakened, and thus is unable to withstand enormous pressure from below since it is incapable of maintaining its control over the people (ibid.: 7–8).

One such group is that of the 'intellectuals', who, owing to travel, or exposure to other societies, want change. These intellectuals 'transfer' their 'allegiance' or 'desert' the cause of existing institutions and point to their archaism (Edwards 1970: 38, 41). The repressors lose faith in themselves and revolutions follow. In this connection Edwards writes, 'So long as the entire body of repressors believe firmly in themselves and in the righteousness of their actions, they cannot be overthrown by revolution' (ibid.: 45, 59). Thus Edwards emphasises also the psychological state of the elite.

Brinton agrees with Edwards about the importance of the psychological faith of the ruling class, and its divisions, but he goes beyond Edwards in that he does not neglect other factors such as the inefficiency of the class, its failure to admit new social groups and its loss of military power (Brinton 1965: 39, 49, 51–3, 55, 60, 65). Here S. N. Eisenstadt and J. D. Green argue that it is not merely divisions within the elite but rather the polarisation of the elite that leads to instability. The elite form two or three coherent groupings, who exhibit sharp differences in points of view about the polity (Eisenstadt 1978, 1999; Green 1984). In the Middle Eastern attempts at revolution in Tunisia and Egypt that are studied here, the military elite deserted the rulers and hence this led to the success of these attempts; whereas in Morocco and Jordan, the military elite stayed loyal and united with the monarchs and their elite, and no revolution, but some reform, resulted instead.

Theda Skocpol, in her 1979 book *States and Social Revolutions*, adds another dimension to the study of revolutions – namely, deterioration of state structures. She spearheaded what Goldstone calls the 'third generation' theories, which drew attention to the 'structural vulnerabilities of regimes as the basic causes of revolutions' (Goldstone 2001: 139). Unlike other theorists, such as Gurr, Johnson, Tilly and Marx, who stuck to the notion that revolutions are purposive and voluntaristic, Skocpol wrote that the analyst should 'take a nonvoluntarist, structural perspective on their causes and processes' (Skocpol 1979: 14–15). According to her, the structures of the state break down before a revolution occurs (Skocpol 1979: 29, 285). For her the basic causes of social revolutions lie 'in the structure and capacities of the state organisations, as these are conditioned by developments in the economy and class structure and also by developments in the international situation' (ibid.: 32). She deals with both domestic and international structures (ibid.: 291). Domestically, she departs from Marx in suggesting the potential autonomy of the state. The state is no longer treated as an instrument of the dominant class. She explores not only class relations but also relations of the state to dominant and subordinate classes (ibid.: 31). In her case studies (France, Russia and China), she shows how the rulers may act against the class of landlords. The upper class would be against reforms and thus would put a strain on the domestic structures of the state (ibid.: 30). This could happen internationally as well where the state may also attempt policies, such as responses to international military pressures and opportunities, which conflict with the interests of the landed class (ibid.: 31).

On the basis of her case studies, Skocpol summarises her theory of revolutions thus: 'caught in the cross-pressures between class structures and international exigencies, the autocracies and their centralised administrations and armies broke apart, opening the way for social-revolutionary transformations spearheaded by revolts from below' (ibid.: 47). Here Skocpol herself spearheaded the 'third generation' theories, for, unlike Marx, who believed that revolutions would occur in the advanced capitalist industrial nations, she shows that revolutions have happened in agrarian countries (ibid.: 292). For her what was important was 'the breakdown and reconstruction of state administrative and coercive organizations from old to new regimes' (ibid.: 42). In my HD hypothesis I refer to the breakdown of state structures when I show that the existing governmental structures or processes were so dysfunctional that they contributed to the feelings of the revolutionaries that they could not get redress through the state structures and had instead to take matters into their own hands through attempting a democratic solution in Tunisia and Egypt, to be realised only through revolutions.

Diversionary methods theories
Even with the deterioration of the elite and state structures, social movements rather than revolutions will occur if the rulers resort to diversionary tactics and methods such as co-optation (reform), repression and/or democratisation experiments. These are discussed in turn.

Reform theories
Co-optation, concessions and reforms are considered by different theorists to be controversial as regards their effectiveness in preventing revolutions. Whereas some writers, like Tocqueville, consider reform a catalyst for revolution (Tocqueville 1856: 214), and whereas others, like H. D. Lasswell and A. Kaplan (1950) consider it a substitute, the truth of the matter lies perhaps in the positions taken by Huntington and Goldstone, that is, that some reforms act as catalysts and others as substitutes for revolution. It is important to note here the nature of

the reforms, their timing, and how they address the members and composition of the revolutionaries. Thus some policy reforms are likely to be interpreted as a weakness of the regime and as such they may lead to revolution (Huntington 1968: 367). According to M. Silver, where reforms are limited they tend to be followed by revolutions. This is because reforms are perceived to show regime weakness and give benefits to revolutionaries which could be used against the regime. Reforms decrease costs and increase rewards, thus increasing the net private benefit from supporting the revolutionaries (Silver 1974: 63–71).

The timing of the concessions and the perceived strength of the regime are emphasised by Goldstone. Where the ruler has already lost his perceived effectiveness and justice, concessions may be seen to be 'too little, too late' and hence increase the people's demands for larger-scale change. Therefore, when the regime undertakes reforms from a position of weakness they will further undermine support for the ruler. If, however, reforms are undertaken from a position of strength, they may prevent revolutions, as Machiavelli advised the Prince (Goldstone 2001: 161).

Leadership reforms, insofar as they 'may drain away the dynamic elements in the revolutionary movement and join to the Establishment', may prevent revolution, according to Huntington (1968: 367). These are especially effective if they are well timed, that is, if they occur when the revolutionary groups are in their intermediate power levels, for in the groups' phase of minimal power the few reforms offered to them appear too little in terms of their aspirations for total change of the system, and in their phase of maximal power the groups are so near to their goal and their intensity of discontent so acute that they will not be deterred by reform (Hoffer 1951: 28).

So far as the composition of the revolutionaries goes, those reforms are effective in preventing revolutions which alter the balance of power in the revolutionary groups. Thus reforms which strengthen the more moderate revolutionaries tend to be beneficial to the incumbents (Huntington 1968: 368). So are reforms directed towards the peasants, especially if they are land reforms. But reforms directed towards the urban intelligentsia, as in the Middle Eastern countries studied here, may act as catalysts for revolution since the needs of these latter groups are utopian and cannot be fulfilled by any government (ibid.: 371, 375–6).

In the attempts made towards revolution in Tunisia and Egypt, last-minute concessions by the rulers did not prevent the revolutions. What about co-optation in the long run, which in the past had contributed to the longevity of the rule of Ben Ali in Tunisia (23 years) and of Mubarak in Egypt (almost 30 years)? Why was co-optation no longer effective in 2011? Co-optation had with time increasingly benefited only the few, who had become more and more greedy and corrupt, which led to perceptions of relative deprivation on the part of young university graduates, who had no prospects of finding jobs without bribes, but who were educated enough to be savvy with social media mobilisation skills and use of cellphones, and were inspired by the 'Twitter Revolution' in Iran and subsequently by the Tunisian uprisings. This occurred even at a time when the macro-economy was improving but corruption was rampant.

In the attempts made towards reform in Morocco and Jordan, the imbuing of pre-emptive reform measures with religion, namely the emphasis placed on the direct descent of the monarchs from the Prophet Muhammad, resulted in the kings' survival. Reforms, however limited, initiated by the monarchs were believed in as the rulers were trusted as commanders of the faithful. Where there is trust in a ruler's intentions to carry out their promises and where the ruler is perceived to be just, transition towards reform rather than towards revolution tends to be preferred.

Repression theories

When facing demands from protesters for political change, regimes have combined repression with concessions. According to Harry Eckstein, concessions which are 'timely' and repression which is based on very good intelligence are essential for the survival of regimes (Eckstein 1965: 153–9). The question ultimately hinges on how to choose the right combination of these two methods.

So far as repression is concerned, Lasswell and Kaplan elaborate on the role of elite force by emphasising the degree of actual control of the instruments of violence by the elite. They suggest that the greater the control, the less the probability of revolution (Lasswell and Kaplan 1950: 266–7). On the other hand, the Feierabends studied the effects of the different levels of exercise of this force and concluded, on the basis of their quantitative cross-national study, that, other factors being equal, predominantly permissive and extremely coercive regimes encounter little violence from the ruled, whereas regimes using a medium level of coerciveness encounter more violence and revolution (Feierabend and Feierabend 1966: 249–71). However, these writers do not deal with the question of why the elite slackens or tightens its control on the use of force. An added dimension to the effectiveness of the use of force by the rulers in preventing revolutions depends, according to C. Kurzman, on whether they are consistent or not in the use of force. Kurzman considers inconsistency as a factor in undermining the ruler's position (Kurzman 1996: 153–70). The role of the military in abandoning the rulers in Tunisia and Egypt in 2011, and in supporting the monarchs in Morocco and Jordan, will be analysed in detail in my case-study chapters of this book.

According to Goldstone, the degree and context of repression need to be analysed too. Where repression is 'not strong enough to suppress opponents, or . . . is so diffuse and erratic that innocents are persecuted, or . . . is aimed at groups that the public considers representative and justified in their protest', it can undermine a ruler's stability (Goldstone 2001: 161). Moreover, Goldstone adds to these conditions the 'perceptions of vulnerability' of the rulers. The more the regime is perceived as losing ground, the more the protesters may bear great risks of increased regime violence and proceed with the toppling of the rulers. But when they perceive the regime as unshakable, they are reduced to silence in the face of indiscriminate repression (Goldstone 2001: 161).

Here, Pitirim A. Sorokin introduced the concept of the 'threshold of revolution' in his original work, *The Sociology of Revolution* (1925). For Sorokin, there is a psychological threshold at which the instinct of freedom is annihilated by severe repression. However, up to this point repression of the most important instincts, or of a large number of them, enhances the will to resist and thus may lead to revolution (Sorokin 1925: 368–9, 380). Rulers in actual pre-revolutionary situations, however, lack information about such matters, are often over-confident, and veer back and forth in their use of repression, which increases their vulnerability to being overthrown (Goldstone 2001: 161).

In the detailed case studies of Tunisia and Egypt covered in this book, it was found that repression by the rulers was counterproductive. Repression, which had been used selectively against extremist Islamists in the past to please the USA in its 'war on terror', was extended to the moderate dissident population at large and became more severe, to such an extent that it had elicited Western public condemnation, as evidenced by the Cairo speech on 4 June 2009 by the newly elected President of the USA, Barack Obama, condemnation subsequently repeated in his numerous other speeches prior to 2011, which had addressed the dictators as being on 'the wrong side of history' (Alianak 2012: 8). This raised the hopes of dissidents and tended to contribute, however indirectly, to the Arab Spring.

Political liberalisation theories

Another method used by the rulers studied here was their 'political liberalisation' attempts. These efforts, urged by the Bush and Obama administrations, were at best half-hearted and resulted in raising the expectations of the population only for these to be dashed over and over again by rigged, tampered-with and controlled elections, which led to frustration, anger, and feelings of mistrust, of injustice and of the hopelessness of redress given the existing governmental structures and processes, along with a determination to transition to democracy. These feelings were reinforced by the lack of clear succession plans for the ageing rulers of Tunisia and, especially, of Egypt. In the case of Egypt, rumours about the grooming of Gamal Mubarak, the son of Hosni Mubarak, to succeed his father were widely resented.

Indeed, the illiberal democracies that Tunisia and Egypt had introduced resulted in what the State Failure Task Force had called a 'partial democracy'. According to its quantitative study, 'partial democracies', which embark on reform and concessions and which have shown some weakness, are extremely unstable. On the other hand, democracies and autocracies were shown to be fairly stable (Goldstone 2001: 166). So by moving in the direction of illiberal democracy, the leaders of Tunisia and Egypt unwittingly brought about the downfall of their regimes.

Methodology of the study

This book is based on a case-study approach to testing the HD hypothesis. The cases covered are discussed in two Parts: I, The Transition towards Revolution and II, The Transition towards Reform. In Part I, the cases of the Tunisian (Chapter 2) and Egyptian (Chapter 3) revolutions are considered. In Part II, the cases of the reforming monarchies, Moroccan (Chapter 4) and Jordanian (Chapter 5), are studied. Chapter 6 concludes by presenting similarities and differences regarding the revolution and reform efforts, and attempts to depict the heuristic value of the HD hypothesis in explaining concisely the Arab Spring region-wide.

My data for arriving at the priorities or hierarchies of values of the rulers and the ruled involves analysing the chants and statements of the protesters, the speeches and actions of the rulers, and most important of all, the very reliable public opinion polls, in particular those conducted by the Pew Research Center and the Abu Dhabi Gallup Poll in 2010 and 2011 and beyond that well into the post-revolutionary era.

Scope and purpose of the study

This study attempts to contribute to reform theories by explaining why reforms occurred in some Arab Spring countries. In addition, instead of separate models for revolution as suggested by Goldstone, one for the rulers and one for the ruled (Goldstone 2001: 174), my HD hypothesis, as presented in this book, shows the dynamic interaction of rulers and ruled. It discusses, in each chapter, the calls for social justice versus the co-optation of 'crony capitalists', and the calls for populist democracy versus the illiberal democracy of the rulers (in terms of limited participation, ineffective political parties, stifled civil society). Also, the book stresses the outcomes of the revolutionary and reform processes up to the summer of 2013. I try to discern whether the Arab Spring was realised in the countries studied by giving a vivid picture of the interactions of the rulers and the ruled.

My HD hypothesis attempts to contribute to the development of what Goldstone calls the needed 'fourth generation' theory (Goldstone 2001: 175). It tries to meet his condition of treating stability as problematic and focuses on the conditions of regime sustainability over time. Moreover, it gives a prominent role to networks and ideology, but shows that the leadership of revolutionaries, although provided for by the HD hypothesis, is not pertinent in the Middle Eastern revolutions studied here. Also, as Goldstone suggests should be the case, my hypothesis deals with the interplay of the multiple actors involved in revolutionary processes and outcomes. In addition, my analysis attempts to unify the case studies with the findings of rational choice models. Further case studies need to be undertaken, of course, to apply my HD hypothesis and test its heuristic value region-wide. Although there are not enough instances of revolutions or reforms in the Arab Spring countries to warrant effective statistically significant quantitative studies, perhaps in the future analysts could be challenged to attempt them anyway.

PART I

The transition towards revolution

The transition towards revolution

The transition towards the Jasmine Revolution in Tunisia: the Arab Spring realised?

Jasmine! How sweet the smell of hope and celebration of this exquisite, fresh, dainty, white national flower! The Jasmine Revolution also started full of fresh hope in Tunisia, from around 17 December 2010 to 14 January 2011, when President Zine El Abdine Ben Ali fled the country. It took a mere 29 days for people power to topple a rule that had lasted around twenty-three years (phase 1). The revolution is still 'dainty', still transitioning with efforts to democratise, resulting so far in the legalisation of banned political parties, including the Islamist Party, *Hizb al-Nahda* (Ennahda), in the election of the Constituent Assembly on 23 November 2011, in projections for parliamentary and presidential elections for the end of 2013, and in direct people power still being active, all in an attempt to realise the aims of the protesters (phase 2).

This Tunisian uprising was the first in the Arab Middle East in the twenty-first century against an authoritarian regime, cascading and spreading region-wide in what became known as the 'Arab Spring'. But have the goals of the Tunisian Arab Spring been realised so far?

Phase 1: The Jasmine Revolution erupts and Ben Ali flees

Why did the Jasmine Revolution erupt and why did Ben Ali flee? Ben Ali's old diversionary methods of co-optation, repression and the promising of political liberalisation, that had served him so well for around twenty-three years (albeit showing underlying fissures and cracks of late), proved to be no longer effective at the start of the second decade of the twenty-first century, when he was confronted with the determined demands of the majority of the Tunisian people.

The contributing and underlying reason was an emerging hierarchical dissonance in values between the priorities of the ruler and those of the majority of Tunisians that persisted, was not bridged, and ultimately undermined Ben Ali's regime. The President emphasised stability and did not resort to religion, unlike in the past, when he had used this soft power successfully (Pendulum Model) when confronted with the earlier crisis of legitimacy resulting from his staging of a bloodless *coup d'état* in 1987 against the then ageing first Tunisian President, Habib Bourguiba. This neglect of the palliative of religion and of this soft power resulted in Ben Ali's not relieving the intolerability of the dissonance in values of the ruled, who emphasised economic improvement and redress of their perceived relative deprivation, and of his own emphasis on stability. Indeed, a Pew Research Center Poll showed that whereas Ben Ali called for stability in the name of attracting investments and tourism through his own rule, the protesters prioritised a strong economy (59 per cent) arrived at through democracy (40 per cent). When asked which was more important, stability or democracy, 55 per cent preferred a democratic government even if it risked instability, whereas only 38 per cent preferred a stable government even if there were a risk of its not being fully democratic ('Pew study' 2012: 2, 5). The resultant intolerable and unbridgeable gap in priorities led to the uprising, which forced Ben Ali to flee the country when the military did not side with him.

Social justice versus the co-optation of the ruling family and crony capitalists

Ben Ali relied on co-opting Tunisians through a tacit 'social contract', initially where the hierarchies of the ruler and the ruled coincided – where the ruler emphasised stability and the ruled acquiesced in it in return for the achievement of the second priority of economic well-being. This was especially so when Tunisian businessmen wished to avoid the instability in neighbouring Algeria, which was caused, they believed, by unchecked Islamist extremists. Initially, Ben Ali's stability came before the economic advancement and contentment of the majority of Tunisians, and indeed was viewed by them as a precondition for these.

Why did a dissonance emerge in the values of the ruler and of the ruled? This depended on the performance of the macro-economy as a whole and its consequences in what Fadhel Kaboub calls the 'neoliberal phase', which started in the late 1980s, and was followed by the ill-effects of the 'plutocracy phase', which started in the early 2000s (Kaboub 2011: 7). Together they contributed to the discontent of Tunisians at persistently high unemployment, especially among the aspiring and educated young, and generated feelings of what J. C. Davies (1962) called 'relative deprivation', a precondition for revolution, with growing corruption among the ever-shrinking elite (Ben Ali's extended family, known as The Family, and crony capitalists) and growing social inequalities, which led to anger and to demands for social justice. This dissonance between the priorities of the ruled and the ruler became crucial to the advent of the uprisings. Ben Ali's co-optation, which had extended to the majority of Tunisians, was reduced to a perceived small elite. Even though the President still theoretically emphasised the co-opting of the majority of Tunisians in his speeches, the reality was perceived to be different.

It is true that the regime's means of co-optation of the population had increased since the economic liberalization, especially in the 1990s. The economic restructuring would theoretically increase benefits for the entire population through privatisation of state-owned enterprises, promotion of export-oriented industry and the encouragement of tourism (Kaboub 2011: 7). Indeed, the macro-economy took off, with 5 per cent average growth each year. The UN's Human Development Index showed an improvement from 0.696 in 1995 to 0.769 in 2009, with 80 per cent of the social strata rated as 'middle class' (Erdle 2010: 138, 362–3). Indeed, Tunisia was commended for having the largest middle class in the Arab world, hence providing a possible foundation for democratic development (Anderson 2011: 2). Also, the tax burden on the population was kept almost constant, at 20 per cent of GDP between 2004 and 2009. Outstanding national debt even declined from 59.4 of GDP in 2004 to 45.4 per cent in 2009. The budget deficit remained almost constant, at around minus 3 per cent between 2004 and 2009 (Ministry of Finance, Republic of Tunisia 2009). Although these represented signs of a robust and bright economic future, there were four hidden problems that were to reduce the contentment and satisfaction of Tunisians.

For one, the European economic crisis of the late 2000s had an adverse effect on the Tunisian middle class since there was a decline in the remittances sent by Tunisians living abroad in Europe; tourism also declined and exports were adversely affected (Paciello 2011: 6–7). Indeed, the total value of Tunisian world exports fell by 22 per cent in 2009 (Joya *et al.*, December 2011: 21). Rising world food prices eroded the income gains that the middle class had made, especially in the urban hubs (Erdle 2010: 367), as seen also by the high level of private indebtedness (Paciello 2011: 6).

A second problem was the geographic unevenness of the macro-economic prosperity (Erdle 2010: 366). According to Sari Hanafi, the 'Tunisian economic miracle' was concentrated in the capital and in the northern coastal cities and not in the interior or the south of the country (Hanafi 2011: 2). It is no wonder that the signs of unrest and protests first occurred in the poorest regions, as was seen as early as 2008 in Gafsa in the southern mining region, where unemployment ran at 30 per cent and where youth unemployment was 40 per cent – all perhaps due to poor infrastructural planning (Paciello 2011: 6–7). As early as the mid-1990s Ben Ali had recognised this problem. For example, in his 1999 speech after he had won the presidential election for his third term, he promised to upgrade infrastructure (Erdle 2010: 120). He repeated this promise again and again over the years, although he produced no tangible results. He therefore raised expectations only to dash them by his inaction, leading to frustration and anger, which was manifested later in the protests.

A third problem with the functioning of the economy was the persistently high unemployment figures, especially among educated young people. Although the macro-economy was growing, the regime was less successful in attracting foreign investment after 2000 and even in convincing the private sector to invest – both being necessary for job creation (Erdle 2010: 116; Zisenwine 2011: 37). This decline in new private investment made the state rely mainly on the momentum from privatisation of state enterprises. According to the World Bank (2010), average real economic growth was still robust at 3.3 per cent in 2009, albeit lower than the 6.3 per cent it had been in 2007. Thus Tunisia did not experience a recession but the relative economic decline led to a government stimulus with promises of the creation of more state jobs, increases in state payrolls and an emphasis on development projects. In September 2010 the International Monetary Fund (IMF) projected a 3.8 per cent increase for 2010.

There was still the gnawing problem of unemployment, however. The expanding export industries had been in clothing and agriculture, which employed low-skilled workers and thus did not generate much further employment for educated young people (Paciello 2011: 6). Moreover, they were not competitive *vis-à-vis* other countries and hence their long-term prospects were uncertain (Erdle 2010: 116).

Ben Ali recognised this problem of unemployment as far back as the 1990s. He proceeded to create two special funds under his immediate supervision: the National Solidarity Fund (FNS) and the National Employment Fund (FNE), set up in 1994 and 1996 respectively. The FNS was set up to finance social and physical infrastructure in under-developed and disadvantaged areas, whereas the FNE was established to support micro-credit schemes and provide for the training of young jobless Tunisians. Unemployment was officially 15 per cent (and 25 per cent unofficially) of the Tunisian workforce, and thought to be twice that among the young. Moreover, Ben Ali depicted fighting unemployment and creating jobs as 'the priority of priorities' in his 15 November 1999 speech (ibid.: 120). He was supported in this by his elite, who prioritised jobs and the avoidance of mass lay-offs as the measure of stable control over economic efficiency in confronting and being ever-watchful of possible Islamist social engineering (ibid.: 359–60).

Many analysts, however, believed that there was a serious discrepancy between the grandiose government discourses and the reality of actual political practices (ibid.: 115). These discourses proved to be counterproductive for the regime as they raised expectations only for them to be dashed once again, resulting in frustration and anger. Since the time of his re-election in 2004, Ben Ali had not instituted substantial new reforms in the internal policy field (ibid.: 125). On the contrary, the National Employment Fund had been reduced in order to decrease government expenditure (Goldstone 2011: 12). The number of jobs created had declined from 80,000 in 2007 to 57,000 in 2009 (Paciello 2011: 5). This was especially significant in that the number of young people entering the job market was increasing dramatically at the same time. Since 1990, the youth population (aged 15 to 29) had grown by 50 per cent, according to Jack Goldstone (2011: 12). Moreover, Ben Ali's modernisation endeavours involving free university studies had led to an explosion in the number of educated young people, making it 'difficult, if not impossible for any government to create enough jobs to keep pace' (ibid.).

The high expectations of educated young people were dashed, resulting in a situation about which Eric Andrew-Gee concluded: 'The absence of work violated an unspoken bargain struck between Ben Ali and the people: You ignore our iron fist and we will supply you with jobs' (Andrew-Gee 2011: 1). The dissonance between the hierarchy of the young for social justice and Ben Ali for stability was coming to a head. Matters reached crisis proportions when Mohamed Bouazizi set himself on fire on 17 December 2010 in desperation, in protest against his enduring unemployment and subsequent unjust treatment. This young man had become a street vendor selling vegetables in the streets of Sidi Bouzid in central Tunisia, but was prevented from plying his trade by a female police officer, who had confiscated his cart and goods, accusing him of not having the necessary legal permit to sell his items, which made matters even worse. Bouazizi became a symbol for young university graduates, who empathised with him since they also suffered from unemployment. He was depicted on the Internet as a college graduate, although according to his sister he had never graduated from high school. Bouazizi's self-immolation was the spark that ignited the protests that engulfed Tunisia. Ben Ali did visit Bouazizi in hospital and promised to send him to France to a treatment facility, but did not follow up on it prior to Bouazizi's death, eighteen days after the immolation, on 4 January 2011 ('Mohamed Bouazizi' 2011: 1–2).

At Bouazizi's funeral in Sidi Bouzid, attended by 5,000 people, many chanted 'Farewell Mohamed, we will avenge you . . . We will make those who caused your death weep' (ibid.). Henceforth he was considered a martyr, to be avenged by protests, which increasingly were morphing from economic discontent to political demands for the stepping down of Ben Ali, since there seemed to be no hope of a solution to the unemployment problem within the existing regime.

It was no wonder that Ben Ali endeavoured, on 9 January 2011, a few days before his abrupt departure on 14 January 2011, to make a last-ditch effort to co-opt these young protesters with promises of investing $5 billion in development projects in order to employ 50,000 university graduates over the subsequent few months. When this had no effect in quelling the protests, he again promised (the very next day, 10 January 2011) to create 300,000 new jobs in the next two years (Paciello 2011: 9). He even went so far as to promise to refrain from shutting down the Internet, so dear to the young people, and not to run for the presidency again. But it was too late. As one youth put it, 'These are the same promises he made last week, that he made a few years ago, that he made in 1987, but on the ground it is always the same' (Kirkpatrick 2011a: 2).

A fourth, and perhaps the most serious, problem with the functioning of the economy was that Tunisians blamed corruption among the elite for their lack of jobs. Indeed, several protesters who had stormed the President's family mansion in Hammamet said that it was the corruption of the first family and not the country's economic problems that was the real motivator of their protests (ibid.: 3).

The conditions for relative deprivation, although dormant and whispered about, had finally surfaced. Ben Ali had managed to co-opt only the shrinking elite in his endeavour to guarantee the stability of his rule, but in the process he had lost the majority of Tunisians, who resented this preferential treatment. Not only were the latter not co-opted but they had become pro-active in calling for social justice, thus creating an intolerable dissonance in the hierarchy of their values and those of the ruler. Tensions were heightened because Tunisians perceived no possibility of redress and no chance of upward economic and social mobility as long as Ben Ali's regime stayed in power.

How corrupt was the regime, in fact? The Corruption Perception Index compiled by Transparency International for 2010 seemed to be at odds with reality. It gave Tunisia a score of 4.3 (down from 5 in 2005) on a 10-point scale (where 10 represented least corrupt and 1 most corrupt), placing Tunisia relatively well internationally at 59th out of 178 countries ('Corruption Perception Index 2010 results' 2011: 12). Perhaps this was due to the fact that the national chapter of Transparency International was not allowed to conduct independent investigations from within Tunisia (Henry 2011: 13).

In reality, corruption had increased in the previous decade, becoming even more intolerable in the last two years of Ben Ali's rule, resulting in the 'plutocracy phase' of the Tunisian economy (Kaboub 2011: 7). At the same time Tunisia seemed to be taking measures against corruption. In 2008 Tunisia had ratified the UN Convention against Corruption. The Ministry of the Interior was assigned to combating fraud. The Audit Office of the Republic of Tunisia was tasked with monitoring financial irregularities in public enterprises. But its effectiveness was limited as it depended administratively on the Council of State, which Ben Ali chaired, and therefore it did not investigate Ben Ali's extended family and its allies for such matters (Henry 2011: 12).

Members of the family of Ben Ali and his wife, Leila Trabelsi, exercised extensive control over the private sector even though the country was undergoing market-oriented reforms. They got preferential treatment in the sale of public holdings during the privatisation efforts. Moreover, they hindered the rise of a competitive and autonomous private sector by such measures as defamation, coercive taxation, selectively redistributing benefits from economic policies to themselves, extorting private and public lands, forcing banks to give them loans amounting to more than $1.7 billion with no repayment guarantees, and receiving 'commissions' to broker business deals in order to amass billions of dollars and to build a gigantic business empire in quasi-monopoly businesses such as retail, telecommunications, media and real estate. Moreover, many of the resources of the '26–26 Fund', designated for impoverished people's welfare, were instead distributed through 'clientelist' networks to co-opt select business people. Nepotism thus became the main channel for the distribution of jobs, which especially frustrated and angered many of the young (Henry 2011: 2;

Kaboub 2011: 7; Paciello 2011: 7–8). Also, the greed of the Family tended to discourage innovation and investment efforts in that entrepreneurs could not be sure they would be able to reap rewards since they risked becoming the targets of family predators (Erdle 2010: 229).

Tunisians gossiped and spread rumours in private about the kleptomania of Ben Ali's extended family. According to Steffen Erdle, writing in 2010, just prior to the toppling of the President, 'Allegations of corruption within the circles of *pouvoir* [have] been rampant since a couple of years to the point of becoming *chose commune* in private conversations with many Tunisians' (ibid.: 228). These popular suspicions about 'crony capitalists' and the Family centred on rumours, as there was no freedom of information law to show the true finances of the government (Henry 2011: 13). Ben Ali's 'Shadow Budget' was used to co-opt whoever he pleased without scrutiny. The presidential palace thus became an informal 'Shadow Government', where actual decisions were arrived at (Erdle 2010: 140, 148).

The Ben Ali extended family included seven clans: the Ben Alis, the Trabelsis (Ben Ali's wife's clan), the Kefis, the Shiboubs, the Mabrouks, the Zarrouks and the Materies. They were only the tip of an iceberg which included several business tycoons, who had managed to marry into the clans, making altogether 60 ruling families bent upon profiteering and amassing great wealth but not actually occupying public office, contenting themselves instead with informally influencing policy through the Palace (ibid.: 145, 146, 149, 445).

Tunisians saw confirmation of their suspicions about the extent of corruption in the well documented secret diplomatic dispatches from the US ambassador, which were created on 23 June 2008 and made public and released by WikiLeaks on 7 December 2010 (WikiLeaks 2010). These confirmed their perceptions of an ever-widening gap between the super-rich (especially the privileged family of Ben Ali's wife, Leila Trabelsi, and 'crony capitalists') and the poor, which spawned and accentuated feelings of relative deprivation, sparking the uprisings. Ambassador Robert F. Godec wrote, 'Although the petty corruption rankles, it is the excesses of President Ben Ali's family that inspire outrage among Tunisians'. He continued, after citing instances of the extravagances of the Trabelsis and other relatives: 'With Tunisians facing rising inflation and high unemployment, the conspicuous displays of wealth and persistent rumors of corruption have added fuel to the fire'. He cited the protests in the region of Gafsa as a case in point of 'the discontent that remains largely beneath the surface'. He warned ominously of the fragility of the regime: 'This government has based its legitimacy on its ability to deliver economic growth, but a growing number of Tunisians believe those at the top are keeping the benefits for themselves' (ibid.: 5). He concluded that as a result of this Tunisia's economic investors were staying clear, because 'Corruption is the elephant in the room; it is the problem everyone knows about, but no one can publicly acknowledge' (ibid.: 6).

The demonstrators wanted the freedom to cross these Red Lines imposed on the media by the regime and to write about the corruption of the Family that had enraged them so (Hanafi 2011: 2). However, there was a growing consensus among Tunisians that WikiLeaks was not the major cause of the uprisings, but that people were nevertheless interested in reading the leaked documents, if only to confirm their suspicions. As one politician put it: 'The Youth of Tunisia were the ones who made the revolution, not WikiLeaks' (Ajmi 2011: 2).

People power versus the power of repression

Repression in the name of stability was prioritised by Ben Ali initially in the 1990s, following an early 'Tunisian Spring' of liberalisation after he had first come to power in 1987. At that time, the President had a period of thawing relations with the main opposition, the Islamists. Ben Ali used religion to consolidate his new position. He saw to the building of hundreds of new mosques and restored religion to its former pre-Bourguiba stature. He even went on the haj to Mecca, which was much-advertised. But he wanted to promote his brand of Islam, the 'true real Islam', an apolitical Islam (Versi 2000: 4; Erdle 2010: 282–3).

Once it became apparent that the Islamists were gaining ground politically in the elections of 1989, he clamped down on them. In line with this, imams were appointed and paid by the state (Henry 2011: 9). Parties based on religion were banned. This dashed the expectations he had raised during his first years in office when he had opened up the system and allowed opposition parties. Especially hard-hit was the newly constituted al-Nahda (Renaissance) Party, born from the openly Islamist *Mouvement de la Tendance Islamique* (Islamic Tendency Movement), the MTI. The Islamist Party resorted to demonstrations and perpetrated a violent attack against an office of Ben Ali's ruling party. The President took on the Islamists from 1990 to 1992, when they were neutralised. He arrested thousands of them and forced others into exile, and many were killed (Halpern 2007: 85).

At first, Tunisians, fearful of the instability in neighbouring Algeria, which was caused by extremist Islamists, acquiesced through a 'national pact' with Ben Ali. However, the President, instead of reinstituting liberalisation after the clampdown on the Islamists was complete in 1992 (that is, after he had been in power for five years), became even more repressive, which led to human rights abuses. He suppressed political discourse in general, including that of the secular opponents of the regime.

Repression was increased even more following the terrorist attack by a suicide bomber in April 2002 which killed nineteen people, including eleven tourists, at a synagogue in the resort of Djerba, for which al-Qaeda claimed responsibility. In 2003, Tunisia, having joined the US 'war on terror', enacted the Anti-Terrorism Law on Support of International Efforts against Terrorism and Money Laundering (known as the 2003 Anti-Terrorism Law), giving itself new powers of arrest, which were used against political and religious freedoms of the people in general because the law was so vague that it allowed for wide inter-pretation by the security forces of the Tunisian state (Mullin and Shahshahani 2011: 124; 'Promises and challenges' 2011: 151–2). Moreover, it allowed the monitoring and disruption of personal communications (Erdle 2010: 306).

In late 2006 and early 2007, fourteen suspected Islamists, reportedly with al-Qaeda links, were killed in a shoot-out with security forces and hundreds of people were arrested. In its final two years, the Ben Ali regime cracked down on Tunisian civil liberties even harder in its endeavour to silence all domestic critics of the regime. In 2010, an amendment to the Penal Code was passed to criminalise any complaints about human rights abuses to foreigners, which were henceforth to be treated as treasonous. It is believed that this was done to create an untarnished image in the eyes of the EU, with which Tunisia wanted to acquire advanced partnership status (Henry 2011: 7).

For Ben Ali, the 'Security-first' approach, a priority expressed to Steffen Erdle (2010: 291), entailed a preponderant police force and pervasive *Mukhabarat* (Intelligence Services). Thus, the power base of the President resided in the secu-rity community and hardly in the civilian or military institutions. 'The security and secret services have . . . become an integral, even essential element, of the regime apparatus – and the use of coercion a normal aspect of political life', wrote Erdle (ibid.: 433). Their disproportionate use of force against a tiny group of opponents, once the Islamists were neutralised and against an opposition whose strength had declined, had increased dramatically since the early 1990s, so much so that there were even protests from within the state elites about the excessive use of repression as being unjustified and counterproductive (ibid.: 308). Perhaps the coercive actions of the security apparatus can be explained by its wish to maintain its *raison d'être*, along with its influence with the state and its position in the society (ibid.: 446).

Indeed, Tunisia was deemed to have become a 'police state' by the 1990s by Clement Henry, who estimated that there were around 80,000–150,000 police in the 1990s, two to four times their number in the mid-1980s. This amounted to one agent for every 110–15 Tunisians (Henry 2007: 301–2). Laila Lalami puts the figure as high as one police officer for every 40 adults (Lalami 2011: 8).

Human rights abuses were perpetrated in the name of the security of the state. There were numerous incidents of torture and other ill-treatment of citi-zens by the security forces, who were involved in the arbitrary arrest, detention (whether incommunicado or otherwise) and interrogation of real or perceived political dissenters (Amnesty International, 24 January 2011: 2). Thousands of Tunisians were detained for indefinite periods of time without formal charges ('Promises and challenges' 2011: 149–50). Although in 2005 Ben Ali began pardoning many Islamist prisoners, and had ordered the release of all al-Nahda detainees by 2008, he continued to repress the former political prisoners, according to Human Rights Watch (2010a). They were prevented from finding work, from relocating for a job, or from travelling, and hence were condemned to a life of poverty. Also, they were subjected to constant police monitoring and questioning of their families and neighbours, thus making them 'social pariahs' (ibid.: 1).

The judicial system was compromised as well. The judges were not independent, especially since their appointment procedures were flawed (Amnesty International 2011: 2). The appointment and dismissal of judges was arbitrary depending upon whether they toed the lines of the state and therefore they were at the whim of the President and his family. Accusations of police brutality were usually suppressed by the judges in violation of Tunisia's international treaty obligations. Defence lawyers, especially those of human rights activists, were often harassed by the police (Henry 2011: 11). Moreover, there was a practice of trying civilians before military courts (Amnesty International 2011: 2).

The peaceful exercise of the rights to freedom of expression, association and assembly was limited by law too. Articles 48 and 51 of the Press Code respectively criminalised defamation of the President and gave a broad definition to defamation. Articles 61 bis and 121–2 of the Penal Code dealt with incitement to rebellion by speech in public meetings or places. Articles 6 and 7 of the Law of Public Meetings prohibited meetings deemed by the Government to disturb the peace and public order and allowed the presence of security officials at the meetings (ibid.).

On the eve of the revolution, conditions for the hierarchical dissonance of priorities between those of the forces of Ben Ali fixated on stability and those of the people alienated by twenty years of repression simmering with the desire for dignity and freedom were ripe. But how did people power come about? The fact that a frustrated individual had set himself on fire prior to Bouazizi and no revolution had occurred (Chomiak 2011: 75) showed the importance of other factors. First, unlike in the past, the regime used unusually excessive force; second, the people had been becoming accustomed to contentions with the state since the early 2000s; third, tech-savvy individuals learned to bypass the state-controlled traditional media through the use of the Internet and social media and through cellphone videos showing the excesses of state repression, which were disseminated regionally and internationally; fourth, the labour union (UGTT) and the lawyers' associations abandoned their passivity and instead became proactive against the regime; fifth, the army refused to fire on the demonstrators. In the following, these factors are discussed in turn.

First, as long as the repression was predictable and sustained in a limited way, it worked over the years in subduing the bulk of the Tunisians. But once it became sudden, unpredictable, unjustifiable and extremely excessive, as exhibited by the regime's use of force against demonstrators (especially in Thala and

Kasserine, where the security forces were aided by snipers, carrying out a series of massacres between 8 and 12 January 2011, and where thirteen people were killed according to Al Jazeera's estimates (Rifai 2011: 3)), it shocked and enraged the masses nation-wide and boomeranged against the regime. The dissonance had become intolerable. The people's dormant hatred of the regime awoke with a vengeance, overcoming their fear. The ratio of regime hatred to regime fear tilted towards hatred on a scale of attitudes. So long as the ratio was fractional (where fear exceeded hatred) no protest action was taken by the people, but when the ratio exceeded 1.0 protests became prevalent and persistent. Henceforth, the more the regime used extreme and unjustifiable repression the more the bulk of the people became determined to exercise what became known as the 'people power' of vast demonstrations. There seemed to be a threshold beyond which increased repression would become counterproductive.

Second, the history of contentious politics, a precedent to people power, albeit not as widespread, was a decade long. According to Laryssa Chomiak, it was this history of contentious confrontations and not the single event of Bouazizi's self-immolation that should be dwelt upon as harbingers of the Jasmine Revolution (Chomiak 2011: 75). A lid had been kept on contentiousness up until around the 2000s. Permits for demonstrations had been applied for but were usually denied. Unrest, albeit on a limited scale, had been increasing since around the early 2000s. The regime responded with moderate repression and contained it easily, but the cumulative effect of the unrest was to break the people's habit of obedience and submission. In June 1999, bloody clashes had occurred during a football match. In the spring of 2000 protesters in the southern provinces had shouted anti-regime slogans while smashing public buildings. In April 2000, there was a hunger strike by a journalist, Toufik Ben Brik. Also in 2000, signs of discontent multiplied, as seen in the spectacular defeats of pro-RCD party candidates in the elections of the Tunisian lawyers' association and human rights league. In July 2001, Mokhtar Yahyoui, a judge from the Tunis Court of First Instance, sent an open letter to Ben Ali about the lack of independence of the judiciary, and when he refused to repent he was dismissed and later expelled from the magistracy. In 2005 there was a hunger strike by fifty lawyers (Erdle 2010: 121, 122, 127).

Also in 2005, labour disputes assumed prominence when clashes occurred between demonstrators and police in the southern mining districts of Redeyef and Feriana over unemployment and rising living costs. The protests were triggered by allegations of corrupt recruiting practices by the national phosphate company, which was the largest employer in the region. So far, the protests had been concentrated in the south and called for changes from above – that is, they demanded reforms. Repression was used on a limited scale, even in the case of the later demonstrations in Gafsa, again over the hiring practices of the state-run Companie Phosphate de Gafsa (Gafsa Phosphate Company or CPG). The workers, unable to rely on the local branch of the General Tunisian Workers' Union (UGTT) as they believed it had struck an unfair agreement with the CPG, took to the streets protesting against gross neglect by the Ben Ali regime. These demonstrations swiftly led to a loosely organised social movement across the Gafsa region. As a result of the sporadic clashes, which continued in the spring of 2008, the President sent the military into Gafsa and Redeyef. The ensuing repression resulted in the fatal shooting of two protesters in June 2008 and the quashing of the demonstrations (Chomiak 2011: 72–3).

Third, as the Tunisian traditional press tended not to cover these occurrences owing to state blockage, Internet-savvy activists started to disseminate information about these events via e-mail and Facebook (ibid.). Although Ben Ali, on 18 August 2008, ordered the shutting down of Facebook, it was unlocked by 3 September 2008 as a result of an international Facebook campaign. Despite this, six young activists called, via Facebook and Twitter, for an organised event called 'Tunisie en Blanc' (Tunisia in White) to take place on 22 May 2010 to demonstrate peacefully, by wearing white and going to cafés, against Internet censorship in Tunisia, this time in Tunis, the capital city. However, security officers detained some of the organisers of this six-day-long Facebook group and did not allow individuals dressed in white to sit in cafés on Avenue Bourguiba in Tunis, which was later to become the site of the Jasmine Revolution (ibid.: 74–5).

Although Article 1 of the Press Code and Article 8 of the Tunisian constitution guaranteed freedom of the press and publication, and, though Ben Ali expressed his support for freedom of expression in his 7 November 2000 speech, the reality was perceived to be different, as revealed by the Tunisian Journalists Association on 3 May 2002 (Miladi 2011: 3). In the same year the regime struck at journalists and bloggers when it arrested the first cyber-dissident Zouhayr Yahyaoui (Erdle 2010: 262). According to Reporters Without Borders, the Government filtered opposition websites and monitored cyber-cafés, and recorded the identities of their users. Moreover, social file sharing sites such as DailyMotion, YouTube and Facebook were regularly blocked (Reporters Without Borders 2010: 1). The Tunisian Internet Agency of the regime was active in this campaign. It censored and monitored Internet users, preventing them from accessing pages containing 'unacceptable' political content (El-Issawi 2012: 5). Moreover, it mounted 'phishing' attacks on Gmail and Facebook accounts, collected passwords and e-mail lists of suspected opponents of the regime and arrested prominent bloggers (Garton Ash 2011: 2).

Thus the Internet was a tool both of the oppressors and of the oppressed. However, according to Timothy Garton Ash, 'On balance it offers more weapons to the oppressed' (ibid.). It offered an avenue for the activists to bypass the controlled traditional media and Ben Ali's press codes, which shaped coverage of the news and imposed fines and prison sentences for violators crossing the Red Lines set by the state against publishing or broadcasting news critical of the regime. Journals were screened before publication. The Ministry of Communication was responsible for the overall media and the Ministry of the Interior approved applications of new print publications. Moreover, the Agency for External Communication, created in 1990 and put under the Ministry of Communication, determined the funding and hence viability of media outlets, as it controlled the distribution of advertising revenue from public administrations to them (El-Issawi 2012: 4).

Although private 'independent' radio and television media were permitted in the mid-2000s, they were controlled by the unwritten rules of the Red Lines of not presenting opposing opinions, especially criticising regime corruption, so much so that the private media exercised self-censorship in order to survive (Miladi 2011: 3). Repression increased to an unprecedented level around two years before the ousting of Ben Ali, contributing to an increase in frustration with the regime and exacerbating the dissonance of priorities between those of the ruled for freedom of expression and dignity and those of the ruler for stability. In fact, after Ben Ali won the presidential election of 2009 by 89.62 per cent of the vote, he instigated regime reprisals against the media, for example against ten independent journalists (Reporters Without Borders 2010: 1).

With the regime censoring and controlling the traditional media, the activists found an outlet for their priority through the new media which had developed over the previous decade. How prevalent was the new media in Tunisia? By June 2010 around 34 per cent of Tunisians were Internet users ('Tunisia: country profile' 2011: 3). An estimated 18 per cent of Tunisians were on Facebook, which Ben Ali had neglected to block in time (Garton Ash 2011: 1). Thus Tunisia had one of the highest Facebook membership rates in the world, according to Marc Lynch (2012: 74). According to another estimate by *e.politics*, roughly 2 million Tunisians were on Facebook, Twitter being less pervasive with perhaps 500 active users within Tunisia's borders, whereas YouTube was not available as it was government-censored. Around 85 per cent of the population had cellphones (and 5 per cent smartphones) ('How social media accelerated Tunisia's revolution' 2011: 1). Activists relied on images taken by cellphones and disseminated via Facebook and the satellite TV network broadcast out of Qatar, Al Jazeera. It is estimated that more than half of Tunisian TV audiences tuned in every night to Al Jazeera (Miladi 2011: 4). Although the Al Jazeera offices in Tunisia had been shut down back in 2006 by the Ben Ali regime, which had also proceeded to close its embassy in Doha, Qatar, in protest at the TV station's 'hostile campaign' against it, the network had built and maintained a strong relationship with online activists. It therefore had the means to cover, and the motive for covering, the protests once they broke out (Lynch 2012: 76).

How did all this new media come together in December 2010 and January 2011? How did the eruption of the protests begin? Here is the story of the man on fire, Bouazizi. He was not the first person to burn himself in protest. Back on 3 March 2010 another street vendor, Abdesslem Trimech, had set himself ablaze in the town of Monastir in the far South but this did not receive any significant media coverage. According to Yasmine Ryan, 'The key difference in Sidi Bouzid was that locals fought to get news of what was happening out, and succeeded' (Ryan 2011: 2). A video clip posted on Facebook by Bouazizi's cousin of the victim's mother peacefully protesting outside the municipality building, happened to be picked up by Al Jazeera's new media team in Qatar and broadcast on TV, giving it a wide audience. Activists were emboldened and planned more protests via Facebook until the protests became national in scope, as the shocking images of police brutality went viral on social media and Al Jazeera (ibid.). Then, people poured into the streets of even the capital city, Tunis, and began to organise themselves via cellphones and Facebook, feeling a sense of solidarity ('How social media accelerated Tunisia's revolution' 2011: 1). Each demonstrator became a citizen 'journalist', embodying 'a reflexive individualism' of carrying a cellphone and filming police brutality and repression, which was later to be posted on Facebook and Al Jazeera, bypassing the official media (Hanafi 2012: 205). One of the popular pages of Facebook, which had over 12,000 members, read 'Your people are burning themselves, Mr. President' (Miladi 2011: 5). Social media facilitated the protests but did not cause them.

The activists were helped by the cyber-activist group 'Anonymous', which in a counter-move struck a number of regime websites with 'direct denial service' attacks by shutting the websites down temporarily by flooding them with traffic. The top five government websites were knocked offline for a substantial period of time. Additionally, 'Anonymous' provided the protesters with methods of circumventing government censorship via proxies (Anonymous Operation Tunisia rages' 2011: 1; 'Operation Tunisia' 2011: 1).

Also fuelling the protests, especially among university students, was the video clip of a song performance, entitled '*Rais el-Bilad*' (O Country's President), sung by a 22-year-old rapper, Hamada Ben-Amor, who was nicknamed El Général, which became the theme song of the revolution but led to his arrest. The uprising had by this time spread from the interior sectors of the country to the capital and from the youth to the older generation and families, far beyond the traditional opposition (Lynch 2012: 77–8).

Fourth, what role did civil society play in the uprising and in the success of people power in overcoming the regime's power of repression? It was perhaps the excessive use of Ben Ali's security forces against the peaceful meetings of the labour union, Union Générale Tunisienne de Travail (UGTT), and the lawyers' syndicate, that precipitated their wrath and made them join the protests in force. Labour unions and professional associations of lawyers had thus far had a chequered, off-and-on history of co-operation wih the regime, alternating with suffering repression at its hands. The UGTT leaders had in the past often marched to the drum of the regime only to be challenged by their rank and file. The local union activists called for protests as early as 17 December 2010. The UGTT held a rally at Gafsa, on 28 December 2010, which was blocked by the security forces, which in turn made the national UGTT break away from the regime and throw its weight behind the protesters. At the same time, around three hundred lawyers held a rally near the government palace at Tunis in solidarity with the demonstrators, which was followed by a rally on 31 December at which lawyers were beaten by the security forces. This made them more determined to link political demands to economic grievances. On 6 January 2011, 95 per cent of Tunisia's 8,000 lawyers went on strike in protest against the beatings and police brutality towards the peaceful protesters (Rifai 2011: 2–3). This, in turn, had a cascading effect when the teachers went on strike as well. The UGTT and the lawyers' association came to the forefront of the protests in 2010 and 2011, putting to use their organisational skills to mobilise the protesters further, swell their ranks and contribute to the effectiveness of people power.

Fifth, what role did the military play in the final analysis in helping people power prevail over Ben Ali's power of repression? Faced with massive people power, the military was overwhelmed by the unprecedented sheer size of the crowds and decided not to intervene on the side of the security forces, which were proving to be inadequate in crowd control. This was one of the factors leading to the passivity, at first, of the military before it sided with the protesters. The other factor was the army's marginalised position in the Ben Ali regime, as a result of which it did not have a vested interest in saving the President, but on the contrary calculated that it had much to lose from the wrath of the people from which came some 20,000 out of a total of 27,000 soldiers in the Army, as conscripts (Brooks 2013: 6). These conscripts identified with the people from which they originated and hence were averse to firing on their fellow citizens.

In fact, the military was deliberately kept small by Ben Ali at around 35,000 soldiers, including the Army, Navy and Air Force, as he was afraid of a coup (Erdle 2010: 144). Moreover, it did not have a stake in the regime, because it was ill-funded, with a mere 10 per cent of the state budget and otherwise it was not involved in the economy – in other words, there was no military-industrial complex in Tunisia (ibid.). Also, it was confined to being a professional force whose top leaders were kept out of political positions in the government (Erdle 2010: 144; Knickmeyer 2011: 2). Further, its corporate identity and responsibility were separate from the highly unpopular coercive police who attempted to control the crowds. The military, not having the bad reputation for brutality of the security forces in the eyes of Tunisians, was propelled to seek and capitalise on popular sentiment in order to enhance further its long-term corporate interests (Brooks 2013: 10).

It thus had much to lose and very little to gain from firing on the protesters. The armed forces did not listen to Ben Ali, who wanted them to use live rounds if needed in Tunis, where the demonstrations had spread. Although the troops had moved into the streets of Tunis, they reportedly had deployed helicopters to stop paramilitary snipers of the regime from shooting from rooftops (Knickmeyer 2011: 1). While it is true that the army had, in the interior of the country, mainly acted as 'power brokers' interposing themselves between the protesters and the police to keep the peace, it is reported that on occasion, for example at Kasserine, it had been active in defending the people from Ben Ali's thugs, snipers and elite militia. But it was after they were deployed to Tunis that they assumed a different role from 'power brokers', taking on 'political' roles in the expediting of the departure of Ben Ali (Brooks 2013: 11–13). Indeed, the leader of the military, General Rachid Ammar, reaffirmed the reasoning behind the military's withdrawal from positions defending Tunis in the final days of Ben Ali's rule, stating 'Our revolution is your revolution . . . The army will protect the revolution' (Kirkpatrick 2011b: 1). People power had triumphed over the power of Ben Ali's repression in large part because of the military's stance.

Populist democracy (aspired to by the ruled) versus illiberal democracy on the part of the ruler

Although Ben Ali had instituted some measures of political liberalisation in an attempt to win over the people when he came to power in 1987, he soon reneged on his 'Tunisian Spring' in the 1990s. He allowed political parties and civil society in principle, but in practice he tightly controlled them, angering many Tunisians. Their hopes had been raised only to be dashed again and again. This was especially the case in 2002 when he called for a revision of the Tunisian constitution to remove his term limit and allow his re-election. The conditions for a hierarchical dissonance in values or priorities between ruler and ruled were being created. Whereas Ben Ali increasingly emphasised reining in freedoms in the name of stability, Tunisians called for achieving dignity and empowerment to deal with the country's economic woes through democratisation. To repeat, a Pew Research Study conducted on the eve of the revolution showed this widening dissonance. More Tunisians, 55 per cent, preferred a democratic government over stability, with only 38 per cent preferring a stable government even if there was a risk of its not being fully democratic ('Pew study' 2012: 2, 5).

Ineffective political parties

Although Ben Ali had instituted a multi-party system (1988 Party Law), he controlled the legalisation of parties, the possibility of their election through quotas, and their independence in participating in the assembly once they were elected, so much so that Tunisia was in effect an illiberal democracy, which was greatly at odds with the priorities of the ruled for a populist democracy. The Tunisian political parties were so subdued, and rendered so weak and ineffective, that they did not play a significant role in the uprising of 2010–11 (Dunne 2011: 1). Demands for more openness and greater political freedom had been made in the past by the intelligentsia, however, as well as by Tunisians living abroad and by Western pro-democracy organisations.

The ruling party, the Constitutional Democratic Rally (RCD), dominated the parliamentary elections. The single-list majority voting system, which provided for the victorious party list to win all the seats, resulted in a de facto guarantee of a quasi-automatic majority for the RCD (Erdle 2010: 104, 295). Even so, Ben Ali weakened the link between the party and the state institutions when he assumed the party chairmanship, exercising direct personal control over the RCD (ibid.: 100). Moreover, the ruling families' prominence contributed further to the de-institutionalisation of the Party. However, the RCD served an important purpose for Ben Ali, since through it the President controlled the National Assembly, which served as a 'democratic façade', a rubber stamp of the regime's policies, an instrument of co-optation, and a 'modern variant of the traditional *Bai'a* [Islamic oath of allegiance] binding the ruled to the ruler', as in other Middle Eastern countries (ibid.: 167–8).

So far as other parties are concerned, most were never legalised. Such was the fate of al-Nahda and the Tunisian Communist Workers Party (POCT) among many others. As legislation prohibited the use of the words 'Islam' or 'Islamic', the Islamist MTI (*Mouvement de la Tendence Islamique*) renamed itself *Hizb al-Nahda* (Renaissance Party). However, Ben Ali refused to allow it to participate in the 1989 parliamentary elections as a recognised party. Consequently, it ran its candidates as 'independents' ('Promises and challenges' 2011: 145). It won more seats than expected, garnering 13 per cent of the votes, which was more than that of all the secular opposition parties taken together. Its popularity indicated to the regime that it would not be as easily co-opted as the secularists (Erdle 2010: 105). Consequently the regime clamped down on it, by jailing many of its members and forcing its leader, Rachid Ghannouchi, to leave Tunisia in exile, only to return after the toppling of Ben Ali. By 1992, al-Nahda had been dismantled and consequently did not play a significant role in the uprisings of 2010–11.

The POCT was banned also throughout the Ben Ali years, and hundreds of its members were imprisoned and tortured. Also, its leader, Hamma Hammami, was eventually sent into exile in 2002. As government repression increased later on, the POCT joined the Islamists, the liberals, the leftists and the human rights activists in 2005 to form the October 18 Coalition of Liberty, Freedom and Human Rights, which called for a civil democratic regime to replace Ben Ali's illiberal democracy ('Promises and challenges' 2011: 142).

The legalised parties were a handful, a mere seven (Erdle 2010: 137). Of these three small opposition parties, the Democratic Progressive Party, the Democratic Forum for Labour and Liberties and the Renewal Movement, did not play a significant role in the 2010–11 uprising, although later they did join the transitional government (Dunne 2011: 1). This was so because Ben Ali did not allow any genuine opposition parties when he was in power. But he did provide a quota of 20–25 per cent of the Chamber of Deputies' 214 seats to be proportionally allocated in accordance with the votes won (Henry 2011: 4). Therefore, the legalised parties were invariably co-opted as they owed their positions in the Parliament and their finances to Ben Ali's regime.

Moreover, the legalised parties tended not to be connected to the man in the street. They had not bothered to campaign with the aim of building grass-roots support. Consequently, they had a very narrow social base. Their membership was concentrated among the intellectuals and the functionaries living in the urban centres of the coastal north and east, and was of an older generation (Erdle 2010: 246–7). Of course, they did not take part in the uprisings, because they deemed them to be too risky an affair.

The first pluralistic election for President took place in 1999. But the opposition candidates were limited by the requirements that they had to be chairmen for five years of the legal parties, already co-opted and represented in the Parliament, and they had to be not older than 70 (later, the age limit was raised to 75). Only two politicians qualified and Ben Ali won with 99.44 per cent of the votes (ibid.: 120). This holding of presidential elections gave a veneer of democracy to an otherwise authoritarian regime. But Ben Ali went further by amending the constitution in 2002 to do away with term limits and make himself eligible for many terms, leading to his being re-elected five times. However, this backfired, because Tunisians, being accustomed to his constant tinkering with the constitution, did not believe him when, days before departing from office, he promised that he would not change the constitution, meaning that he would step down in 2014 owing to his age, but to no avail. Moreover, the whole question of succession to an ageing leader, who was then 74, and the fear that a corrupt member of his despised extended family, or even his detested wife, might take over, did not bode well for Ben Ali. Tunisians wanted democracy, some even calling for a parliamentary system of government. How were they to achieve this? If the legalised parties were not effective, was civil society then the answer?

Civil society stifled
Freedom of expression and association and the right of freedom of assembly were guaranteed according to the Tunisian constitution in Article 8 and Tunisia's international obligations in the International Covenant on Civil and Political Rights (ICCPR), which it had ratified on 18 March 1969, and the African Charter for Human and People's Rights (ACHPR), to which the country was also a signatory. Both treaties reaffirmed Tunisians' obligations to meet these rights (Human Rights Watch 2010b: 37). Associations had to be legalised,

however, through registration – which according to a 1959 law required them to be apolitical and according to amendments to a 1969 law were confined to such government-approved specialisations as sports, culture, science, the arts, charity, social aid, women's issues and development (Henry 2011: 5). However, it was the practice of the regime to bypass the legalisation procedure by denying the receipt of applications from 'undesirable' associations. This was especially so in the case of 'independent' labour unions, which were attempting to break away from the co-opted Tunisian General Labour Union (UGTT) in spite of the fact that Article 250 of the Labour Code provided that the mere notification to the regime of an intent to found a union, a list of its officials and its constitution, would be sufficient for an organisation to operate legally (Human Rights Watch 2010b: 7, 36). Those not recognised but independent organisations were allowed neither to publicly criticise the regime nor to hold public meetings (Paciello 2011: 1).

Moreover, though the number of legally registered civil society organisations increased during Ben Ali's rule from 1,776 in 1987, when he came to power, to around 9,350 in 2009, only a dozen or so of them were independent (Henry 2011: 5). Also, the Government monitored the legal associations very closely. Articles 6 and 7 of the 1969 Law on Public Meetings allowed the presence of security officials at their meetings and prohibited non-governmental organisations (NGOs) from activities deemed by the regime to disturb the peace and public order (Amnesty International 2011: 2). Subsequent amendments to the law made it more difficult to form an independent association, and specifically the law of 1992 instituted a 'general' category, which opened an organisation to general public participation and hence to the danger of its being flooded by regime-loyal RCD activists (Henry 2011: 5).

Ben Ali controlled and co-opted most of the legal associations. The Tunisian Union of Industry, Commerce and Crafts (UTICA), the National Union of Tunisian Women (UNFT) and the Tunisian Union of Agriculture and Fishing (UTAP) were controlled by the ruling party and hence promoted the regime's interests (Henry 2011: 9, 10). According to Steffen Erdle, the business association, UTICA, and the labour federation, UGTT, prioritised stabilisation over democratisation; whereas the forces for democracy included the students, the Islamists and many of the free professionals, who wrote editorials, organised demonstrations and served in the Tunisian human rights movement (Erdle 2010: 225). It was this priority for democratisation and preference for a populist democracy by these forces that was a factor in challenging Ben Ali's illiberal democracy with its emphasis on stability and contributed to his overthrow.

The General Union of Tunisian Students (UGET) had a long history of opposition to the regime's efforts to restrict basic freedoms. For example, in 1993, UGET condemned the Government's campaign against Islamists and al-Nahda; in 1995 students struck against the regime's proposed reforms of higher education; in 1998, students demonstrated in protest over the Government's university policies; in 2006, they organised sit-ins and protests to pressure the officials of the University of Tunis Mahdia to change their minds and allow UGET to launch a federal office at Mahdia; and in 2009, they conducted a peaceful sit-in at al-Bassatine women's dormitory of the University of Manouba against unfair discrimination in its admission policy concerning housing denied to women from the impoverished southern regions of the country. The regime attempted to quell UGET student activism by police surveillance, harassment, arrests, and arbitrary detainment and torture of UGET leaders and activists. The Government even went so far as to attempt to maintain control of UGET by promoting pro-government students as the legitimate representatives of the student union (Human Rights Watch 2010b: 25–35). Moreover, according to UGET members, the pattern of repression increased since 2006 (ibid.: 26). It is, therefore, no wonder that students were at the forefront of the protests leading to the success of the revolution.

Although Ben Ali had promised pluralism when he had come to power in 1987, from 1990 this was not to include the Islamists. The Government henceforth imposed total control over the religious institutions. Mosques were required to remain closed outside prayer times and to be opened only for certain religious activities; and prayer leaders were to be subject to authorisation by the regime. While it is true that Islamic heritage organisations were created, they were supervised and financed by the Government (Erdle 2010: 301). Control over the religious institutions was so complete that, although Islamists were critical of Ben Ali, they 'did not play a prominent role in the protests that unseated Ben Ali' (Arieff 2011: 16). They were, however, to play a significant role in the post-revolutionary period.

Professional associations, such as the Tunisian Bar Association and the Journalists' Union, were, on the contrary, active in the protests against the Ben Ali regime. The judicial system lacked independence as it was manipulated by Tunisia's Superior Council of Magistrates, which nominated, assigned and disciplined the judges (Paciello 2011: 2). The Association of Judges was essentially shut down in 2005 when its leadership was replaced by docile judges. The Tunisian Bar Association was discouraged from holding meetings since the police surrounded and invaded them. Defence lawyers of human rights activists had their telephones tapped (Henry 2011: 10–11). Incensed by the repression it suffered, the Bar Association played a significant role by utilising its mobilisation capabilities in spreading the protests from the peripheries to the capital and from the young to all age groups (Hanafi 2012: 207).

The media civil society groups suffered a neutralisation process by the 1975 Press Law (Law 32-1975) and especially by its amendments in the Press Codes of 1988, 1993, 2001 and 2006, which, although they guaranteed freedom of the press provided for under Article 1, in practice exercised pervasive censorship in the name of security (El-Issawi 2012: 7). Also, the state, being the largest provider of advertising revenues, influenced the viability of the media. The Tunisian Press Law permitted the suspension, confiscation and closing of any 'unwanted' publications and even provided for fining and issuing jail sentences to journalists crossing the Red Lines of criticism of the regime, enabling the regime to move cases from the Press Code to the realm of the Penal Code (Erdle 2010: 301–2; El-Issawi 2012: 8).

The first and only legally recognised Tunisian journalists' union held its first founding Congress on 13 January 2008 with a membership of approximately one thousand print, radio and television journalists, encompassing both state-run and private media. Surprisingly, its elections resulted in a majority of six independent journalists over three pro-Government members for its nine-member board, thus portending an autonomous future, much to the chagrin of the regime (Human Rights Watch 2010b: 14). Accordingly, the Union proceeded with controversial reports on press freedom in Tunisia. Especially significant was its second report, which it released on 4 May 2009 and which criticised the Government for harassing and persecuting journalists, constricting their work and censoring the media. This prompted the regime to take measures that undermined the Union and led to the ousting of its democratically elected board. On 24 August 2009 the outgoing displaced executive board denounced the illegality of the electoral violations, but to no avail (ibid.: 17). Thus on the eve of the revolution no love was lost between the Government, which prioritised stability through controlling the media, and the majority of journalists, who emphasised freedom of the press.

Human rights associations were also critical of the regime. The Tunisian League of Human Rights (LTDH) did succeed in maintaining its independence in 2000 by preventing the RCD from electing its members to leadership positions on the LTDH board; but the organisation suffered consequences, being harassed by break-ins by unidentified thugs (believed to have police connections), by frivolous lawsuits and by the inability to hold a new congress, solicit new members or collect dues from its 3,500 members. Another organisation, the Association of Democratic Women (ATFD), was legally recognised and was believed to be a genuinely independent human rights association. A further organisation, the National Council for Tunisian Liberties (CNLT), although it was denied official recognition by the Government, continued to operate and even fielded a radio station, Kalima, and an online newspaper. When the regime shut down Radio Kalima in January 2009, it resumed broadcasting criticisms of the human rights abuses of the Government from Italy (Henry 2011: 5–6). As a result, all these human rights associations played an auxiliary role to the syndicates in the revolution. They supported the uprisings by providing documented information about death tolls and casualties in an attempt to influence international powers to take firm positions against the Ben Ali regime (Hanafi 2011: 3).

The civil society organisations which played a direct and decisive role in fuelling the uprisings were, as seen, the labour unions. However, this anti-regime
stance had not always been the case. The Tunisian General Labour Union
(UGTT), comprising some 600,000 members and 15,000 unions nationwide,
was often split over its support of the regime. The national leadership of UGTT
was co-opted by Ben Ali (Erdle 2010: 316). This led some of its independent
dissidents to wish to form the Tunisian General Labour Confederation (CGTT)
in order to better represent the interests of the workers in 2007. However, it was
prevented by the police from holding a press conference to announce its formation. Despite this and other difficulties, the union continued to hold meetings
for the next five years and supported the protest in 2008 over high unemployment in the Gafsa mining region. In this connection, Habib Guiza, one of the
founders of the union, expressed his union's priority thus: 'We are fighting for
the principle of pluralism. It is extremely important to continue to stand firm
in the face of government harassment and dismissal' (Human Rights Watch
2010b: 10). The CGTT's situation was made more difficult as the UGTT had
to approve, according to Article 376 of the Tunisian labour code, decisions by
unions to strike. Workers participating in unauthorised strikes faced possible
prison sentences from three to eight months in duration (Human Rights Watch,
October 2010: 11).

This authoritarian rule by the UGTT national leadership was challenged in
late 2010 too. Whereas in northern Tunisia, especially in the capital Tunis, the
UGTT leadership was negotiating with the regime, their counterparts in the
south were opposing the Government (Hanafi 2012: 207). Indeed, following
Bouazizi's self-immolation, people had gone to the union office in Sidi Bouzid
to demand that it show its opposition to regime corruption and had got a positive response ('Promises and challenges' 2011: 141). The spontaneous protests
were henceforth to be organised and to be spread from one periphery town to
another by these unions (Hanafi, 23 January 2011: 3). The national leadership
of UGTT changed its course, followed the directives of its rank and file and
took a strong anti-Ben Ali position once it realised that excessive force had been
used by the regime. Henceforth it supplied logistical support to the protesters
(Henry 2011: 9). This contributed to the organisation, spreading and ultimate
success of people power, and to demands to replace the illiberal democracy of
Ben Ali, with its emphasis on stability to the detriment of freedom, by a populist
democracy, which was prioritised by the majority of Tunisians.

Phase 2: Transition to democracy? The Jasmine Revolution in transition

How were the goals of the revolution to be achieved through people power?
Was the amorphous, leaderless people power to be stabilised, galvanised and

institutionalised, or was it to continue to be rudderless and directionless and not achieve the realisation of the revolution at all? In Tunisia two simultaneous trends emerged. First, there was people power attempting to be translated into democratic institutions through traditional politics, such as elections, and the replacement of the authoritarian government by a democratic one, albeit one tailored to Tunisian needs. Second, there was people power attempting to continue to exercise pressure on the Government through continued mass gatherings generated by the new media, much according to the adage 'Once the *jinni* is out of the bottle, it is hard to put it back'. Should another bottle be created? What form would it take? What shape would it take, and how long would it take to construct it in order to accommodate the *jinni*? And would it ever suit the *jinni* who has just achieved his/her independence and freedom?

Elections for the national constituent assembly

Tunisians were intent on achieving their priority, democracy through elections, as a first step. They turned out in large numbers on 23 October 2011 for the elections of the National Constituent Assembly, which was to appoint a new transitional government and draft a new constitution. According to the National Democratic Institute's electoral observation mission, 90 per cent of the registered voters, who comprised approximately 54 per cent of the Tunisian population, braved the sun, waiting for up to five or six hours to cast their ballots (Parker 2011: 1). Tunisians believed in the fairness of the election, which was monitored from start to finish by a truly independent election commission, the Independent High Authority for the Election (ISIE), which was perceived to be transparent, unlike its tainted counterparts in Ben Ali's Ministry of the Interior, and hence the people felt encouraged and emboldened to participate. Besides, the army, their defender against Ben Ali, was deployed to protect the polling stations, although the military itself did not vote (Muasher 2011: 1–2).

The initial enthusiasm for democracy was also reflected in the attempt to accommodate the many and diverse opinions of people power through political parties. It is estimated that around a hundred and ten parties were legalised and participated in the elections (Fisher 2011: 4). Moreover, the electoral system, based on proportional representation, was designed to include as many parties as possible in the drafting of the constitution and to prevent any one party from winning a landslide victory ('The Islamist conundrum' 2011: 58; 'Tunisia: Islamist party sweeps election' 2011: 1). The diverse parties ranged from the Islamist al-Nahda Party to the sundry secular parties and even the organisations of the remnants of the old regime, which after the dissolution of the RCD on 9 March 2011, regrouped while looking at small parties and independent lists, even adopting opportunistically the vocabulary of 'democratic transition' ('The Islamist conundrum' 2011: 58). However, a dampener was put on this scholarly optimism when a poll conducted on the eve of the election found that 61.4 per cent of Tunisians 'ignore political parties in the country' ('Ennahda movement' 2012: 3). So what did guide people power in the enthusiasm for democracy? Which parties would be the winners?

The election resulted in five parties moving far ahead of the pack. Al-Nahda won 90 seats, becoming the largest party in the 217 member Constituent Assembly; the Congress for the Republic (CPR) came in second with 30 seats; the Ettakatol was third with 21 seats; the Aridha Chaabia populist party was fourth with 19 seats (Ayari 2011: 2–3); and the Progressive Democratic Party (PDP) with 16 seats was fifth ('Tunisian Constituent Assembly election, 2011' 2012: 4). It appeared that the three frontrunners would divide the spoils since no single party had won a majority of seats.

The leading party, the Islamist al-Nahda, had assumed its name in 1989 but was never granted legal status and was even persecuted under Ben Ali, who declared in 1992 that he had succeeded in dismantling it completely. Al-Nahda was only to be legalised after the start of the revolution on 1 March 2011. Within a period of six months or so it had managed to garner an impressive number of votes. Perhaps this was due to its having in the past maintained, despite Ben Ali's repression, networks linking its members and supporting the families of political prisoners, and more immediately to provide charitable services to poor prospective voters (Brody-Barre 2012: 216).

Also, as an unemployed young college graduate put it aptly, 'religion is the source of Ennahda's [al-Nahda's] credibility' (Wolf 2011: 1). Accordingly, al-Nahda became, following the ousting of Ben Ali, the most organised party, owing to its grass-roots appeal. As a moderate conservative Islamist party, which purported to support workers' rights and women's education, al-Nahda was 'generally described as socially centrist with mild support for economic liberalism' ('Ennahda movement' 2012). According to Moncef Marzouki of the Congress for the Republic Party (CPR), the electoral success of al-Nahda, within the context of the 23 October elections, can be summarised thus: 'Tunisians want centrist politics . . . They want an Arab-Muslim identity (Ennahda) and also democracy and human rights represented by the two parties CPR and Ettakatol' (Watson and Shair 2011: 2).

The next party to consider, that came second in the elections, is the CPR, founded in 2001 by Moncef Marzouki, a medical doctor, who was also the founding member of the human rights National Committee for the Defence of Prisoners of Conscience. Although the party was not legalised and was even harassed by Ben Ali's security, it remained active in the human rights realm abroad and also at home, until finally it was granted legal status on 8 March 2011 after the revolution (Brody-Barre 2012: 217–18). Its election platform called for the abolition of Ben Ali's hated political police, the promotion of human rights, transparency and democracy through a civil state, and the creation of a constitutional court (Ayari 2011: 1).

The third party to consider is Ettakatol (The Democratic Forum for Labour and Liberties), which is led by Mustapha Ben Jaafar, who founded it in 1994. Ettakatol was legalised by Ben Ali in 2002 but stood 'outside' the parliamentary process, mainly because it did not want to add to the veneer of pluralism with which Ben Ali chose to mask his authoritarian regime. In the 23 October 2011 elections the party projected itself as a left-of-centre party. It emphasised gender equality and transparency using both traditional media and social media to mobilise its grass-roots supporters, especially among the young (Brody-Barre 2012: 218).

A deal was struck among these top three parties to form a governing alliance. In this deal, the Speaker of the Assembly was to be the Secretary-General of the Ettakatol Party, Mustapha Ben Jaafar, and the President of the Republic was to be the renowned human rights activist and CPR leader Moncef Marzouki. In this power-sharing arrangement, al-Nahda reserved for itself the Prime Minister's office by appointing Hamadi Jebali, its Secretary-General, to this post. Jebali had been the editor of *Al-Fajr*, the banned al-Nahda newspaper, and had been sentenced to sixteen years' imprisonment in 1992, having been charged with membership of an unauthorised organisation and with an intention to change the regime ('Ennahda movement' 2012: 2).

The ease with which the Islamists and secular liberals formed the 'Troika' can be attributed to their having begun to create a political society of mutual trust and of rules for democracy, as far back as eight years before the end of Ben Ali's regime. Al-Nahda's ideologue, Rachid Ghannouchi, and CPR's human rights activist, Moncef Marzouki, had met while in exile no fewer than twenty times in London over this eight-year period, as they knew each other well (Stepan and Linz 2013: 23–4).

Indeed, after the results of the election were known, Ghannouchi struck a conciliatory and all-inclusive note, telling a crowd of supporters:

> We will continue this revolution to realise its aims of a Tunisia that is free, inde-
> pendent, developing and prosperous, in which the rights of God, the Prophet,
> women, men, the religious and the non-religious are assured because Tunisia is
> for everyone. ('Tunisia: protests erupt' 2011: 2)

He was enunciating al-Nahda's stance of support for a 'civil' state. In its ideal form this would result in what Alfred Stepan summed up as 'twin tolerations', which are needed in a situation where both religion and democracy flourish, where 'religious authorities do not control democratic officials who are acting constitutionally, while democratic officials do not control religion so long as religious actors respect other citizens' rights' (Stepan and Linz 2013: 17). Neither a forced secularism nor an imposed theocracy would lead to democracy.

What about the opinion of Tunisians? Polls conducted both before and some time after the 23 October election showed approval of the Islamists. In

Al Jazeera's poll of 6 July 2011, 47 per cent of the respondents said that they strongly identified with Islamism, 19 per cent that they identified with liberalism and 19 per cent that they identified with Arab nationalism, with only 6 per cent strongly favouring communism or socialism ('Tunisians undecided ahead of October vote' 2011). A Pew Research Center Study, after the election in mid-2012, continued to show that Tunisians had a favourable view of al-Nahda, with 65 per cent approval. Also, two in three Tunisians viewed the party's leaders, Rachid Ghannouchi and the then Prime Minister Hamadi Jebali, favourably ('Pew study' 2012: 5).

A poll conducted a year later, in March 2013, by the market research company Sigma Conseil, showed that this enthusiasm had waned. Tunisians' trust in political leaders had declined, 59 per cent of the respondents stating that they did not trust any politicians or refusing to comment. Those who indicated trust ranked al-Nahda's former Prime Minister, Hamadi Jebali, third and the founder of the al-Nahda's Party, Rachid Ghannouchi, fourth behind the new Prime Minister, Ali Laarayedh (second), and, surprisingly, Beji Caid Essebsi, the founder of the opposition Nidaa Tounes Party and former interim Prime Minister during the immediate post-revolutionary period, as the most trusted. When people were asked 'What active politician would you choose for President if the elections were held tomorrow?' Essebsi again came first, with Jebali second with 29.1 per cent, Hamma Hammami, the Secretary-General of the Workers' Party, third and Laarayedh trailing in fourth place. Around 47.7 per cent did not agree with the choice of former Interior Minister Laarayedh to replace outgoing Prime Minister Jebali, because according to his critics Larrayedh had not performed well as Interior Minister, especially since he had not pushed for security reform adequately. Moreover, in contrast to the voters in the Constituent Assembly elections of 23 October 2011, respondents, when questioned about the upcoming 2013 elections for Parliament and the presidency, showed little enthusiasm. Around 61.1 per cent stated that they were unsure or did not intend to cast a ballot in the upcoming elections (Yaros 2013b: 1–3), now slated for late 2013.

This projected potential apathy of Tunisians concerning the traditional avenues of politics, namely elections, may be the result of several factors, including the nature of Tunisian party politics and the state of socio-economic developments or shortcomings to date, and may signal in large part a resort to, if not a return to and a reliance on, direct people power instead by the frustrated populace.

To overcome this potential apathy, generated, it is believed, by the plethora of political parties, many of the small political parties attempted to form coalitions for the elections of 2013. But these were often marred by a 'tradition of mistrust, discord, and personal interests' (Brody-Barre 2012: 225). An example of recent coalition-building is the coalition formed by the old elite in mid-April

2013. In the face of the ongoing debate about whether to exclude former RCD members from participating in future governments, the old elite attempted to come back, albeit without Ben Ali, by forming a coalition of six parties, reminiscent of Bourguiba's Destour, to continue the legacy of the parties that had ruled Tunisia prior to the 2011 revolution. Their immediate, though vague, aim was not to let al-Nahda 'give vain promises without taking real action' and to push for their own participation in politics as 'it is not right to exclude everyone else for his [Ben Ali's] errors' (Haffar 2013b: 2). This confrontational attitude towards al-Nahda is also reflected in other coalition-building efforts. According to Andrea G. Brody-Barre, Tunisian political parties tended to concentrate on the secular-versus-religious issue and on the role of Islam in the new state and to ignore other policy areas, a stance which was detrimental to party politics (Brody-Barre 2012: 225). Perhaps this neglect to offer choices on multiple other salient issues, especially concerning the economy, which sparked the revolution in the first place, was a reason for the alienation of future would-be voters and made them want to take matters into their own hands through direct people power.

Direct people power in action

Even though elections were taking place, Tunisians resorted to direct people power, which continued to remain vibrant. For example, demonstrations were held in front of the Media Centre, in Tunis, on 25 October 2011 by the families of the martyrs and the wounded. The crowd did not wait for the political parties to redress their grievances, as instanced by one woman who shouted: 'This is a wake-up call for the Tunisians who are engrossed with the political parties . . . We did not come to talk about parties, you keep yourselves busy with that' (Melki 2011: 1).

Politicians were not exempt from harnessing people power to circumvent parliamentary and governmental channels and to push their agendas by taking matters to the street. Notable here is the rally on 23 October 2012 staged by Beji Caid Essebsi, of the new Nidaa Tounes Party, the former interim Prime Minister during the post-revolutionary period. He declared that the new government had forfeited its legitimacy because it had not completed the constitution on time, within a year of the election of the National Constituent Assembly on 23 October 2011. Accordingly, he called for a fresh mandate to govern, to be arrived at by round-table talks outside the parliamentary venues and avenues. Essebsi was supported by anti-coalition secularists and wealthy Ben Ali loyalists and former ruling-class members who wanted to make a political comeback (Stepan and Linz 2013: 25).

Countering these groups, and also using people power was the organisation named the Leagues for the Protection of the Revolution (LPR). As a group with a cultural focus, the LPR claimed to prioritise the protection of the revolution's principles of dignity and human rights. However, it was accused of violating these very rights. Notably, it was accused by the opposition parties, the unions and journalists of threatening the critics of the Government in order to promote al-Nahda's interests, a connection which al-Nahda strongly denied. It was also accused by the opposition party, Nidaa Tounes, of involvement in the death of Lotfi Naguedh, a regional leader of the secular Nidaa Tounes Party during a demonstration called for by the LPR in the southern town of Tatouine in October 2012 (Dreisbach 2013: 2–3).

Another organisation criticising the LPR and also using people power was the UGTT. In its 6 April 2013 report, the UGTT accused the LPR of involvement in the 4 December 2012 demonstration, which led to attacks on its headquarters (Masrour 2013d: 2). Moreover, the Union resorted to people power by going on strike to protest against the violence against it by the religious right, most notably by the Salafi groups, which labelled UGTT an 'enemy of God' during demonstrations which resulted in the burning down of several UGTT regional offices in February 2012. The UGTT had asked the Government to investigate the violence but no immediate action was taken in bringing the perpetrators to justice. Perhaps the Union's resort to people power can also be explained by their not winning significant parliamentary representation in the 2011 National Constituent Assembly elections. Moreover, the UGTT was resisting the January 2013 appointment of al-Nahda members to key positions in the south for the largest mining facility plants (Stevenson 2013: 2).

People power was, however, most pronounced and reached unprecedented levels following the assassination of the secularist leftist politician, Chokri Belaid, on 6 February 2013. This had dire repercussions for traditional politics and for the path of orderly transition to democracy.

Belaid, the Secretary-General of the Democratic Patriots Party, was a critic of the Government. He specifically blamed al-Nahda for not doing enough to stop the violence by ultra-conservatives, like the Salafis, who targeted individuals and events, which they deemed to be against their strict interpretation of Islam. At a news conference the day before his murder, Belaid had prophetically warned against political violence (Doucet 2013: 2). As it turned out, an extremist Islamist, who claimed he was executing a *fatwā* (religious ruling) issued against Belaid, was among the four individuals later arrested in connection with the assassination (Samti 2013b: 2).

The Popular Front coalition (composed of twelve political parties, including Belaid's party, along with associations of environmentalists, leftist nationalists and independent intellectuals) and the newly formed (29 January 2013) Alliance for Tunisia (composed of five political parties, Nidaa Tounes, al-Massar, al-Joumhouri, the Socialist Party and the National Democratic Party) immediately called for a general strike. Their decision to rely on people power was accompanied by an attempt to circumvent the National Constituent Assembly, when they also proposed to suspend opposition membership in the Assembly (Masrour 2013a: 2).

Labour unions participated in the general strike and demonstrations. The demonstrators chanted for the resignation of the Prime Minister, Jebali, threw stones, and even set fire to a police station in the town of Boussalem. The violent protests spread across the country, with police resorting to warning shots and tear gas ('Strike called over Tunisia killing' 2013: 2).

After three days of mass protests and the setting on fire of some local head-quarters of the al-Nahda Party, pro-Nahda counter-demonstrations took place, attempting to reaffirm the legitimacy of the Government. Here, al-Nahda too resorted to people power. Ghannouchi, the ideologue of the party, warned that a counter-revolution by former regime elements was behind the unrest by attempting to deepen political divisions in the country. He stated 'The past is not dead' and called for reconciliation: 'Dialogue with words is better than dialogue with bullets . . . We have no choice, we are all on the same boat' (Yaros 2013a: 2).

The same reconciliatory note was struck by the Prime Minister, Jebali, who stated: 'We are different but should unite in the love for this country . . . We will not kill each other just because of our differences' (Haffar 2013a: 2). Accordingly, he called for the establishment of an apolitical technocratic government. He was supported in this by the UGTT, UTICA, and many members of the National Constituent Assembly. In this camp was the articulate dean of the Tunis Law School, Fadhel Moussa, who urged the reprioritisation of stability by stressing the need 'to stop this political mess and achieve a better stable political scene'; and instead of unruly people power, he continued to urge that Tunisia should 'not deviate from the democratic path we are working on' (ibid.).

People power was, however, not going to be neglected by any group that did not agree with the official line, including al-Nahda members who disagreed with Jebali. The hardliners in the party refused to give up key portfolios in the cabinet and threatened to take to the streets of the capital, which they did, insisting on the right of the party to govern as mandated by the 23 October 2011 election ('Ennahda says it may leave power in Tunisia' 2013: 2). Thereupon, the party overruled Jebali in its Shura Council meetings of 16 and 17 February 2013. He resigned on 19 February 2013. But while the Shura Council rejected the idea of an entirely apolitical technocratic government, it moved towards a cabinet that would include both politicians and technocrats as a compromise (Khlifi 2013: 2). It was revealed that, even before the assassination of Belaid, Jebali had been pressured by the opposition to consider the reshuffling of his cabinet, but had settled on the entirely technocratic government option after the murder of Belaid (Samti 2013a: 2).

In the ensuing negotiations al-Nahda preferred a five-party cabinet, with Wafa and the Islamic Block of Freedom and Dignity added to the Troika

members. These two opposition parties withdrew, however, after lengthy negotiations. But both the other two Troika members insisted on the neutrality of the
Ministries of the Interior, Justice, Defence and Foreign Affairs. They had their
wishes met in the new cabinet under the new Prime Minister, Ali Laarayedh,
who was the former Interior Minister and who had been the spokesman of the
Islamic movement from 1981 until his arrest in 1990. Al-Nahda was pressured
by the crisis and the ensuing people power to move towards making good on
the idea of a more inclusive government (Masrour 2013c: 2). According to
al-Nahda's post on its Facebook page, 28 per cent of the ministers of the new
cabinet were drawn from al-Nahda (down from 40 per cent in the previous
cabinet), and Independents formed 48 per cent of the new government ('Tunisia
PM Ali Larayedh unveils new government' 2013: 1).

Has the Tunisian Spring been realised so far?

'A revolution is like an earthquake. It takes time to form a new landscape', said
Ghannouchi in December 2012 (Doucet 2013: 1). The landscape has not been
fully constructed yet. The hierarchies of the values or priorities of Tunisians
have not been fully met. Indeed, this continuing challenge was behind, and was
a contributing factor in, the extensive scope of the demonstrations that erupted
after the Belaid assassination in February 2013.

What were the priorities of Tunisians after the revolution of January 2011?
A poll conducted by the International Republican Institute (IRI) in May 2011
shows the respondents' 'first mention' in the following hierarchical order:
security-sector reform, 36 per cent; job growth, 27 per cent; development and
reform of the economy, 9 per cent; organising of elections, 7 per cent; improving
living standards, 6 per cent; social reforms, 3 per cent; anti-corruption measures,
2 per cent; inculcating good values in government, 2 per cent; regional development, 1 per cent; achieving the goals of the revolution, 1 per cent; other, 3 per
cent; don't know/refusal, 1 per cent (Pickard and Schweitzer 2012: 4).

More recent polls, conducted around six months later in early 2012, indicated that the economy had risen to be the number one concern of Tunisians.
Specifically featured here were the job market and the need to strengthen the
sectors that had, prior to the revolution, led to 5 per cent growth per annum
(Laaribi 2012: 3).

The expectations of Tunisians had been raised by the revolution, but people
were confronted with harsh realities. The views of the young unemployed, who
were impatient for results and who wanted quick economic relief, were ones of
frustration going on two years into the revolution. One of them depicted their
plight: 'Nothing, nothing has changed . . . There are no jobs. All the revolution
gave us was freedom of expression' (Doucet 2012: 1). It was apparent that conditions conducive to unrest, if not another revolution, were ripe. It was no wonder

that the Tunisian President, Moncef Marzouki, warned that if the new number one priority, the Tunisian economy, was not fixed there would be a 'revolution within the revolution' (Lawrence 2012: 1).

Indeed, growth for the fiscal year 2011 declined to 0–1 per cent. The recession in Europe, which had accounted for 80 per cent of Tunisian trade, was a contributing factor. Further, with Tunisian instability, tourism dwindled by 50 per cent and foreign direct investment (FDI) declined by 20 per cent, with more than 80 foreign companies leaving Tunisia. The number of the unemployed increased to 700,000 (as against 500,000 at the end of 2010), owing to lay-offs, the return of Tunisian migrant workers fleeing the unrest in Libya, and the increased number of unemployed university graduates, who made up around 70,000 of the 120,000 persons entering the workforce each year. Therefore, unemployment rose to 17 per cent from 14 per cent prior to the revolution, and stayed officially at 17 per cent in 2013. Unemployment for the best educated individuals rose to an estimated figure of around 30 per cent in 2012. Moreover, poverty was worse than in 2010 and corruption in the bureaucracy and in the police force remained a serious grievance (Achy 2011: 5, 7; Le Nevez 2012: 2; Milne 2013: 2–3).

However, the Government started to take measures to reverse the rise in unemployment figures and to shift spending to the impoverished regions of the interior of the country. Also, al-Nahda leaders talked of a hybrid, a 'social economy' of free-market capitalism and socialism without clarifying the details. But the Government faced a dilemma. Should it accede to the IMF-endorsed policies and cut fuel and food subsidies and resume privatisation, which would run the risk of alienating further, and thwarting the short-term aspirations of, the youth who spearheaded the revolution, or not? (Milne 2013: 2–3).

Indeed, only 11 per cent of the respondents of a Pew Research Center Poll in the spring of 2013 believed that the Tunisian economic situation was 'good'. But they were more optimistic about their personal economic situation, with 42 per cent reporting that they expected it to be 'good', responding in the spring of 2013 (Pew Research Center 2013a). The Government needed to capitalise on this.

However, in another survey in 2013, this time by Transparency International, Tunisians reported that the level of corruption in their country had risen in the two years following the uprisings of 2011, with 80 per cent saying that it had worsened. Christoph Wilcke of Transparency International attributed this to the social and economic turmoil following the Arab Spring, which did not give the Government enough time or energy to push for reforms. This frustration with corruption could very well undermine the efforts of the Government to restore stability (Torchia 2013: 1).

Thus, there was a growing recognition among the Troika members that for a vibrant economy to emerge, they needed to re-stabilise the country and prioritise this. According to a poll released on 30 April 2013 by the Pew Research Center, 75 per cent of respondents still preferred democracy as a means of solving the country's problems, with only 22 per cent opting for a strong leader to do so. But when asked about the actual realisation of empowerment by April 2013, 61 per cent believed that they still did not have any say in their government (Pew Research Center 2013b: 60, 174). Clearly, the Tunisian Government needed to prioritise the development of democratic institutions too. But fifteen months after the election of the National Constituent Assembly, the country faced a prolonged deadlock over the drafting of the constitution, although there was talk of elections for Parliament and President projected for late 2013. A further destabilising factor was the rise of the Salafis, who were accused of deadly attacks ('Ennahda says it may leave power in Tunisia' 2013: 2). On the other hand, al-Nahda's foot dragging on the cancellation of the anti-terrorism law had antagonised prospective coalition members, for example the Wafa Movement, from joining a new, more inclusive cabinet (Masrour 2013b: 2).

In December 2012, Ghannouchi summed up the Government's stance thus: punishing acts of violence that break the law, but also reaching out to 'moderate' elements in all political groups. The result was, according to Ghannouchi, a government of 'moderate Islamists and moderate secularists' coming together. For him 'The revolution is not in danger', but he acknowledged that 'there was a battle about the post-revolutionary model' (Doucet 2013: 2).

The transition towards revolution in Tunisia: viability of the HD hypothesis and Pendulum Model

The HD hypothesis and the Pendulum Model are viable in explaining the transition towards revolution in the toppling of Ben Ali. As we have seen, conditions for the hierarchical dissonance of values prevailed in 2010 and 2011, with Ben Ali increasingly emphasising stability and Tunisians prioritising economic justice and a solution to the youth unemployment problem, which spawned feelings of relative deprivation. The injustice of the regime was not mitigated by its resorting to religion, even though Ben Ali had used this approach in the past (he had used it successfully when he had come to power in a bloodless coup). In fact, he clamped down on religion and used excessive force against his own people, over-stressing stability *vis-à-vis* the dignity of Tunisians, thus creating an intolerable gap in the hierarchies of values. The lack of a viable successor when he was ageing (he was 74), and the prospect of his being succeeded by a corrupt member of his despised family, dashed the hopes of the people too as regards their priority of transitioning towards democracy. Tunisians perceived no possible redress for their grievances via existing governmental institutions, and so they revolted and Ben Ali fell from power.

CHAPTER 3

The transition towards revolution in Egypt: the Arab Spring realised?

'Bread! Freedom! Social justice!' was the cry of enraged Egyptians as they protested at Tahrir Square in Cairo and in other cities, beginning on 25 January 2011. President Hosni Mubarak was toppled only eighteen days later, on 11 February 2011. In phase 1, the revolution erupted and Mubarak fell. Phase 2 represented a transition towards a second revolution as the country went through populist ownership and military management; tried to transition to democracy through parliamentary elections; experienced its first democratically elected President; and finally, in 2013, underwent a summer of upheaval engulfing the whole social fabric through a counter-revolution. But was the Arab Spring realised?

Phase 1: Revolution erupts and Mubarak falls

Why did the revolution erupt and why did Mubarak fall? Mubarak's old methods of co-optation, repression, and promises of political liberalisation, that had served him so well for almost thirty years, though showing some serious cracks of late, were no longer effective in saving his rule. Emboldened by the success of the Tunisian revolution against Ben Ali, the determined masses lost their fear of the regime and demonstrated, demanding the ousting of Mubarak too.

The underlying reason for the revolution was a hierarchical dissonance in values between the priorities of the ruler and those of the majority of Egyptians; this persisted, was not bridged, and ultimately undermined Mubarak's regime. The revolutionary groups of the ruled considered economic improvement to be their highest-priority value, as illustrated by the respondents to a Pew Research Center Poll in 2011, conducted on the eve of the revolution, in which 82 per cent considered this value to be 'very important', surpassing that of the law-and-order priority of the Egyptian President, which scored 63 per cent (Pew Research Center 2012). It is therefore no wonder that the first cry of the protesters was for 'bread', while Mubarak continued to emphasise his usual appeals to stability with security as his highest-priority value, and relegated the divisive neoliberal economic measures to second priority. This dissonance became intolerable, since, unlike the rulers of Morocco (Chapter 4) and Jordan (Chapter 5), who successfully reformed their monarchies, Mubarak did not resort to the palliative of religion, which could perhaps have saved his rule. At a time of crisis, when his legitimacy was questioned and the pendulum of his rule was out of equilibrium, he did not try to draw it towards equilibrium by using the soft power of Islam, as depicted by my Pendulum Model in connection with other rulers who enjoyed longevity and survived (Alianak 2007: 5).

Having given up hope of redress from the existing regime, the ruled gave vent to their frustrations, overcame their fears, and emphasised their dignity in attempting to secure on their own the economic and social justice denied them over the years, demanding the liberty to do so and demonstrating at the aptly named Liberation Square (Tahrir Square) in Cairo.

Social justice versus the co-optation of elites

In the face of the revolutionaries' first-priority demand for economic improvement, Mubarak's efforts to co-opt the ruled were perceived as being too limited, too late and at best inadequate, and also as further alienating many Egyptians. Economically, co-optation encompassed limited measures directed at the various classes of Egyptians, but in the end it was actually perceived as flagrantly favouring the small elite at the expense of the rest of the population at large.

Mubarak's economic co-optation, during his almost thirty-year rule, ended up concentrating resources on the ever-shrinking corrupt small elite at the expense of the middle class, who at best saw their chances of aspiring to the upper class considerably diminished and at worst saw their continued middle-class status jeopardised. While at times giving the increasingly strike-prone public workers small wage concessions, which were only gobbled up by the petty corruption of his appointed state managers, Mubarak completely lost touch with the Arab street, and neglected and antagonised the poor.

The Egyptian macro-economy had been thriving with the 1990s privatisation of state industries. Yet this carried with it the seeds of instability, which were compounded with the global economic crisis of the late 2000s. But the Egyptian GDP continued to grow by 4.6 per cent in 2009 and 5.3 per cent in 2010, according to the CIA Factbook ('Turmoil in N. Africa' 2011: 2). Yet this bounty benefited only the few, namely the powerful businessmen in Mubarak's National Democratic Party (NDP), the Government and the People's Assembly, in line with the maxim of the time that 'wealth fuels power and political power buys wealth' ('2011 Egyptian revolution' 2011: 7).

All this was confirmed by the Abu Dhabi Gallup Center Poll conducted in 2010. During that year, only 9 per cent of Egyptians classified themselves as 'thriving', down from 2007, and only the richest Egyptians, those in the top 20 per cent income bracket, considered their lives to be better than in 2009. Also, in spite of a 5.3 per cent growth in GDP, only a fifth of Egyptians said in 2010 that economic conditions for them were getting better (Abu Dhabi Gallup Center 2011a: 2–3). The rise in GDP in 2010 was accompanied by an actual decline in the perceived possibility of accessing this new wealth. This led to the conclusion that, on the eve of the Egyptian revolution of 25 January, economic growth occurred without perceived prosperity, and without a perceived opportunity to lessen the gap between the super-rich and the rest of Egyptians (ibid.: 2, 4). This, spawning feelings of relative deprivation without (given the existing Mubarak regime) any possibility of redress, led to the January–February 2011 revolution. According to telecom billionaire Naguib Sawiris, 'They [the protesters] see the nice buildings we live in and they have to live in this [squalor] . . . That is why they are doing this' (Worth 2011: 11).

The situation was aggravated by the protesters' feelings that this wealth was amassed illegally and unjustly by the few. According to a Pew Research Center Poll published in 2011, 53 per cent of the respondents cited corruption as a top concern, as against the 43 per cent who cited lack of economic prosperity (Pew Research Center 2011a: 9). In the face of this anger, it is no wonder that suspicions of official corruption helped fuel the uprising ('Egypt's magnate Ezz hopes for fair trial' 2011: 1). According to Transparency International, Egypt's 2010 Corruption Perception Index, using a scale where 10 was very clean and 0 highly corrupt, was quite low at 3.1 (Transparency International 2010: 12).

Egyptians knew the country's anti-corruption laws, which prohibited financial corruption of public officials. But they were also aware of the existence of structural limitations, which were mainly due to the fact that the executive branch, that is President Mubarak, exercised his discretion to intervene and prevent investigations of offenders. This had led to the insulation of Mubarak and his cronies, the individuals he wanted to co-opt, from the law. The result was that his cronies were seen not only as corrupt, but as flaunting their immunity to boot (Fadel 2011: 294, 299). This process aggravated feelings of social injustice. It is no wonder that 'social justice' was the third slogan of the uprising. This sense of injustice perpetrated by the regime was so entrenched that a poll conducted in Egypt among Internet users by the Google executive Wael Ghoneim in June 2011, four months after Mubarak fell, showed the persisting scepticism. Around 14,049 respondents did not consider the new government to be serious about tackling the issue of social injustice, and only 1,797 readers said they believed it was (Madbouli 2011: 1).

The result was continuous pressure by the protesters to deal effectively with the corrupt officials, which included Mubarak himself, his wife, Suzanne Mubarak, his sons Alaa and Gamal Mubarak, their relatives, the former Prime Minister Ahmed Nazif, several ministers such as the Finance Minister Youssef Boutros-Ghali, the Housing Minister Mohamad Ibrahim Soliman and others, as well as prominent businessmen such as Ahmed Ezz, the steel magnate who was the richest man in Egypt (Baldwin 2011: 2; Detter and Hertog 2011: 1; 'Ex-housing minister' 2011: 1).

On 17 May 2011, Suzanne Mubarak was released by the Illicit Gains

Authority in exchange for relinquishing her amassed wealth, and on the same day Mubarak did the same concerning all his assets and properties in Egypt, which he bequeathed to the country. However, he was not released, and faced trial in August 2011 for allegedly securing illegal profits from selling Egyptian natural gas to Israel via his business associate Hussein Salem. According to media reports, Mubarak had amassed between $9 and $11 billion, while Alaa Mubarak had bank deposits of LE 220 million, excluding extensive and valuable property holdings, and Gamal Mubarak had $180 million made from private business deals on the Egyptian and various European stock markets (El-Din 2011: 2; 'Egypt's ruling military will not consider Mubarak amnesty' 2011: 1). In May 2011, Switzerland followed suit and froze 410 million francs (around $463 million) in funds abroad linked to Mubarak and his associates ('Mubarak, wife questioned over wealth' 2011: 1). This perceived corruption, along with Mubarak's ordering of a violent crackdown on protesters, led later, in June 2012, to a court sentence of 25 years, to be served in Tora prison. However, on 19 August 2013, in an about-face measure, the court decided to release Mubarak from prison having granted his appeal against his sentence, and he was put under house arrest pending his retrial.

The former prime minister Ahmed Nazif, with an estimated wealth of LE 150 million, was also remanded into custody by the Ministry of Justice's Illegal Gains Authority (El-Din 2011: 2). The former finance minister Youssef Boutros-Ghali, who had managed to flee the country, was handed a sentence of 30 years in prison on corruption charges by an Egyptian court (Massad 2011: 3).

Corruption charges were also brought against several cronies of the Mubarak family. These 'crony capitalists' were of the worst kind, as they had enriched themselves through privatisation deals in the selling of state properties. The neoliberal economic policies urged by the IMF in the restructuring adjustments of the Egyptian economy in the name of macro-economic stability had resulted, back in the 1990s, in an 'economic and class apartheid', with an elite that was bent on living in luxury while plundering the nation, a reality to which the IMF was at best indifferent (Dahi 2011: 4; Fadel 2011: 300; Massad 2011: 3; 'The world revolution' 2011: 2).

But the people felt otherwise. Accusations that businessmen were forced to give both the sons of Mubarak a cut in local partnerships with foreign companies abounded ('Mubarak, wife questioned over wealth' 2011: 1). This particular Egyptian market-driven economy lacked transparency and enraged the otherwise patient and stoical Egyptian people, who ultimately could not take the injustices any longer and revolted (Ajami 2011: 2).

The middle class felt that, in the pre-2011 economy, Mubarak had to a large extent not attempted to co-opt or win them over, or at worst had neglected them completely. This perception was held not only by professionals, but also by state employees and, especially, by educated young people. Lack of prosperity as a top concern and worries about the economy plagued 50 per cent of middle-income-range respondents to the Pew Research Center Poll, as against 38 per cent of poor and 41 per cent of rich respondents (Pew Research Center 2011a: 10). Desiring upward mobility but frustrated because they were politically disconnected, the professional middle class saw the prevailing corruption as an immediate threat to their greatest asset, their human capital (Fadel 2011: 294).

The increasingly bulging youth population exhibited high scepticism about the Egyptian leaders' concern for the young. They constituted a large number. At least 50 per cent of the population of Arab countries were under the age of 25 (Al Sharekh 2011: 2). According to a poll conducted in 2010 by the Abu Dhabi Gallup Center, only 29 per cent of respondents believed that the regime was concerned about the young, considerably down from 41 per cent in 2009 (Abu Dhabi Gallup Center 2011a: 4). This was perhaps because unemployment, especially among young university graduates, was substantially higher than the 9.7 per cent national figure for 2010 reported by the CIA World Factbook ('Turmoil in N. Africa' 2011: 2). One young protester stated that he was even facing difficulties entering the middle class, as he was unemployed with no prospect of improving his lot. He blamed Mubarak for not being able to attract a spouse. 'No marriage, no kids, no apartment, no money', he lamented (Grier 2011: 31). His college degree had raised his expectations, only for them to be dashed by the stark reality. According to one estimate, the unemployment rate for college graduates was ten times as high as that for elementary school graduates ('2011 Egyptian revolution' 2011: 7).

According to the Abu Dhabi Gallup Center Poll findings, it was this 'perceived difference between what should be and what was which created the driving force for the country's historic uprising', rather than plain unemployment and poverty. The driving force behind the revolt was the 'moral anger and a sense of social injustice [that the] . . . societal distribution of pain is unfair and the suffering is not inevitable' (Abu Dhabi Gallup Center 2011a: 1). Hence the protesters' repeated calls were for 'Bread, freedom, social justice' (El-Ghobashy 2011: 9).

Bread had been hard to get at times or else was too expensive. In 2008, inflation in urban areas stood at 19.7 per cent and the price of basic foodstuffs had risen by 25 per cent to 51 per cent ('Egypt's rich cannot escape from real world' 2008: 4). This especially hurt the poor. On the eve of the revolution 40 per cent of Egyptians lived on $2 per day ('2011 Egyptian revolution' 2011: 7). They depended on subsidies and social programmes to survive. There were major widespread bread shortages in 2008. Mubarak tried to co-opt the poor. He ordered the military, which ran its own bakeries to feed the troops, to start selling subsidised bread to the public. He also sought to crack down on the black market for wheat. Bakers who got government-subsidised flour were in the habit of selling it at a huge profit on the black market, taking from poor people's mouths. This petty corruption, based on *baksheesh* (bribes), pervaded Egyptian life, where individuals sought to supplement their meagre pay-checks to make ends meet (Michael 2008: 1–2).

The bargain between rulers and ruled, based on a system of subsidies and promises of redistribution of wealth in return for popular quiescence, instituted by the first Egyptian revolution in the 1950s and 1960s, had begun to unravel, chiefly around a decade previously when the Government had no longer been able to keep its side of the bargain of subsidies (Ajami 2011: 2). This was the result of a swelling of the population, which had grown from 30,083,419 in 1966 to 79,000,000 in 2008 and thus entailed the feeding of many more mouths ('2011 Egyptian revolution' 2011: 7–8). The IMF's restructuring policies had also discouraged government subsidies. Reform measures that were instituted involving privatisation had, as noted above, aggravated matters further for the poor in having given rise to 'crony capitalism' (Ajami 2011: 2).

Also, during the global economic downturn, Egyptian public debt had in 2009 stood at 76 per cent of the GDP, indicating that there were limited reserves left for fiscal policy manoeuvring (Hamzawy 2009: 2). All this was manifested in the Abu Dhabi Gallup Center Poll, which showed that public satisfaction with public services provided by the Egyptian Government in 2010 had sharply declined since 2009. Public transportation services satisfaction declined from 78 per cent in 2009 to 48 per cent in 2010; housing availability satisfaction from 39 per cent in 2009 to 26 per cent in 2010; educational system satisfaction from 61 per cent in 2009 to 56 per cent in 2010; and environmental preservation efforts satisfaction from 39 per cent in 2009 to 26 per cent in 2010 (Abu Dhabi Gallup Center 2011a: 5). Also, in the capital city of Cairo the services the Government did provide were so unevenly distributed that they perpetuated inequalities and contributed to instability (Liotta and Miskel 2010: 5, 7).

Wages were miserably low, even for the employees of the largest single employer, the public sector, further widening the gap between rich and poor (Olster and El-Tablawy 2011: 2). Consequently, there were labour protests related to bread-and-butter issues by government employees, labour sit-ins by industrial workers, and demonstrations by the general public during the global economic crisis of the Mubarak era. In 2009, there were approximately a thousand strikes and other forms of industrial protests, with over 300 labour strikes in the first half of 2010 alone (Ottaway and Hamzawy 2011: 3).

Responding to popular demands and to a court order to review the pay scale, Mubarak tried to co-opt the workers, and had his National Council for Wages deal with the matter. They raised the minimum wage, which had been set at LE 35 back in 1984, to LE 400. This, however, was deemed to be inadequate by the 2011 protesters, who demanded further rises. The post-Mubarak military government responded by raising the minimum wage to LE 700 ($117.8) on 1

June 2011 ('Egypt sets minimum wage at $117' 2011: 1). Further demands by the striking public workers included the removal of Mubarak-era bosses, who allegedly had pocketed many of the workers' benefits (Worth 2011: 3).

Mubarak had completely lost touch with the Arab street and the poor. However, owing to their preoccupation with basic survival and hence their inability to take time off from work, many of the Egyptian poor did not join the protesters at Tahrir Square. This task was undertaken by students, professionals, businessmen, and even middle-class couples ('2011 Egyptian revolution' 2011: 2). Hence it was the middle class and its aspirants who demonstrated, because they were the most concerned about the economy shown by the Pew Research Center Poll (Pew Research Center 2011a: 10).

If economic co-optation failed to appease most Egyptians, the very limited, half-hearted and last-minute political co-optation measures undertaken by Mubarak did not mollify their sense of an affront to their dignity, which had been violated, they believed, for over 29 years. Indeed, their recovery of a sense of dignity through overcoming of their fear proved to be a linchpin of the revolution.

Faced with the 25 January 2011 protesters, Mubarak tried to appease them by dismissing his unpopular Prime Minister. And on 31 January, six days after the start of the uprising, he swore in his new cabinet. This measure included the added concession of replacing the despised Interior Minister, Habib el-Adly, whose command of Egyptian security forces, it was believed, had led to the brutality of some of his officers (he was later tried for this offence in an Egyptian court in August 2011 after the fall of Mubarak). But the President's gestures in early 2011 had not gone far enough, according to the protesters. Still, 15 out of the 29 newly appointed cabinet ministers had been ministers before. Even though 14 of the new faces were not members of the ruling National Democratic Party (NDP), they were nevertheless perceived to be the trusted cronies of Mubarak (Contenta 2011: 2). Mubarak's directives to the new government to control inflation, to preserve the subsidies and to provide more jobs were not believed to be genuine by the protesters, who scoffed at him and continued to gather and demonstrate at Tahrir Square ('2011 Egyptian revolution' 2011: 17).

Mubarak nevertheless continued his political appeasement measures by releasing around a thousand prisoners who had completed at least three-quarters of their sentences, on 2 February 2011, but to no avail. Additional measures included the release of 34 political prisoners, including some members of the Muslim Brotherhood, as well as 840 prisoners from the Sinai province. And although promises were made to lift the emergency laws which had been instituted in 1981 after the assassination of Mubarak's predecessor, Anwar al-Sadat, they were never believed to be genuine given the repressive nature of the regime ('Egypt "frees political prisoners"' 2011: 1–2).

People power versus the power of repression

Having come to power as a result of the assassination of President Anwar al-Sadat in 1981 by Islamist extremists, Mubarak always had a penchant for repression to guarantee 'security' and the stability of his rule, which became his first priority. The repressive state of emergency was reinvigorated with the amended Law no. 162 of 1958, the Emergency Law of 1981 (Amnesty International 2005a: 2), which gave temporary police powers to the Government, only to be renewed again and again throughout Mubarak's presidency.

The general Egyptian public acquiesced at first in this battle of Mubarak with the remnants of Islamic extremists. What created an intolerable dissonance of values with the population was, on the one hand, Mubarak's increased dose of repression resulting in excessive human rights abuses, beginning in the late 1990s and widening in scope beyond the Islamist extremists to include elements of the population at large whenever Mubarak suspected them to be against his economic and foreign policies. On the other hand, this increased and pervasive repression coincided with the awareness of the Egyptian people of these abuses through modern communication media, whether through independent satellite television channels, such as Al Jazeera, beginning in the 1990s, or through mobile phones, the Internet and social media in the 2000s.

The June 1995 assassination attempt made against Mubarak by the al-Gama'a al-Islamiyya while he was abroad visiting Addis Ababa intensified his resolve to ensure 'security' by clamping down further on extremist Islamists. This determination was reinforced by subsequent events, such as the terrorist attacks aimed at tourists at Luxor in 1997 and similar attacks on tourists on 7 October 2004 at Taba and 23 July 2005 at Sharm el-Sheikh, both resorts in the Sinai. This terrorism antagonised a large number of Egyptians too, who believed it threatened tourism in general, a mainstay of the Egyptian economy (Goldschmidt 2004: 198), especially when Mubarak had al-Azhar condemn the terrorists for causing economic havoc (Alianak 2007: 192, 202).

There followed a public relations campaign by the Mubarak regime through the state media in the form of television programmes, films and posters warning of the perils posed by the terrorists and extolling the virtues of the Government. The latter was depicted as already propagating Islam in an atmosphere of personal religious freedom, thus undermining the militants' intended imposition of their own interpretation of Islam through their slogan 'Islam is the solution' (Sullivan and Abed-Kotob 1999: 89). And to prevent further criticism, Mubarak had Parliament pass Press Law 93 of 1995, which imposed the heaviest sentences of steep fines and even imprisonment for up to five years on journalists 'publishing false information'; this was reinforced by a bill in early 1996 making it a crime for journalists to criticise Mubarak and/or his family (ibid.: 130).

However, in time the repression targeted, beyond the extremist Islamists, the population's large moderate Islamist components too, so much so that in 2001 it was estimated that there were between 15,000 and 20,000 Islamist political prisoners in Egypt (Kassem 2004: 156). In 2007 there were around 18,000 administrative detainees, and in 2009, according to Amnesty International, these included peaceful critics of the Government (2008: 1; 2010: 3).

Although Mubarak did acknowledge the need to improve human rights and promised reforms during his Police Day Address in 2004, he did not follow through on this. Instead he pushed for the extension of the Emergency Law (Alianak 2007: 192–3), and proposed amendments to 34 articles of the constitution, including the controversial Article 179, which was designed to be the basis of a new, more repressive anti-terrorism law. This law would give the police sweeping powers of arrest, of monitoring private communications, and of violating the privacy of homes, correspondence, telephone calls and other communications, all designed to go against individual freedoms. Further, it would give the President power to bypass ordinary courts and refer terrorism suspects to military and special state security courts, denying defendants a fair trial and giving them no right of appeal (Amnesty International 2007b: 1; Human Rights Watch 2010: 1). These constitutional amendments were pushed through by a national referendum, which passed them in 2007 (Amnesty International 2008: 2). Also, in 2010 Amnesty International reported 'grossly unfair trials of civilians continued before military courts in breach of international fair trial standards' (2010: 3).

Repression was detected especially in the actions of Habib el-Adly, Mubarak's interior minister, who launched several arrest campaigns under the pretext of defending the country from terrorism and had thousands of Egyptians sent to the notorious Tora prison, where they were tortured and subjected to other inhumane behaviour, notably after the Luxor attacks of 1997 and again following the Dahab and Sharm el-Sheikh bombings in the mid-2000s. However, most of the detainees were not considered or perceived to be linked to these attacks, according to an NGO report ('Tora prison' 2011). Some of those cleared of terrorism-related charges by the courts even ended up being continuously held under Administrative Detention orders, involving a practice by the Interior Ministry of circumventing the release orders by issuing new detention orders (Amnesty International 2007a: 2–3; 2011: 2). The provision of Administrative Detention, the indefinite detention ordered by the Minister of the Interior, also resulted in detainees being held in prison without charge or trial, sometimes for years in appalling conditions (Amnesty International 2009: 2–3). This prompted the August 2006 creation of the Egyptian Network for the Defence of Detainees by NGOs and human rights activists to train lawyers on the issue of Administrative Detention and mobilise civil society, especially at a time when many of these detainees went on hunger strike (Amnesty International 2007: 2–3).

The authorities failed to properly investigate and prosecute those responsible for the pervasive torture, even going so far as to reinstate some of the police officers who had been tried and found guilty, according to Human Rights Watch (2010: 2). This was also significant in terms of the rendition programme of the CIA involving Egypt, and raised concerns of possible human rights violations relating to those sent to Egypt from Guantánamo. According to the US State Department, 'torture and abuse of detainees . . . remained common and persistent' in Egypt (Amnesty International 2005b: 1).

Matters got worse on the eve of the Arab Spring. Amnesty International reported the death of four detainees in 2010, allegedly as a result of torture and other ill-treatment (2011: 3). It is no wonder that the Egyptian police received ratings worse than those of military and religious leaders in a 2011 Pew Research Center poll. Respondents stated that the police had a 'bad effect' (61 per cent), with only 39 per cent reporting that they had a 'good effect' (Pew Research Center 2011a: 13).

Whereas in 2004 Mubarak had raised Egyptian expectations for reform, he had dashed them later with his increasingly expanding repressive measures, which led to the frustration of the population. Egyptians took Mubarak's reform efforts as not being serious at best, and as an affront to their dignity at worst, which contributed to their heightened sense of anger and even rage, all preconditions for protests and uprisings, much in accordance with James C. Davies' classic J-Curve Theory of Revolutions (Davies 1962). Further, as Mubarak did not dwell upon the palliative of religion to seek an increase in and further justification for his repressive measures to be implemented by al-Azhar, matters got worse for him, especially since the severity of the human rights abuses became more apparent owing to modern communication methods and media from outside Egypt.

The mobilisation, intensification and spread of people power in confronting this increased repressive power also took several years, namely from 2003, before coming to a head in the attempted revolution in the spring of 2011. The anti-Iraq War demonstrations in 2003, the Kefaya rally in 2004, the April 6th Youth Movement's protests in 2008, all led to confrontations with the repressive power of the state and utilised online activism with offline street activism (Lim 2012: 235–41), which are prime characteristics of people power. The trigger in 2011 was the successful revolution in Tunisia, which emboldened Egyptians and made them overcome their fear of repression. Several factors contributed to the enormous numbers of demonstrators, who, unlike in the past, turned out in unprecedented numbers in Tahrir Square in Cairo and also in other cities such as Suez City and Alexandria, which led to sustained demonstrations for eighteen days until Mubarak was toppled. This involved important roles played by social media, mobile phones, satellite TV, private media (before the state media changed sides), word of mouth, post-prayer gatherings at mosques on Fridays, conversations with taxi drivers, and youth activism involving football players and fans, the Muslim Brotherhood's Youth Wing, and various other groups and masses in the street.

It was this 'overlapping of networks of various media', which Merlyna Lim calls 'Intermodality', that was 'necessary for a social movement to move beyond online following to a larger audience' (2012: 240–1). The overlapping sources of information included informal networks such as word-of-mouth communications by family and friends (72 per cent), mobile phones engaged in SMS texting (28 per cent), Facebook (15 per cent), e-mail (2 per cent) and Twitter (1 per cent), as well as TV (97 per cent) and Internet news sites (13 per cent) (Zhuo et al. 2011: 7). Similar results were recorded by the Abu Dhabi Gallup Center polls, conducted in late March and early April 2011, which asked about the sources of information Egyptians relied upon for news during the protests. Respondents cited Egyptian State TV (81 per cent), Al Jazeera (63 per cent), and Facebook and Twitter (8 per cent) as their sources of news (Abu Dhabi Gallup Center 2011b: 6).

In spite of the fact that social media were not the prevalent source of information, they did provide the spark that ignited the cascading volume of demonstrations. According to Wael Ghoneim, the Google executive, cyber-activist and leader of the anti-regime protests, 'Without Facebook, without Google, without You Tube, this [the revolution] would have never happened', and 'If there was no social networks it would have never been sparked' ('Social media, cellphone video fuel Arab protests' 2011: 1). Social media created awareness at low cost, enabled mobilisation, planning, communication and sustainability of protests, along with mobile phones, both before and during the events. As one activist put it, 'We use Facebook to schedule the protests, Twitter to coordinate, and You Tube to tell the world' (Howard 2011: 1). Concerning Twitter's role in 'contentious collective action', Marc Lynch wrote: 'Twitter does not cause revolutions, but revolutions are tweeted' (Lynch 2011: 304). It was rather people power that made the difference. It was 'the committed Egyptians occupying the streets of Cairo [that] did that [the ousting of Mubarak]' (Howard 2011: 1).

Although the April 6th Youth Movement had organised through Facebook a 'Day of Mourning' for Police Day (25 January 2010) to protest against police brutality, which had long been much-touted by bloggers since the early 2000s, it did not elicit the same response as in 2011 and it was not focused on overthrowing the regime. What was different in 2011 and emboldened the masses was, in the words of Ahmad Maher of the April 6th Youth Movement, the following: 'After the revolution in Tunisia, we are able to market the idea of change in Egypt. People now want to seize something' (Fleishman 2011). Social media provided the 'momentum', which had Tunisian roots, as Egyptians watched YouTube, joined Facebook groups, read tweets, and watched on TV Ben Ali being overthrown (Sheedy 2011: 33–4). Whereas earlier attempts at organising such protests had failed, the 25 January 2011 Facebook protests succeeded owing to the news coverage about Tunisia (Lynch 2011: 305).

Accelerating the pace of change across the region, social media provided the trigger for the Egyptian revolution. 'Technology served as an accelerant', said Alec Ross, a leader of the US State Department's social media efforts, adding that 'a movement that historically would have taken months or years was compressed into far shorter time cycles' and that 'having connected online they [protesters] were more likely to come together offline' ('Social media, cellphone video fuel Arab protests' 2011: 2).

It was the nature of the online message, too, that created a sense of 'shared victimisation' and hence a 'sense of community' and 'social convergence' that brought people out in masses offline (Kavanaugh *et al.* 2011: 9; Zhuo *et al.* 2011: 8; Lim 2012: 242). The weak ties created virtually were transformed to strong ties between converging Egyptians, casting doubt on Malcolm Gladwell's 2010 thesis that social networks tend to create weak ties and not the strong ties needed for real action (Sheedy 2011: 2, 22–3).

Central to the mass protests were two viral social media efforts, 'We are all Khaled Said', and Aasma Mahfouz's video. The Facebook-page memorial to Khaled Said, a summer 2010 victim of police brutality, had 473,000 users as of 6 February 2011. It was accompanied by YouTube pictures contrasting the once-healthy Said with his morgue images. Its use of 'we' created a feeling of 'shared victimisation' concerning a problem that was perceived to be universal (Sheedy 2011: 36–7, 43; Lim 2012: 242). After 14 January 2011 and the fall of the Tunisian dictator, Facebook announced a revolution in Egypt to start on 25 January 2011. Aasma Mahfouz, one of the founders of the 2008 April 6th Youth Movement, a Facebook group, also called for revolution by boldly uploading a video of herself on Facebook on 18 January 2011, calling for people to reclaim Egyptian 'honour' and 'dignity' by going to Tahrir Square 'to demand our rights, our fundamental human rights' (Sheedy 2011: 36–8). Both calls were repeated under hashtag #Jan25 on Twitter, too.

The Internet blackout initiated by Mubarak's government on 27 January 2011 that continued for five days and shut down close to 97 per cent of Egypt's Internet traffic, did not dampen the resolve of the determined masses of Egyptian protesters (Kavanaugh *et al.* 2011: 9). The momentum had been established; the planning had already gone forward; the time for real action had come. As one young activist put it, 'when the government shut down the web, politics moved on to the street, and that's where it stayed' (Lynch 2011: 303). The blackout, which involved the regime's invoking licensing agreements between the Egyptian Government and individual Internet service providers, and which also involved orders to Vodafone to switch 'off' mobile phones and flood cellphones with pro-Government text messages, came too late ('Internet is easy prey for governments' 2011: 1). The Government had waited too long, according to some analysts (Glanz and Markoff 2011: 2). Instead of diminishing the protests, the blackout enflamed them further. The protesters adapted quickly. For example, they gave interviews to news organisations in return for access to their satellite Internet connections (Sheedy 2011: 42). They made use of Al Jazeera, the regional/global satellite TV channel, to post their mobile phone videos as 'citizen journalists'.

Egyptians had become addicted to free expression fanned by the convergence of satellite TV channels and social media. According to IRI, 84 per cent of the population acquired their information from TV and only 6 per cent from Facebook (Borkan 2011: 1). Also, they were influenced by some prominent state TV journalists who joined the protesters, such as Shahira Amin, the senior news anchor of Nile TV, who resigned on 3 February 2011 in protest against her network's siding with the Mubarak Government, and Hala Helmy, a TV host, who did not appear on the air following 25 January 2011 and who co-founded the Media Revolutionaries Front made up of journalists protesting against state media policies. They were followed by journalists working for state TV. Indeed, in some state media outlets there were demonstrations by employees either in support of the revolution or in protest against the perceived corruption of their media (Brown 2011b: 2). Further, three government papers, *Al-Ahram*, *Al-Gomhoria* and *Al-Akhbar*, changed their coverage during the uprising from supporting Mubarak to supporting the protesters (Chammah 2012: 1).

Although the protests were planned online, many people who participated in the street activism of 25 January 2011 learned of them through word of mouth (Sheedy 2011: 42). Family and friends were called (Giglio 2011: 1); taxi drivers were enlisted to spread the word, and coffee shops were frequented along with football fields and mosques. The April 6th Youth Movement distributed some 20,000 flyers in the mobilisation effort (Lim 2012: 243). The word of mouth was especially important in the poorer neighborhoods of Cairo, whose people could not afford the Internet or computers, with demonstrations starting simultaneously in twenty locations before proceeding to Tahrir Square (Sheedy 2011: 40). The activists walked down the streets, even calling on onlookers from the balconies of densely populated apartment buildings to come down and join the march, with much success.

The mass demonstrations were sustained also by post-prayer protests following Friday mosque gatherings as the Government could not close down the places of worship or distinguish would-be protesters from those who congregated there just to pray (Giglio 2011: 2). The protests were also sustained, communications established and coordination achieved by the use of mobile phones, which could easily be concealed and carried and charged by being tapped into street lights (Zhuo *et al.* 2011: 7). Mobile phone penetration in Egypt well exceeded the 72 per cent figure reported in 2009 (Ghannam 2011: 25). Face-to-face encounters were supplemented by texting. However, mobile phones were at times jammed or shut down by the Government in some areas, such as Tahrir Square in Cairo ('The new media' 2011: 8).

The actual on-the-spot confrontation in the Square with the state police was sustained also by militant football supporters, who had been hardened previously by regular battles with the security forces and rival fan groups in the past, and by members of the Muslim Brotherhood's Youth Wing, who contributed their expertise in providing social services and survival skills in the face of the Mubarak regime, although the parent Muslim Brotherhood did not join officially at first. They were joined by activists from other political groups and parties in mobilising online agitation along with offline demonstrations (Lim 2012: 243).

The protesters included secularists, Islamists, communists and ultra-left-wingers (Ungerleider 2011: 1). A disproportionate number of the activists were aged under 30, energised by D. McAdam's 'biographical availability', that is the absence of personal constraints such as marriage, family or full employment (Lim 2012: 235). It was mainly lack of employment that propelled participation in the protests. According to a poll conducted by the US-based International Republican Institute, participation in the demonstrations of 25 January 2011 was due mainly to 'low living standards and lack of jobs'; 64 per cent said this, only 19 per cent citing 'lack of democracy and political reform' (Borkan 2011: 1).

People power triumphed over the power of repression as the protests could be maintained and sustained over eighteen days until Mubarak was toppled, perhaps in large part because the military refused to side with him and did not intervene against the demonstrators. Indeed, in February 2011 the popular chant was 'The military and the people are one hand' (*al-gaish wa'l shaab humma wahed*). Further, there was a lack of major overt opposition from the elites (Zhuo *et al.* 2011: 6). Also, the US government sided with democracy. But was people power to translate into or lead to a populist democracy, which had been denied to Egyptians under Mubarak, who had instituted an illiberal democracy at best, in the long run? What was the actual role of the military to be in the post-Mubarak era?

Populist democracy versus illiberal democracy
Mubarak depicted himself as a strong leader who disciplined his people as a father figure in order to bring about his highest priority, stability, while permitting and promising at times democracy, albeit in the very limited fashion of an illiberal democracy at most. The majority of Egyptians had a different hierarchy of values from the President's. In recent years, according to a Pew Research Center Poll, 53 per cent of respondents had mentioned democracy as being their top concern, while 33 per cent had cited political instability as their top fear. These fears of political instability were more pronounced among the wealthier Egyptians (41 per cent), than among middle-income (32 per cent) or low-income (30 per cent) individuals (Pew Research Center 2011a: 9–10). The wealthier Egyptians were the base of support for the Mubarak regime, and

hence were more inclined towards his highest value, stability. The preference for democracy over political stability was more pronounced among lower-income individuals (64 per cent) than among middle-income participants (48 per cent) or high-income interviewees (55 per cent) (ibid.: 18).

As to Mubarak's claim that a strong leader was preferable to democracy as regards solving the country's problems, Egyptians were evenly divided in 2007, with 47 per cent favouring a strong leader while 50 per cent preferred democracy (Pew Research Center 2011b: 50). But on the eve of the revolution this preference had shifted more towards democracy. In the spring of 2010, 60 per cent stated that democracy was preferable to any other kind of government, whereas only 22 per cent preferred a non-democratic government in some circumstances, with 16 per cent exhibiting no preference (ibid.: 41).

Egyptians had increasingly given up hope of gaining redress for their conditions under the existing system of government and hoped that an alternative form of government under their own control, namely a populist one, might prove a better bet. Therefore the priority of most Egyptians was shifting more towards democracy, whereas Mubarak's hierarchy was shifting away from liberal democracy towards stability, albeit with a grudgingly illiberal democracy at best. The increased rigging of parliamentary elections in the autumn of 2010 compared to that in 2005 contrasted sharply with Mubarak's continued promises of 'free and fair elections' prior to the elections. Mubarak raised the people's expectations only to dash their hopes later. Clearly, conditions for an intolerable hierarchical dissonance of values gap between the values of the regime and those of the people was being created – a precondition for revolution.

Faced with what they believed to be a hopeless situation as regards redressing their economic grievances under the Mubarak regime, people pushed for taking matters into their own hands via a populist democracy at the least. Their rejection of the Government's illiberal democracy was manifested in low levels of voter participation, anger at rigged elections, which unfairly limited opportunities for political parties, and dissatisfaction with the regime's restrictions on civil society organisations.

Declining political participation
The Mubarak regime went through the motions of encouraging participation in the parliamentary elections of 2005 and 2010 and the presidential election of 2005, only to meddle with participation and actually limit it. On 25 November 2010, for example, three days prior to the start of the 28 November parliamentary elections, the Higher Election Commission (HEC) urged Egyptians to vote by stating: 'All Egyptians with the right to vote are asked to cast their ballots in the parliamentary elections on Sunday in exercise of their legal and constitutional rights . . . In order for the elections to express the will of Egyptians, they

are urged to positively take part' (Mohamed 2010: 1). Yet the ensuing voter turn-out was very low. This was very much at odds with the democratic aspirations of many Egyptians and certainly did not reflect the general interest of the Arab street, especially of the tea and coffee house frequenters, in political discussions.

In the 2005 parliamentary elections voter turn-out was around 28 per cent, with only 8.7 million of the 44.5 million Egyptians of voting age (more precisely, of the 31.2 million who had the proper documentation) actually voting. The situation was worse in the presidential elections of the same year, with only 22.9 per cent, or 7.3 million of the 44.5 million, voting as the voters saw no meaningful choice. In the 2010 Shura Council (Upper House of the Egyptian Parliament) elections the turnout was even lower, at only 14 per cent (Soliman 2010: 1), whereas in the elections to the Lower House of Parliament, also in 2010, only 35 per cent of eligible voters turned out to cast their ballots, although rights groups claimed that actual participation was no more than 15 per cent ('35 Pct voter turnout in Egyptian elections' 2010: 1; Nasrawi 2010: 2).

Why was voter turn-out so low? The large number of non-voters believed that the elections would be rigged, that they would involve violence, and that they would not offer choice or change anything (Soliman 2010: 2). In fact, bribery of those voters who did turn out discounted the value and fairness of elections, giving short shrift to the significance of actual issues. This vote-buying happened in spite of an official ban on using money to affect voters' decisions, as stipulated by the People's Assembly Law and the regulations of the Higher Election Commission (Emam 2010b: 1–2). According to Youssri el-Gharabawi, an independent political researcher with the semi-official newspaper *Al-Ahram*, 'People vote for the candidates who offer them cash bribes', as money remained the only tangible and immediate benefit of the elections for poor people, who saw an opportunity to sell their votes (Sadek 2010: 1).

Notable here was food bribery, designed to lure even a whole impoverished neighbourhood by offering its inhabitants free breakfast and lunch (Emam 2010a: 1). Here the ruling NDP outdid the opposition parties, who distributed free meals consisting of only basic staples such as *fuul* (fava beans) and *taamiya* (fried bean sprouts), by offering more substantial hot *kofta* (meatball) sandwiches in the poor streets of Cairo's Abbassiya, for example (Mohamed 2010b: 1–2). Other forms of bribes included blankets for the poor, free medicines, and medical check-ups by doctor candidates of the NDP, among other inducements (Madbouli 2010: 2).

Cash payments were not uncommon either. For example, in 2005 some candidates were known to have paid up to LE 500 (almost $87) to convince voters to vote for them (Emam 2010b: 2). In 2010, according to the Independent Coalition for Monitoring Elections, a coalition of NGOs, voters were being paid LE 20–150 (roughly $3.50–26.00) each for their ballots at the polling station of Cairo's Matariya district (Nasrawi 2010: 2).

Apart from tainted bribery, another reason why many Egyptian voters stayed at home was the fear of violence erupting at the polling stations. Violence was especially pronounced in 2005 when mobs of voters tried to break into polling stations that were closed by the police to keep out the NDP's opposition voters, resulting in fourteen deaths. This dissuaded many people from going to the polling stations in 2010, which resulted in a reduced number of deaths: nine people ('Egyptian parliamentary election, 2010' 2011: 6; Michael and El Deeb 2010: 1–2).

An additional reason for low voter turn-out was the danger posed by the hired thugs of the NDP, who bullied and prevented Muslim Brotherhood campaigners, for example, from monitoring the elections. Other irregularities, according to human rights groups, included the stuffing of ballot boxes and the using of photocopied ballot papers (Emam *et al.* 2010: 1–2).

A final reason for low voter turn-out was the inordinate advantage enjoyed by the NDP over the other political parties, thus limiting the voters' choices. Although the legal spending limit for candidates was raised from LE 70,000 in 2005 to LE 200,000 in 2010, candidates ended up spending more (Sid-Ahmed 2005: 1–2; Emam 2010b: 2). In 2010, candidates and their parties spent LE 515 million on elections to the Lower House of Parliament. Mubarak's NDP spent the bulk of the money, estimated at LE 500 million as against the meagre spending by the al-Wafd and Muslim Brotherhood group of LE 15 million (Sadek 2010: 1). This gave an overwhelming advantage to Mubarak's party over the other parties and contributed to weakening the opposition parties, thus offering limited choice for the electorate.

Ineffective political parties

What made the NDP so strong? Why was it perceived to have an unfair advantage over the other parties? The regime was the first to deny that the NDP's strength was due to an unfair advantage. The Government pointed to the subsidies it gave to encourage other political parties and insisted on the 'fairness' of the elections. But the situation was far otherwise. While it is true that the regime allocated an annual subsidy of LE 100,000 to each party, it placed conditions on the spending of it. The money was largely to be earmarked for haj pilgrimage trips for the party's members, except when the Secretary-General of the NDP, Safwat al-Sherif, ordered the party to spend the funds on campaigns praising President Mubarak (El-Shobaki 2011: 1; 'Party time' 2011: 2).

Where did the NDP actually stand *vis-à-vis* the other parties in the political system? Since its inception in 1979, the NDP had won majorities of 75–95 per cent in every parliamentary election, with a membership of only 2 million out of around 79 million Egyptians, according to its official website prior to the 2010 elections. In 2005 it had won 311 seats, which included 166 Independents who later joined the NDP after the election ('Meet the players' 2010: 1–2). However, its victory in the 2010 parliamentary elections, winning 424 seats, was a land-slide, gaining it 86.4 per cent of the 508-seat People's Assembly. The combined strength of all the opposition parties stood at only sixteen, or only 3 per cent, and there were 65 'Independents' ('Official results' 2010: 1). But this inordinate 'success', especially since it was perceived to be arrived at unfairly, carried with it the seeds of its own destruction.

After the first round of elections, on 28 November 2010, the two major opposition parties, the Muslim Brotherhood (MB), running its candidates as Independents, and the secular al-Wafd Party, had decided to boycott the second round of elections, which was to be held on 5 December 2010, citing gross irregularities and fraud. While they, especially the Brotherhood, had cried foul in previous elections but nevertheless participated in them, they were incensed by the magnitude of the irregularities in the 2010 elections. For the Brotherhood it was its first boycott since the 1990s; whereas for the al-Wafd Party, which had had usual working ties with the Government in the past, it was new ('Polls open in Egyptian run-off vote' 2010: 1).

This decision of the two parties to withdraw signalled and added to the legiti-macy crisis that faced the regime. Amr Hamzawy, of the Carnegie Endowment for International Peace, said of the decision: 'It means the opposition are no longer buying into the system'; and Hassan Nafaa, a columnist writing in the independent daily *Al-Masri Al-Youm*, added: 'What happened in the first round confirms that the ruling party is determined to completely monopolise power, even if it must resort to fraud' ('Ruling party "damaged" by opposition boycott' 2010: 1–2).

Not only did the NDP's behaviour discourage the existing opposition parties, but it also limited potential challengers by controlling the establishment of new parties and hence their entry into the political system. According to the 1977 Political Parties Law, the decision about new parties was left solely in the hands of the Political Parties Committee. This body included Mubarak appointees, such as the head of the Shura Council, the Parliamentary Affairs Minister, the Justice Minister and the Interior Minister, in addition to three judges. In 2005, some cosmetic amendments were introduced to the law, such as reducing the number of ministers from three to two, adding three public figures, and raising the number of members required for founding new parties from 50 to 1,000. But Mubarak's supporters still controlled the Committee by possessing the right to decide on new parties (El-Hennawy 2011: 1). It was no accident that in 2010 the NDP's Secretary-General, Safwat El-Sherif, as Speaker of the Shura Council, was also a member of the Committee (Meet the players' 2010).

The criteria the Committee was to go by included the exclusion of religious parties, which instantly disqualified the Muslim Brotherhood, and any party whose programme was not completely distinct from that of the existing parties, to be determined solely by the Committee. As a result of this, and as a result also of a labyrinth of complicated procedures, new party aspirations were usually and systematically quashed. The lucky permit recipients were the founders with ties to the regime. However, it was understood that if they crossed the Red Lines, their parties would be disqualified ('Party time' 2011: 2).

Therefore, it was no wonder that a major request of the opposition groups and civil society activists had been the amending of the Political Parties Law of 2005 in order to facilitate the formation of new parties ('Egyptian parliamentary election, 2010' 2011: 3–4). But it was not until after the 2011 revolution that a new political parties law was instituted. The notorious Political Parties Committee was abolished. In its stead a seven-member judicial committee was set up to decide on a party's eligibility within 30 days, if it had at least 5,000 members from at least ten of Egypt's 29 provinces. Should the new committee raise any objection, it should, within eight days, refer the matter to a court, the Supreme Administrative Court, which had a month to act otherwise the party would automatically acquire official status. Also, the new law lifted the stipulation about proving a distinction between the applicant party's platform and those of the existing ones (El-Hennawy 2011: 1). But while it banned overtly religious parties, it did not prevent the Muslim Brotherhood from forming a political party, the Freedom and Justice Party (FJP), as a 'civil party' with a religious background ('Party time' 2011: 1–2).

While it was true that the Muslim Brotherhood had not fielded candidates as a political party and only ran candidates as Independents, it had suffered inordinately during the 2010 parliamentary elections under the Mubarak regime. The regime crackdown on it had begun on 9 October 2010, as soon as the Brotherhood had announced that it would field Independent candidates for the 28 November 2010 first round of elections. This crackdown involved arrests of several candidates and supporters prior to the elections. The candidates were charged with the illegal use of religious slogans, namely 'Islam is the solution', while campaigning ('Egypt frees arrested opposition candidates' 2010: 1). According to international rights groups, the intimidation and repression of opposition candidates ahead of the election had made a fair vote improbable ('Egypt's NDP complains of 52 candidates' 2010: 1). Further, the police had arrested over 1,000 Muslim Brotherhood supporters prior to voting in the first round ('Polls open in Egyptian run-off vote' 2010: 1).

As a result, the elections were depicted as 'the most acrimonious in the nation's parliamentary history', with seven deaths, of which two were reported by the authorities to have had health causes ('Egypt's ruling party heading for solid win' 2010: 1). Rights groups accused the regime of bullying, ballot stuffing and other dirty tricks in the first round ('Islamists, secular party withdraw from poll' 2010: 1). The Government had neither allowed international monitors nor permitted supervision by the national courts ('Egyptian parliamentary election, 2010' 2011: 5).

On the day of the election, 28 November 2010, all electronic websites of the Muslim Brotherhood's senior members were blocked for many hours (Emam *et al.* 2010: 1). According to Hassan Nafaa, the irregularities were enormous: 'This time, it was more hideous and on a larger scale than in any other election' ('Opposition party to abandon seats won in vote' 2010: 1).

As a result, the Muslim Brotherhood did not win a single seat in the first round, which was in stark contrast to its winning of 86 seats, around one-fifth or 20 per cent of the total parliamentary membership, in the 2005 parliamentary elections ('Opposition takes to the street' 2010: 1; 'Role and make-up of Parliament' 2010: 2). Perhaps this was due more specifically to the fact that the fortunes of the Brotherhood had risen since 2000, and that the regime was more adamant and determined to limit it by resorting even to fraud on a large scale.

Moreover, much more was at stake in 2010 – namely the upcoming 2011 presidential elections. To prevent any meaningful opposition to the NDP candidate for President, be it the ailing and as yet undecided Mubarak or (presumably, and more likely) his son Gamal Mubarak, the party was determined to prevent the opposition from garnering the 5 per cent threshold needed in the parliamentary elections in order to be allowed to field an opposition presidential candidate. The 5 per cent restriction was imposed by Article 76 of the constitution, which allowed multi-candidate presidential elections in 2005 ('Egyptian parliamentary election, 2010' 2011: 8). Analysts confirmed this calculation of the NDP, which entailed disqualifying the Islamists and other critics, who would otherwise end up at the assembly, in order to deny them a platform before the presidential elections. According to Ashraf Balbaa of the al-Wafd Party, 'The first round showed that the government was not going to give any space to the opposition', and that 'The new people's assembly is not for the people. It is simply another NDP committee with a single purpose: securing presidential succession in the 2011 vote' ('Egyptians vote in run-off' 2010: 1).

The near absence of opposition parties in the finally elected Parliament of 2010 ensured that no competition would be possible in securing the bigger plum, victory in the upcoming presidential elections of 2011. This raised the question of the President's legitimacy. On the streets of Cairo many expressed disappointment about a future where the ruling party had a 'total political monopoly' on political change (Emam 2010c: 1). A more extreme view was held by Ayman Fahim, a member of the Nasserite Party, which did not win a single seat: 'The ruling party is managed by a group of businessmen who want to control everything in Egypt, and by these polls they will' – these businessman having, according to Fahim, a major say, via the party, as 'bloodsuckers of the poor' (Emam 2010c: 1).

Frustration was rife among many former MPs and groups following the election in December 2010, leading them to demonstrate, protest and make demands, all ominously portending the revolution that was to come early in

2011. Protesters were adamant about insisting on their priorities of democracy and dignity, which conflicted with the priorities of the regime, stability and security. Clearly, the conditions for hierarchical dissonance in values, a precondition for revolution, prevailed in December 2010.

On the very same day as Mubarak's post-election speech on 12 December 2010, hundreds of protesters from opposition parties and groups gathered in front of the Supreme Court to demonstrate. In a rare spirit of solidarity, they included former MPs representing all opposition parties such as the al-Wafd Party, the Muslim Brotherhood, Ghad, Tagammu and the would-be El-Karama Party, and other protesters such as the April 6th Movement, the Kifaya, the National Association for Change (NAC) and the newly formed leftist movement, Hashd. This entire political spectrum of the opposition carried a model of the Parliament with the word 'null' written on it and chanted the slogan 'The parliament is null' (Shukrallah 2010: 1). It is significant that they still, at that point, embraced Mubarak by asking him to take action and dissolve the newly elected parliament.

The demonstrators were more concerned about proving wide-scale vote rigging and election irregularities by gathering evidence. The Muslim Brotherhood, for example, alleged that the voting results in more than 92 electoral constituencies (out of a total of 222) were void. They resolved to resort to legal action by alerting international human rights groups and basic civil protection agencies of the UN and Human Rights Watch ('Brotherhood seeks international support over elections' 2010: 1). NGOs such as the New World Foundation concurred, calling the election 'least representative' of the desire of the Egyptian electorate; and other NGOs started legal action against the Higher Election Commission, which monitored the vote, and the NDP (Emam and Madbouli 2010: 1). The protesters asked the local courts, including the Constitutional Court, to rule in favour of dissolving Parliament and calling for a rerun election ('Opposition takes to the street' 2010: 1).

The opposition even went so far as to propose the setting up of a shadow parliament with representation from all opposition groups and parties. At least 120 former MPs, who had been excluded from the 2010 elections, expressed their intention to participate in it. The planned parliament would be a 'real' parliament, according to Mustafa Sherdi, a member of the al-Wafd Party. He echoed the sentiment of the demonstrators: 'This is just the beginning for us. We want a real parliament. Egypt deserves a democratic parliament.' He continued: 'It is just unacceptable that Egypt's parliament is basically an appointed rather than an elected one' (Shukrallah 2010: 1). It was not until after Mubarak's resignation that Egypt's Supreme Council of the Armed Forces dissolved the parliament of 2010 and scheduled new elections for November 2011.

Another key demand of the demonstrators of December 2010 was for a new constitution 'that would guarantee democratic practice and free and fair elections', according to Mustafa Bakry, a former MP (ibid.): the protesters wanted to amend Article 88 of the constitution so as to restore full judicial supervision of the elections in order to combat election fraud and vote rigging. Other demands included amendments of Article 76 of the constitution to facilitate party and independent candidates to get onto the presidential ballot, and of Article 77 to establish term limits for the President, which had been removed in 1981 ('Egyptian parliament election, 2010' 2011: 3–4).

After Mubarak's resignation on 11 February 2011, the Supreme Council of the Armed Forces (SCAF) called for a referendum on the constitutional amendments, which was passed on 19 March 2011 with a 77 per cent vote (Wing and Kassim 2011: 305). SCAF then, on 23 March 2011, decreed a Provisional Constitution of Egypt, whereby Articles 39 and 40 stipulated that the judiciary was to determine the legality of elections under a Supreme Commission's supervision of elections and a Court of Cassation's subsequent determination of the integrity of Members of Parliament once the election results were announced ('2011 Provisional Constitution of Egypt' 2011: 8).

Dealing with the provisions for presidential election, Article 27 provided that a presidential candidate must be 'supported by 30 members at least of the elected members of the People's Assembly and Shura Council, or . . . at least 30,000 citizens who have the right to vote, in at least 15 provinces whereby the number of supporters in any province is at least 1,000' (ibid.: 6). Term limits were also instituted for the President, according to Article 29, namely two four-year terms (ibid.). These provisions, discussed more fully below, would, it was hoped, guard against the rise of another Mubarak, and possible authoritarianism, and ensure presidential democracy in Egypt in the future.

Civil society stifled

Unlike in a populist democracy, in Mubarak's illiberal democracy civil society groups (NGOs) were stifled in terms of their freedom to be constituted by strict registration rules, in their dissemination of political opinion (if allowed to form) by official Red Lines, and in their functioning and implementation by restrictive public assembly laws.

According to Law no. 84 of Associations of 2002, the Ministry of the Interior was empowered to accept or reject NGO registration. This process involved excessive scrutiny by the State Security Investigations Sector (SSIS), which reviewed applications even though technically it did not have any legal authority to do so (Human Rights Watch 2012a: 31). The SSIS often invoked Article 11 to block registration in cases it deemed did not fit the state's narrow margins of interest. For example, on its recommendation the Ministry of the Interior blocked, because of 'security concerns', the registration of human rights organisations such as the Civil Observatory for Human Rights, the Egypt Initiative for Personal Rights, the Egypt Association against Torture, the Egypt Center for Housing Rights and the World Center for Human Rights, to name a few. Further, membership of an 'illegal association' attracted a punishment under Article 98 of Law no. 635 of 1954 for five years for joining and for one year for communicating directly or indirectly with such an organisation. Mubarak imprisoned political opponents, invoking 'membership in an illegal organization' under Article 86, for simply expressing views sympathetic to the Muslim Brotherhood (ibid.: 29–33).

Civil society was also restricted in its operation. NGOs needed clearance from SSIS for activities that were deemed sensitive to the state. Should NGOs be involved in activities that were critical of the regime, their reputations were subjected to besmirching by SSIS, which was also known for fostering rifts within opposition groups. According to Michele Dunne and Mara Revkin, 'SSIS perpetuated and enforced a police state culture in which Egyptians involved in political and civil society were called on to inform on their neighbors and colleagues in one way or another' (Dunne and Revkin 2011: 2). It was therefore no wonder that Egypt's transitional leaders dismantled the hated SSIS after Mubarak's fall.

In addition, under Mubarak, should an association transgress the official Red Lines, it was subject to dissolution, although in some cases it had recourse to city Administrative Courts, which overturned the governors' decisions to dismantle organisations, for example in Cairo and in Gaza in 2008 (Human Rights Watch 2012a: 32). State control was also exercised through requirements for participation in corresponding state organisations such as mandating trade unions to join the state Trade Union Federation (ibid.: 29).

Freedom of assembly was restricted by Laws on Public Assembly, such as Law 10 of 1914, which restricted the right to assemble of more than five persons, and Law 14 of 1923, which called for three days' advance notice of a planned public gathering, demonstration or procession to be given to the governor, who could then decide to approve it or ban it on the grounds that it might lead to 'public disorder'. Mubarak invoked these laws frequently against peaceful demonstrators. For example, in 2003, following the anti-Iraq War demonstrations, the regime arrested 800 protesters; in 2008, following the Mahalla textile workers' strike and the demonstrations by the April 6th Youth Group, the Government cracked down on the protesters. On 26 and 27 January 2011, prosecutors charged several hundred peaceful protesters with *tagamhur* (gathering) and gave them fifteen-day detentions each, after the state had arrested some 1,200 protesters for 'illegally demonstrating' ('Human Rights Watch' January 2012: 36–7).

Phase 2: The transition towards revolution and democracy

The transition towards revolution and democracy met with challenges by the military (SCAF). It was perceived to have been 'hijacked' by the Islamists through parliamentary and presidential elections, and it underwent a counter-revolution by the military-backed, mostly secularist, 'liberals', with a dose of Salafists and stalwarts of the former Mubarak regime thrown in. The street was manipulated by three groups – the Islamists, the Tamarod (Rebel) coalition, and the military – in an intense and often bloody competition for power.

Either everybody is in charge or SCAF is: populist ownership and military management

Having been held back for almost thirty years by the dam of an illiberal democracy by Mubarak, the revolutionaries were certainly exhilarated and perhaps even flabbergasted by his being toppled in a mere period of eighteen days. It was as though the raging waters of Egyptian dignity, which had been dammed and held back for so long, suddenly, with the breaking of the Mubarak dam, rushed freely through the valley of Egypt and flooded it, with no set plan for an orderly irrigation. Little thought had been given by the revolutionaries to a liberated post-Mubarak state beyond their ad hoc protest coordination and their united desire to rid Egypt of Mubarak. Suddenly everybody felt in charge; they were empowered at last and felt free to flow in different streamlets. After all, according to Professor Galal Amin, they now owned the revolution; but the management ended up resting in the hands of the military (Bohn 2011: 1). The protesters had succeeded in toppling Mubarak because the army had refused to side with the President and had refused to fire on the demonstrators at Tahrir Square when deployed there starting on 28 January 2011 since Mubarak realised that the police alone could not handle the massive crowds. The military had thus 'earned' a managerial role initially.

How was the inherent authoritarianism of a military intent on stability to coordinate with the liberty extolled by the revolutionaries? This pluralistic 'street' lacked a united leadership (Masoud 2011: 117; Muasher 2011a: 1). The makings of a possible hierarchical dissonance of values between the priorities of the military and those of the masses was in the offing, and was to preoccupy Egypt for the next year and a half, beyond the parliamentary elections of late November 2011 and well into the first free Egyptian presidential elections of June 2012 and beyond.

The nineteen-member Supreme Council of the Armed Forces (SCAF) was ill-prepared to govern the country directly. This may account for its hesitancy, its inconsistencies and, at times, its reversals of policy in the post-Mubarak era. Under Mubarak, the military had been increasingly kept out of national internal politics, while it is true that its chairman, Field Marshal Mohamed Hussein Tantawi, had experience in foreign affairs as he had served as defence minister since 1991 at a time of 'cold peace' with Israel when no war occurred (Brown 2011a: 2).

The loyalty of the high-ranking officers had been bought by the patrimonial rule of Mubarak, by providing them with ample arms via purchases from the USA, amounting to $1.3 billion annually, by making them stakeholders in the economy (by encouraging them to become capitalist entrepreneurs of the numerous military factories and businesses, amounting to around one-third of the Egyptian GDP), and by appointing them local governors in around three-quarters of the governorates (Saldanha 2011: 7–8; Newton-Small and Hauslohner 2012: 33). But Mubarak miscalculated. Among the reasons why they abandoned him, and the reasons for their neutrality commencing on 2 February 2011 at Tahrir Square and when they intervened against the regime 'thugs' who had attacked the peaceful protesters at the 'Battle of the Camel', was their human rights training in the USA and their conception of themselves as defenders 'of all the people' (Kinsman 2011: 41–2). Further, there had been a falling-out of the officers with Mubarak's son, Gamal, who, they believed, had presidential ambitions, and with his rising crony capitalists, who were seen as threats to the military enterprises.

In fact, the ordinary soldiers, sitting in tanks on guard at Tahrir Square, felt a special sympathy with the demonstrators and were even delighted often to pose for pictures with crowd members who had climbed on the tanks – contrasting sharply with a similar situation in Tiananmen Square in China in 1989, which had ended in a massacre. Indeed, the Egyptian soldiers were mostly conscripts and as such were the fathers, sons, brothers and uncles of the people themselves. They had always considered themselves heroes bent on self-sacrifice, and men of the people from which they sprang (Newton-Small and Hauslohner 2012: 31). It is no wonder that they fraternised with the Tahrir protesters up until 11 February 2011, when Mubarak stepped down after thirty years of misrule. The demonstrators responded by chanting the slogan '*al-gaish wal-shaab humma wahed*' ('The army and the people are one hand').

This was corroborated by a Pew Research Center Poll which showed that in 2011, 88 per cent of interviewees considered the influence of the military to be 'very or somewhat good', with 90 per cent viewing Tantawi favourably. However, this figure, although still very favourable, had declined somewhat in 2012 to 75 per cent, and Tantawi's favourable rating had declined to 63 per cent and SCAF's was the same (Pew Research Center 2012: 10). This was mainly due to the fact that although SCAF and the revolutionaries had cooperated in the early post-Mubarak months they soon diverged over the speed of the reforms, the sequencing of democratic transition efforts, the retention of the remnants of the old regime such as the Prime Ministers and some cabinet members, the start of the trials of Mubarak and his cohorts, the timing of the expiration of the Emergency Law of 1981, the trial of civilians before military courts, the guaranteeing of freedom of expression and of assembly against the Red Lines drawn by SCAF, and the arrest of 12,000 detainees (and torture of some and the subjection of some women detainees to 'virginity tests').

The diverse revolutionary groups used street demonstrations at Tahrir Square in Cairo and also in other cities, such as Alexandria and Suez City, as political leverage (Dunne 2011: 1). Their demands were so numerous and the crowds so immense that at one point, on 27 November 2011, Tantawi warned 'No one can pressure the armed forces' (Sayigh 2011: 2). Increasingly, however, SCAF utilised the carrot-and-stick approach in the face of new demands, for which new protests were organised on a weekly basis on Fridays after prayers, resulting in a 'protracted state of protest' (Kandeel 2012: 2).

The military-backed government proposed a law in March 2011 banning protests, 'partly because everybody is protesting' (Kristof 2011: 1). SCAF seemed inclined to prioritise stability in the name of law and order. But the people believed otherwise. They wanted to exercise their newly won freedom, which they considered consisted of healthy democratic debate and which entailed some postponement of stability of the political order. The protesters settled instead on SCAF taking ad hoc measures to satisfy the peaceful street (Muasher 2011b: 1–2).

Indeed, according to a Pew Research Center Poll, Egyptians rated 'law and order' (stability) fourth in importance (63 per cent in 2011 and 60 per cent in 2012), jointly with 'free speech' (63 per cent in 2011 and 60 per cent in 2012), after 'improved economic conditions' as the first priority (82 per cent in 2011 and 81 per cent in 2012), after 'fair judiciary' (social justice) as the second priority (79 per cent in 2011 and 81 per cent in 2012), after 'uncensored media' as the third priority (62 per cent in 2012 with no figures given for 2011) and 'honest multiparty elections' (procedural democracy) as fifth in importance (53 per cent in 2011 and 58 per cent in 2012) (Pew Research Center 2012: 2). As it became feasible to realise parliamentary and presidential elections, actual voting, and elimination of foreign influence (in NGOs, for example), the figures rose from 53 per cent all the way up to 58 per cent, which fuelled the revolutionaries' energy and willingness to risk their lives and limit what they suspected to be SCAF's ambitions to perpetuate military rule.

Among these general priorities there emerged often conflicting sub-priorities. For example, there were different definitions of democracy among the secularists and Islamists during the debate over the sequencing of the writing of the new constitution and the holding of elections. Specifically at the time leading up to the 19 March 2011 SCAF-mandated referendum on eight amendments to the Egyptian constitution of 1971, the Islamists and non-Islamists had different views. For the Islamists, who campaigned for the holding of the referendum first, followed by elections and then by the writing of a new constitution, democracy needed to be instituted quickly as they were confident of winning, seeing that they already had organisations in place. For the Muslim Brotherhood, among the Islamists, who campaigned using religious slogans and who made voting for the referendum a religious duty, freedom must be defined in being bounded by God's law. For the liberals, freedom should lead to the 'right' results of a secular political order, which should not be hurried as they did not trust the *demos* (people) to do the 'right' thing given that the liberals had not had enough time to organise in order to win the Egyptian people over. They therefore wanted to write a whole new constitution first, to be followed by elections later on. Therefore, both Islamists and liberals sought 'to limit democracy according to their own normative commitments' (Masoud 2011: 126).

SCAF had weighed in too via a mass text message, which read 'Referendum on constitutional amendments equals democracy'. The turn-out for the referendum was the highest ever at 41 per cent, with 77 per cent voting 'yes' (Stacher 2011a: 1–2). Having won a popular legitimacy for its guidance, SCAF issued, on 30 March 2011, a new 'Constitutional Declaration' intended to replace the constitution of 1971.

Concerning another priority, a 'fair judiciary', which in 2012 tied for first place along with 'improved economic conditions' with 81 per cent (up from second place in 2011 with 79 per cent, according to the Pew Research Center (2012: 2)), the revolutionary movements called again and again for the observance of human rights, to which SCAF, increasingly intent on emphasising stability, paid lip service at best. Indeed, the demands of the revolutionaries on human rights were very often ignored, and the protesters seemed at times to be 'condemned to the fate of Sisyphus compelled to roll a huge rock up a hill, only to watch it roll back again' (Gabr 2012: 1).

According to Human Rights Watch, writing in May 2012, SCAF's abuses of human rights in 2011 involved the subjecting of 12,000 civilians to 'unfair military trials', which did not provide the basic due-process rights of civilian courts. This figure amounted to more than the total number of military trials during the thirty years of Mubarak's rule (Human Rights Watch 2012d: 1). Other abuses by SCAF that were cited included the torture of prisoners and the subjection of some women detainees to 'virginity tests' (and then the acquittal of the doctor involved). Also listed were the killing of protesters, for example at the march of Copts on the Maspero State TV Building in October 2011 where 27 were killed, as well as the demonstrations at Mohamed Mahmoud Street in November 2011 where 40 were killed (Human Rights Watch 2012b: 1; 2012c: 1–2; 2012d: 2). Further, instances of 'eye-hunting' were denounced, whereby armed police aimed rubber bullets at head level, causing eye injuries, which seemed to be the speciality of the Central Security Forces in their SCAF-ordered crackdowns. There were 60 cases of eye injuries between 19 and 27 November 2011 alone (Human Rights Watch 2011: 1–2).

A study published by *Ahram online* in December 2011 and subsequently updated, entitled 'SCAF: a history of injustice', cited at least fifteen major incidents that needed to be properly investigated. It concluded that the investigations conducted under SCAF's rule had fallen short of standards for open and transparent scrutiny (Eskandar 2012: 1–2). In addition, Human Rights Watch summed up the year on 25 January 2012, on the eve of the first anniversary of the revolution, by stating, 'Mubarak's repressive legacy has been preserved and even strengthened' (Human Rights Watch 2012b: 1).

SCAF had clearly shifted its priorities in the direction of securing stability and security. A content analysis by Rime Naguib of the rule of SCAF based on the 93 letters it wrote during its first year in power revealed this. Naguib concluded that 'the perceived duty of SCAF and the armed forces shifted from protecting the revolution and furthering its demands, to ensuring stability and "the unity of the national fabric" and finally to safeguarding the entity of the state and what is referred to as "the higher interests of the country"' (Naguib 2011: 1).

In answer to the rhetorical question implicit in the title of the second section of this chapter, 'Either everybody is in charge or SCAF is', it can be concluded that SCAF, rather than everybody, ended up being in charge. The managers (SCAF) took over from the owners of the revolution (the revolutionaries). SCAF became 'disproportionately in charge' as a result (Stacher 2011b).

Parliamentary elections: Parliament thwarted

In possession of their newly found freedom, Egyptians embarked on the road of transition to democratic institutions, ever-suspicious of the real intentions of SCAF so far as the formation of a truly civilian government was concerned. It is significant that once elections for Parliament started and Egyptians were satisfied with their fairness, initially, the level of mass protests and ensuing violence against SCAF subsided (Weiss 2011: 3).

In the parliamentary elections, liberals won only 20 per cent of the parliamentary seats, whereas the better-organised Islamists won over 62 per cent of the seats (Fadel 2012: 2), which in turn fanned the secularists' deep-seated feelings of resentment. The Brotherhood had had a lengthy experience under Mubarak of running candidates as Independents, because they were not allowed to form a political party. Further, they had won the hearts and minds of many Egyptians through the charities they ran as social organisations; whereas although the Salafists had not participated in Egyptian politics in the past under Mubarak, they were energised by the revolution and won over many Egyptians via their charities as well. As one taxi driver put it aptly, 'The Islamists cater to our needs and understand our traditions while the liberals and secularists are talking to each other on Facebook'. He continued, 'We tried socialists, nationalists, leftists, liberals, secularists and military rule and they all let us down and failed to take Egypt forward', concluding like a true democrat: 'So maybe it's about time to try the Islamists, and if they fail, we will vote against them next time' (Ghannam 2011: 2).

The ensuing battle lines between Islamists and liberals were ominously set. The revolutionary youth movement faced an uphill battle in winning over the

Egyptian public, as it was not well organised or unified. The April 6th Youth Movement had lost its lustre (Fadel 2012: 2) by not delivering the stability that many Egyptians had come to long for once again as a result of their numerous clashes with the security forces and the lack of results in lessening the economic woes of the country, which had been the first priority of the 25 January 2011 revolution. Egyptians wanted enduring stability, which, they believed, could only be achieved in a democracy.

As a result, they turned out in large numbers to vote. In the first of the three phases of parliamentary elections for the Lower House, around 60 per cent of eligible voters cast their ballots ('Egyptian legislative elections 2011–2012' 2011: 1). Perhaps this was due to Egypt's new Law on Exercise of Political Rights (LEPR), that called upon all eligible Egyptians to vote or face a fine of up to 500 Egyptian pounds (about $83), which was very steep for the average citizen (Weiss 2011: 1). Even in the third phase, voter turn-out was high, at 62 per cent ('Egyptian parliamentary elections 2011–2012' 2012: 5). Voters were to choose from a total of 2,746 candidates for 150 seats, with 100 on the electoral list and 50 for individual seats.

Ever-zealous members of the parties, like the Muslim Brotherhood's FJP, had also competed for seats intended for individual independent candidates, which were to comprise one third of the seats of the Assembly. The final tally of election results showed that the FJP had secured an extra 108 seats in this way, apart from the 127 seats it had won on party lists, giving it 235 seats (47.18 per cent) in an Assembly which was to have 498 elected and ten appointed seats; whereas the Salafist al-Nour Party had won 121 seats, or nearly 25 per cent ('Egypt's Brotherhood wins 47 per cent of parliament seats' 2012: 1). This led the Supreme Constitutional Court of Egypt to rule, on 14 June 2012, that the November 2011 and January 2012 parliamentary elections were unconstitutional and that specifically one third of the winners were illegitimate, which happened to be mostly Muslim Brotherhood members, since they had competed for seats designated for independents. The first freely elected parliament was in peril. It was dissolved by SCAF amid angry protests aimed at the court, which was made up of judges all of whom had been appointed by Mubarak. In a separate ruling issued at the same time, the court threw out the Political Exclusion Law passed by the Parliament, which had excluded the former members of the Mubarak regime from running for office ('Egyptian parliamentary elections 2011–2012' 2012: 13–14). This was a double blow to the Islamists, as their majority in Parliament was questioned and it opened avenues for former regime members to compete as independents in subsequent parliamentary elections.

The first democratically elected president, Mohamed Morsi

Were presidential elections to fare any better? In a continuum ranging from authoritarianism at one end, which SCAF had come to espouse given its highest value, stability, to, at the other end, perpetual revolution, which entailed endless demonstrations and ceaseless demands, Egyptians were to choose the middle ground, the institutionalisation of reform, which encompassed a programme of priorities for an elected President. Were these priorities going to lean towards stability, as espoused by Ahmed Shafiq, the last Prime Minister to serve under Mubarak and hence entail a possible return to the Mubarak-era priorities? Or would they entail a return to the Nasser-era economic *étatisme* of the Nasserite Dignity Party candidate, Hamdeen Sabbahi, or else a complete departure from the past, as advocated by the moderate Islamist Abdel Moneim Aboul Fotouh, a former Muslim Brotherhood member, or as presented by the Renaissance Programme of the 'civil party', the Freedom and Justice Party (FJP) of the Muslim Brotherhood proper, and its candidate, Mohamed Morsi? Numerous other programmes were put forward by other parties, such as the al-Wafd Party, and their candidates.

The results of the first round of presidential elections pointed to two front-runners, Mohamed Morsi of the FJP, who had picked scales as a voting symbol to facilitate the casting of ballots, and Ahmed Shafiq, who had chosen a ladder symbol to simplify voting by his supporters. With no outright winner, a run-off election between these two was mandated in June 2012. The election was seen as a competition between the remnants of the old regime, emphasising stability, as represented by Shafiq, and the erstwhile opponents of at least the last thirty years of Mubarak's rule, the Muslim Brotherhood, as represented by Morsi. The young revolutionaries felt left out as they were not well organised or unified in campaigning for grass-roots votes across the spectrum of the Egyptian electorate. They had not developed a narrative that had a realistic chance of being actualised as opposed to the chaos and instability that might come, as SCAF had warned, if the radical change that they called for was attempted at once (LeVine 24 June 2012: 3). Thus they did not succeed in reaching the man in the street in a realistic, simple way and were perceived by ordinary Egyptians as elites detached from the socio-economic hardships of mainstream life (Mohamed 2012: 1). Further, they did not coalesce around one candidate, but instead fielded multiple presidential candidates and hence divided their supporters, which proved to be a fatal mistake in their attempt to win the presidency (Levine 2012: 3). These three groups, the secularist remnants of the old regime, the liberal young revolutionaries, and the Islamists, were set on a collision course, to be played out in the courtyard managed by SCAF.

Judging from a Pew Research Poll conducted just prior to the presidential elections, namely between 19 March and 10 April 2012, which rated the Egyptian parties and organisations, the results of this game could well have been predicted. The Muslim Brotherhood received 70 per cent favourable views, ranking first. Second came the April 6th Youth Movement, the loose organisation of mostly young and secular activists, with 68 per cent, then the

Freedom and Justice Party with 56 per cent, followed by the secular al-Wafd Party (legalised since 1978) with 52 per cent, then the Islamist al-Wasat Party (a 1990 breakaway from the Muslim Brotherhood) with 46 per cent, then the Islamist Salafi al-Nour Party with 44 per cent, then, last, the secularist coalition of political parties, the Egyptian Bloc, with 38 per cent (Pew Research Center 2012: 1, 12).

So far as Islam is concerned, it seemed that at a time of crisis, Egyptians exhibited a penchant for trusting religion, as my Pendulum Model suggested (Alianak 2007). This is corroborated by the favourable ratings accorded by the Pew Research Poll to the Islamists, namely the Muslim Brotherhood, the FJP, the al-Wasat Party and (to a lesser extent) the al-Nour Party. Also, according to the poll 'Egyptians . . . want Islam to play a major role in society, and most believe the Quran should shape the country's laws, although a growing minority express reservations about increasing influence of Islam in politics' (ibid.: 1). Specifically, the poll showed that 60 per cent wanted laws to strictly follow the Qur'ān, 32 per cent wanted laws to follow the values and principles of Islam, and only 6 per cent wanted laws not to be influenced by the Qur'ān, with 3 per cent 'don't knows' (ibid.: 17). This was in spite of findings that showed an increase in negative ratings of the role of Islam in politics – from 2 per cent in 2010 to 25 per cent in 2012, as against the positive ratings of 82 per cent in 2010 and 64 per cent in 2012 (ibid.).

So far as secularism is concerned, perhaps the increase in secularist feelings may be detected in the divided electorate in the presidential run-off elections, with Morsi barely winning with 51.7 per cent of the poll, as against the 48.3 per cent of Shafiq, with only half of the electorate (51.6 per cent) voting (Hussein and Borger 24 June 2012: 1). Given that only half (54 per cent) of 18- to 29-year-olds, and only 55 per cent of those educated to college level or above, responded that laws should strictly follow Islam, and the rest that they should not do so (Pew Research Center 2012:17), secularism seemed to be on the rise among educated young people, something which would have ominous consequences later, in June 2013.

Also, among voters casting their ballots for Morsi, some were lukewarm. The politically active April 6th Youth Movement, for example, who rightly feared a possible Shafiq win and a return to Mubarak-era politics as Morsi had received only around one-quarter of the vote on the first ballot (slightly more than Shafiq, which was hardly a mandate), urged its followers to vote for Morsi as the lesser of two evils. However, it informally exacted a promise from Morsi that should he win he would not institute an Islamic state, modelled on Iran, but would instead institute a 'civil state'. Accordingly, upon winning, he immediately resigned from the Muslim Brotherhood and the FJP, which he headed.

So far as SCAF is concerned, in whose managed courtyard the secularists and Islamists competed, it was sceptical of Morsi's promises of a 'civil state'.

Indeed, sensing the FJP might very well win the run-off elections, SCAF issued a Supplementary Constitutional Declaration on 17 June 2012 (the last day of voting in the run-off elections) limiting the powers of a future President by reserving for itself considerable powers, even though it had on occasions in the past cooperated with the Brotherhood. Indeed, a SCAF member had emphatically stated, 'If they [the Muslim Brothers] want to impose Islamic *sharia*, the army will save the country. The army won't allow the country to be taken in the wrong direction', and had gone on to outline the military's intention to steer Egyptian politics in the direction of stability: 'They [the Brothers] should know that the armed forces are the pillar of stability and the constitution should say so' (Nakhoul 2012: 3). The military was to do so a year later on 3 July 2013, when it deposed Morsi by siding with the enraged secularist 'liberals' who believed the Islamists had 'hijacked' their revolution. The stage was set for an inevitable future confrontation between the President and SCAF and later in July 2013 with the military, but this was postponed for the time being.

This one-time 'spare tyre' of the Muslim Brotherhood (second to their first choice, Shater), Mohamed Morsi, came into his own as the first freely-elected President of Egypt – of 'all' the Egyptians, as he stated as he took a symbolic unofficial oath of office in front of a sea of thousands gathered in Tahrir Square, the day before his official inauguration on Friday 29 June 2012. Tahrir then saw the birth of a President who saw himself as the 'defender of the revolution' ('Egypt President Morsi's first speech' 2012: 1). As President-Elect, he promised to be 'President for all Egyptians', adding, 'You are the source of all authority and legitimacy.' He continued by affirming that he would not give up the people's revolution: 'The revolution must continue until all its objectives are met.' To do so, he promised, 'I will not give up any of the powers given to the president' ('Egypt President-elect Mohamed Mursi hails Tahrir crowds' 2012: 1). He added: 'The revolution continues . . . with an elected president who leads the ship of the nation and leads the revolution' (Michael 2012a: 1).

By squarely siding with the revolutionaries Morsi was challenging SCAF. He was cheered by the crowd, which chanted, 'A full revolution or nothing. Down, down with military rule. We, the people, are the red line' (Fayed 2012: 1). Morsi also reached out to Egyptians as a whole, whether they voted for him or not: 'I will keep in touch with everyone, and I do not differentiate between supporters and opposition. I will seek advice from you and from Allah almighty' ('Egypt's President-elect promises to put power in hands of the people' 2012: 1). He called for national unity: 'This national unity is the only way to get Egypt out of this difficult crisis' ('Muslim Brotherhood's Morsi urges "unity" in first speech as Egypt's president-elect' 2012: 1). Unlike SCAF, Morsi would not prioritise stability over democracy. Instead he was for both – with democracy leading to long-term stability. He stated, after the court ceremony: 'Today, the

Egyptian people laid the foundation of a new life – absolute freedom, a genuine democracy and stability' (Hendawi 2012: 3).

Later, at an opportune moment, when Morsi perceived that SCAF had reneged on maintaining security in the Sinai, which endangered the very stability it stood for, he 'retired' several SCAF members, cancelled SCAF's controversial Supplementary Constitutional Declaration, and consolidated civilian control of the military. The 'retired' SCAF members included the powerful Minister of Defence, Field Marshal Mohamed Hussein Tantawi, chief of staff Lt Gen. Sami Anan, and three commanders – of the Air Defence Force, the Air Force and the Navy. In their place Morsi elevated a younger generation of officers, who supported his move, and hence divided the upper echelon of the once-powerful SCAF. It is believed that Morsi had consulted with SCAF before taking his surprise decision and had taken advantage of the simmering discontent among the younger officers with the more senior ones in SCAF. According to the retired general and strategic expert Qadri Saeed, 'The lower ranks were not happy with their superiors' recent performance and their excessive involvement in politics at the expense of the army. And they were especially demoralised following last week's Sinai border attack' (Rashwan 2012: 1–2). Indeed, Morsi had taken these measures on a pretext, based on the unexpected attack by jihadists on 5 August 2012 that had left sixteen Egyptian border-guard troops in the Sinai dead and had endangered the peace treaty with Israel, as the jihadists had crossed over into Israeli territory before having been gunned down (Ahmed 2012: 1–2).

What Hamdi Qandil, a prominent television presenter, dubbed a 'civilian coup' was probably staged to pre-empt a possible military coup against Morsi planned on social media for 24 August 2012 by anti-Brotherhood and anti-revolution figures, who had called for mass protests on that date. Morsi had issued his own constitutional declaration asserting civilian control over the military and introducing other prerogatives. Hamdi Qandil added: 'If SCAF had really protected the revolution, Egyptians would have taken to the streets to demand that they be kept in their jobs' (Ali and Mourad 2012: 3). They did not take to the streets against Morsi.

Already a Pew Research Center Poll, conducted between 19 March and 10 April 2012, showed that most Egyptians supported civilian control over the military, with 62 per cent calling it an important priority and 24 per cent considering it very important (Pew Research Center 2012: 2). But the respondents considered a civilian-controlled military to be less of a priority than improved economic conditions, a fair judiciary, law and order, free speech, honest elections, gender equality, religious freedom, and an uncensored Internet, in that order (ibid.).

Perhaps the civilian–military control issue assumed more importance following SCAF's 'soft coup' of 17 June 2012, that is, after the Pew Poll was taken from

March to April of that year. Certainly Morsi, the new manager, the self-styled populist President, considered this uppermost in his mind. Having settled it to his advantage, he was freer to deal with his other priorities, necessary in realising what he deemed to be the goals of the revolution. But was he headed towards an imperial presidency? Not according to him, as he had stated previously that 'the presidency will be an institution', and that 'the Superman era is over' (Knell 2012: 2). However, his new Constitutional Declaration had given him tremendous power, albeit temporarily ('Text of President Morsi's new Egypt Constitutional Declaration' 2012: 1).

Morsi started to implement the Renaissance Project – his campaign platform – under the watchful eyes of the April 6th Youth Movement, which had transformed itself from a revolutionary protest movement into a lobbying group, so necessary in the institutionalisation of a democracy. Its spokeswoman declared, after the Morsi election results in June 2012: 'The time now is to help dismantle the old corrupt system not through street protests but to offer a hand.' As a lobby group the Movement would be involved in 'monitoring the performance of the president. If he deviates from the path, we will be the first to oppose him, and return to the streets' (Michael 2012: 4). Accordingly, the activists set up a website, 'Morsi Meter', to measure the President's success in meeting his campaign promises, all 64 of them, grouped into five categories, Bread, Security, Traffic, Fuel and Cleanliness, to be achieved in his first 100 days ('Morsi's one-hundred day plan' 2012: 1; Murphy 2012: 2; Sayed 2012: 1). Morsi himself summed up his goals as 'stability, security, justice and prosperity' (Knell 2012: 1).

In an effort to placate his critics, Morsi saw to it initially that only five out of the 35 ministries were to be given to the Muslim Brotherhood's FJP, namely Information, Higher Education, Youth, Labour and Housing. Twenty out of the 35 ministers had no publicly declared political affiliations. The ten ministries that went to pro-change political forces were in the low-cost and soft-power realms, perhaps as a reward for these pro-change groups, because these institutions exhibited potential for the mobilisation and strengthening of unofficial networks on the ground (Ashour 2012: 1–2).

Tackling the first priority of Egyptians pertaining to the economy, Morsi took several initial steps. He announced that he would grant 750,000 government employees permanent contracts doing away with the uncertainty of their years-long temporary status (Hussein 2012: 2). He also gave a 15 per cent pay rise to all public-sector employees. Further, he reached out to a million and half citizens by increasing their minimum social security pensions from EGP 200 to EGP 300 (Enein 2012: 1). However, Morsi's future attempts to tackle the poverty problem would conceivably be faced with a lethargic, inefficient bureaucracy, with its vested interests, that could slow down these efforts. In spite of this, Morsi promised to clear bottlenecks in the distribution of subsidised bread, gas for cooking and petrol (Saleh and Pfeiffer 2012: 1).

How many had Morsi achieved of the 64 goals he set for himself in his 100-day plan? According to the Morsi Meter, in his first 50 days he had progressed in two of the five major goal groupings, namely Bread, the first demand of the revolution, and the Environment (Morsi Meter 19 August 2012: 1).

Morsi had also agreed to six demands presented to him just prior to the run-off presidential elections by the National Front for the Protection of the Revolution, which included, among many others, the April 6th Youth Movement. While Morsi had accomplished demand number four following his election by 'flatly refusing the addendum to the Constitutional Declaration [by SCAF] reducing the presidential authorities', by the time of his 12 August 2012 move to assert civilian control over the military he still needed to fulfil the other demands, according to the Front. Now that the President had full authority, the Front stressed that it expected him to proceed towards the freeing of all political prisoners facing military trials, going through with a national unity project which included the setting up of a socially and politically inclusive consultative presidential team, the restructuring of the Constituent Assembly to draft the new constitution, and the holding of parliamentary elections as soon as possible ('Pro-revolution coalition' 2012: 1–2).

The counter-revolution: 'the people' and then 'the people'

Morsi was, however, not to last beyond one year and three days, which did not give him enough time to achieve the various demands of the revolutionaries. While he prioritised stability, to be arrived at through democratic elections, his opponents settled for 'people power' to remove him from office prematurely with the help of the military, and unwittingly were led towards the priority of stability, to be achieved, as it turned out, through an authoritarianism reminiscent of the Mubarak era. Was this a counter-revolution?

Whereas at the end of his 100 days in power Morsi's approval rating was 78 per cent, by the end of May 2013 it had fallen to 42 per cent, according to a poll conducted by the Egyptian Center for Public Opinion ('Baseera') (Osman 2013b: 1). An earlier poll, conducted between 3 and 23 March 2013 by the Pew Research Center, had put his approval rating at 53 per cent, with 43 per cent seeing him in an unfavourable light (Pew Research Center 2013d: 10). On the other hand, Zogby Research Services, in a poll conducted between 4 April and 12 May 2013, reported that overall one quarter of respondents were satisfied with Morsi's performance, whereas three-quarters were dissatisfied with his creating of economic opportunities, his maintaining of safety and order, and his guaranteeing of rights and freedoms (Zogby Research Services 2013: 14).

Egyptian society was very polarised into pro-Morsi and anti-Morsi camps. The results of a 'Baseera' poll in May 2013 indicated that only 30 per cent would re-elect Morsi if elections were held then, with 54 per cent calling for early elections. Morsi enjoyed more support among people of lower economic status, people with less than intermediate education, the older generation, and inhabitants of rural and Upper Egypt (Osman May 2013b: 1–2). Beyond these demographic lines, the deeply divided society was reflecting ideological and religious differences, as seen by the Zogby poll of June 2013. The two main Islamist parties (the Muslim Brotherhood's FJP and the al-Nour Party) secured the confidence of just under 30 per cent of adult Egyptians, whereas the major opposition groups (the April 6th Movement and the National Salvation Front, the NSF) enjoyed the confidence of almost 35 per cent; beyond that, 40 per cent of the population had no confidence in either grouping (Zogby Research Services 2013: 1). To make matters worse, each side embarked on narrative campaigns demonising the other side, with each claiming to be the true 'people' (*ashaab*). Therefore 'the people' were pitted against 'the people', which ultimately degenerated into a fight between the so-called 'infidels', who were depicted as being 'immoral and hostile to Islam', and the 'terrorists', who were characterised as being 'incompetent, inferior and unfit to rule' and consequently as 'un-Egyptian' (El-Dabh 2013: 2; Mogahed 2013: 1–2).

Why did Morsi's approval ratings fall so sharply? Criticisms were levelled against him by the opposition and the military, and, in hindsight, by his own Muslim Brothers.

Morsi's 'mistakes' were enunciated by Gehad el-Haddad, a spokesperson for the Muslim Brotherhood and a senior advisor to its political arm, the FJP, on 18 July 2013 at the Rabaa el-Adaweya sit-in four weeks before it was brutally dismantled by the military on 14 August 2013. El-Haddad believed that Morsi had not gone far enough, listing five major criticisms: (1) he had not carried 'the revolutionary spirit into governmental reforms'; (2) 'He wasn't as forceful as he should have been'; (3) 'He decided to respect the corrupt heritage that was left for him', such as the 'corrupt police' and the 'corrupt judiciary', including the 'corrupt constitutional court' and the 'corrupt set of rules and laws', and he did not exercise 'a carrot and stick rule over the bureaucracy'; (4) 'He should have been more confrontational, more revolutionary and forceful against the old regime'; and (5) 'He was blamed for Ikhwanizing [Brotherhoodising] the state, although he didn't do so'. El-Haddad concluded: 'I think he should have' (Attalah 2013: 3).

The disparate coalition of liberals and the mass of Egyptians was frustrated by the economic stagnation, that did not show any signs of improvement under Morsi. The economy was the top priority of Egyptians in 2013, with 83 per cent emphasising it. However, 56 per cent of respondents to a Pew Research Center poll conducted between 3 and 23 March 2013 believed that their standard of living was 'getting worse', with only 12 per cent saying that it was 'getting better' and 30 per cent reporting that it was 'staying the same' (Pew Research Center 2013a: 1). In comparison to five years previously, 61 per cent believed that they were 'worse off' in 2013 (as against 46 per cent in 2011 and 24 per cent in 2009), according to Zogby Research Services (2013: 5). Also, the Pew Research Center reported that respondents perceived their 'personal economic situation' to have declined during the Morsi year, with only 21 per cent calling it 'good' in 2013, down from 23 per cent in 2012 (Pew Research Center 2013b: 1). Further, the 'national economic situation' was perceived to have deteriorated, with 76 per cent saying it was 'bad' as against 71 per cent in 2012, 64 per cent in 2011, and 80 per cent in 2010, just preceding the Arab Spring (Pew Research Center 2013d: 2, 6). Indeed, during Morsi's year in office the country's economic situation was perceived to be 'good' by 23 per cent in 2013, as against 27 per cent in 2012 (Pew Research Center 2013a: 1).

Egyptian GDP grew only by an annual 2.2 per cent in the first quarter of 2013, when it needed to rise at least 6 per cent in order to absorb the growing population's needs for employment and dent the unemployment figures, which were factors leading to the original protests of the Arab Spring in 2011. In turn, the increasing number of protests during Morsi's rule had discouraged much-needed tourism and foreign investment for development. Most of the oil-rich Gulf Arab monarchies had cut their aid to Egypt fearing possible perceived destabilising effects of the Muslim Brotherhood on their rule – except for Qatar, which had spent 4 per cent of its GDP to help Egypt before Morsi's downfall. Moreover, wealthy Egyptian businessmen, such as Naguib Sawiris, a Morsi opponent, had taken funds abroad and stored their money there instead of investing in their own country (Werr and Torchia 2013: 1–2).

Further, in 2012 the Morsi Government had projected a deficit of 135 billion pounds for the year to June 2013 but by the end of May 2013, with the June figures not yet reported, the deficit had already reached 202.9 billion pounds. The budget deficit was exacerbated, when Morsi tried to quell civil service discontent and keep unrest to a minimum, by a 21 per cent rise in civil service labour costs in the eleven months to May 2013 (Werr and Torchia 2013: 1–2). But the salaries of these officials were perceived to be threatened because of the generous subsidies to fuel and food, which accounted for one-third of total public spending in Egypt, which Morsi insisted on providing as a populist measure to appease the street (Rohac 2013: 1).

However, this very street was threatened by shortages in fuel, which resulted in long queues at petrol stations and in electricity cuts every day, phenomena caused by 'a little bit of foot dragging' and 'willful inefficiency', according to David Kirkpatrick, the *New York Times*' Cairo bureau chief. Kirkpatrick elaborated, indicating that these shortages were miraculously corrected the day after Morsi's downfall ('You know, a lot of people, who were making decisions on a day-to-day basis below him [Morsi] throughout the bureaucracy hated him'), and continued: 'I think they sort of passively or actively resisted him throughout, and so, you know, after a year perched uneasily . . . on top of this government it basically swallowed him up.' He summed the situation up this way: '[Morsi was] not in full control of his government . . . he was sort of perched on top of the machinery of the old regime – the bureaucracies of the old regime, the security forces of the old regime – and he was gradually trying to change that', and continued, 'But there was always an element of at least foot dragging in every part of the bureaucracy and open revolt among the security forces' ('Morsi's ouster in Egypt' 2013: 2–3). The Muslim Brotherhood itself acknowledged this problem, when it reported its fear that the 'deep state' (entrenched interests in the army, the security services, some of the judiciary and the bureaucracy) would not cooperate with the Morsi regime and would not let him 'wield real power, even with a democratic mandate' (Reuters 2013: 1).

What about the demands of the protesters of 2011 for democracy? Morsi tended to prioritise democracy arrived at through elections, as he believed in the then-scheduled parliamentary elections. With this in mind, he had pushed through a new constitution by temporarily assuming extraordinary powers in November 2012 since he was afraid the judiciary made up of Mubarak-era appointees would dissolve the Constitutional Assembly tasked with the writing. This controversial constitution, which was perceived to have unduly favoured Islam, was passed through a popular referendum in December 2012. Morsi tended to believe that his party's struggle with the opposition should shift from street protests to the ballot box and the resulting halls of a parliament. This, according to him, would ultimately produce much-needed stability.

Egyptians too tended to prioritise democracy over stability, back in March 2013, although the percentage favouring stability was on the rise according to a Pew Research Center poll, because Egyptians tended to believe that 'law and order' was 'getting worse' (44 per cent) rather than 'getting better' (26 per cent) – this at a time when they considered 'law and order' to be very important, close behind their first priority of improved economic conditions. Egyptians tended to be evenly divided on 'personal freedoms', with 33 per cent saying that they were 'getting better' and 36 per cent that they were 'getting worse'. Overall, 56 per cent of respondents were not satisfied with the way democracy was working under Morsi, but they still had a favourable view of the Muslim Brotherhood (63 per cent in 2013, down from 70 per cent in 2012) and the FJP, although with a smaller margin (with 52 per cent favouring it and 44 per cent against it). While Egyptian opinion tended to be about evenly divided over the FJP, it was also split for the opposition National Salvation Front (NSF), with 45 per cent reporting a 'favourable' view and 52 per cent an 'unfavourable', reflecting major political divisions that were intensifying. A major source of division came over the nation's new 2012 constitution, with 49 per cent favouring it and 45 per cent opposing it. A further cause of the split was divided opinion over the then-upcoming parliamentary elections, with 46 per cent expressing confidence that they would be fair and 40 per cent expecting they would be unfair (Pew Research Center 2013d: 2–6). The latter group tended to believe that the elections would be unfair since they would be based upon a rushed-through and hence unpopular constitution, and since they would be conducted by the Brotherhood. An even more pessimistic view was reported by Zogby Research Services in its 4 April–12 May 2013 poll: 63 per cent opposed the constitution, with only 30 per cent supporting it (Zogby Research Services 2013: 19).

Clearly, matters were coming to a head, which would result in a major confrontation, peaking on 30 June 2013, the first anniversary of the instalment of the first freely elected President of Egypt, organised by the Tamarod (Rebel) youth group via massive street demonstrations in Tahrir Square in Cairo calling for Morsi to step down. Tamarod included younger pro-democracy people, who were determined as far back as 15 April 2013 to get rid of Morsi at any cost via social media, volunteers and old-fashioned petitions. By mid-May 2013 it had 8,000 volunteers in fifteen of Egypt's twenty-two governorates, which made it a popular movement. By mid-June 2013 it claimed to have received more than 20 million petition signatures (Chulov and Kingsley 2013: 2, 4). It is believed that most of the Tamarod group may have been unaware that they were bank-rolled and supported in other ways, such as through private TV channels by the biggest millionaires, like Naguib Sawiris. The opposition supporting Tamarod consisted largely of an elite that was still in power, such as wealthy businessmen, who were referred to as the *fulul* (beneficiaries of the old Mubarak regime), who sought to reclaim authority and preserve their privileges, high court judges, most of whom had been appointed by Mubarak and who were afraid that they would be retired by the Morsi Government, ambitious politicians, and politicians like Mohamed El-Baradei of the NSF and Hamdeen Sabahi, the third-place finisher in the presidential race, television directors and famous newspaper journalists, the Coptic Pope, Shaykh al-Azhar, and so forth (Asad and Cubukcu 2013: 1–3).

Among the mobilisation slogans used by the opposition were those demonis-ing the Muslim Brotherhood and the FJP. They accused Morsi of Islamising Egypt, 'Brotherhoodising' state institutions, appointing seven governors from the ranks of the Brotherhood and one from the extremist Islamist group, the Gamaa Islamiyya, and, especially, issuing his 22 November 2012 constitutional decrees that immunised presidential decisions from judicial review, sacking the prosecutor-general and shielding the dominant Islamist Constituent Assembly and Shura Council from dissolution, failing to fulfil election pledges to reform the security sector – the intelligence services, the police and paramilitary forces – that formed the pillars of the pre-revolutionary state, and, most importantly, failing to build consensus (Black 2013: 1–2, 4–5).

However, Morsi's supporters insisted that from the beginning of his presi-dency he had been rebuffed: he had tried to reach out to the opposition by calling them to the presidential palace for negotiations but the NSF leaders had refused to accept his invitation to attend and had rejected all his over-tures, preferring instead to resorting to 'people power' in the form of street demonstrations in Tahrir Square ultimately culminating on 30 June 2013, this time organised by Tamarod. According to the 'Baseera' poll, 59 per cent of Egyptians were aware of the Tamarod campaign and half of those who were aware of it were amenable to signing to what amounted to an informal 'recall' referendum calling for the President to step down immediately and not wait for the completion of his four-year term. Awareness was greater in Lower Egypt (59 per cent) and the urban governorates (80 per cent) (Osman 2013a: 1). Moreover, Egyptians were polarised, with around 50 per cent supporting the 'recall' and around 50 per cent opposing it. So, 'the people' were pitted against 'the people'. The division was not along 'simplistic religious fault lines', according to Dalia Mogahed, since the Salafists supported the millions of protesters, who came from 'all walks of life; secular and devout; liberal and leftist; revolutionary and reactionary' including the *fulul* (the remnants of the old regime) (Mogahed 2013: 2). They got support from the military, which was highly regarded by Egyptians, according to the Pew Research Center poll of March 2013 which showed that 67 per cent of respondents had a 'favourable' view of the Supreme Council of the Armed Forces, with only 33 per cent holding 'unfavourable' views (Pew Research Center 2013d: 12).

Why did the military take sides and topple Morsi? There was no love lost between the army and the Muslim Brotherhood. The army disliked the Brotherhood on account of its ideology and its country-wide grass-roots organisation giving it the potential to be the most popular opposition; whereas the Brotherhood was suspicious of the army because of its past role in repressing it (Asad and Cubukcu 2013: 3). But beyond this historical animosity, Morsi and General Abdel Fattah al-Sisi, who headed the military, had an axe to grind. Indeed, al-Sisi had exposed their differences on 24 July 2013 in a speech at the graduation ceremony for the Navy and Air Defence academies: 'I told him [Morsi] six months ago that his project is not working out and that he should go back on it before it is too late' (*Egypt Independent* 2013: 1). What were the details and the chronology of the disputes between Morsi and the military general that led to the military's ousting of Morsi? According to Hamza Hendawi of the Associated Press, who researched the situation, the profound differences between Morsi and al-Sisi had lasted over a year, and included the worries of the general that Morsi had dangerously mismanaged the wave of protests that had resulted in dozens being killed by the security forces earlier in the year; that he was giving a free hand to Islamic militants in the Sinai by ordering al-Sisi to stop the crackdown on the jihadists; that he had alliances with Hamas and Islamist groups; that he was more interested in a regional Islamist agenda than whatever the military saw as Egypt's interests; that he had called for support to Syrian jihadists, who might one day return to Egypt and threaten Egyptian security; that he had, during a visit to Sudan in April 2013, shown flexibility over the fate of a border region claimed by both Egypt and the Sudan; and that he was trying to co-opt commanders to turn against al-Sisi (Hendawi 2013: 1–5).

Accordingly, as early as April the army had drawn up contingency plans to take charge of security should the street violence escalate out of Morsi's control, but it did not then plan to replace the President. However, towards the end of April and the beginning of May 2013, information was leaked that Morsi's aides were trying to co-opt senior army officers and Guard officers in order to replace al-Sisi. Thereupon, al-Sisi took an interest in Tamarod and worked through third parties to connect it with opposition-linked businessmen and the liberals so that they could bankroll Tamarod. The military's protection plan for the ensuing mass rallies of 30 June 2013 was widely believed to be a development of the original contingency plan of April 2013, according to Hendawi. Al-Sisi gave a 48-hour ultimatum to the President. Thereupon, Morsi tried to sound out the 2nd Field Army's Major-General Ahmed Wasfi, who was based in the Suez Canal area, with a view to installing him in al-Sisi's place, but to no avail (ibid.). The military takeover was complete.

Was the Arab Spring realised in Egypt?

Even before the ousting of Morsi, Egyptians had been pessimistic about realising the Arab Spring. Whereas 82 per cent had said that they were hopeful of its being realised in 2011 when it had begun, only 36 per cent were still hopeful in 2013, with 41 per cent expressing their overt disappointment and 22 per cent stating that they were neither hopeful nor disappointed, as reported by Zogby Research Services in June 2013 (2013: 7–8).

But after the fall of Morsi, were 'the people' the winners? 'I don't think so', wrote Khaled Abou El Fadl, a Distinguished Professor of Law at UCLA. He elaborated: 'After the coup, hundreds of people have been injured, killed and imprisoned, many more are yet to come.' According to El Fadl, 'Force begets force and despotism has a remarkable way of perpetuating itself, like lethal cancer. The military, as always, emerges with its traditional privileges and powers intact. The horrendously savage security forces of Egypt emerge as winners' (El Fadl 2013: 2).

Concerning democracy, El Fadl considered that events in Egypt heralded a 'death blow' to moderate Islamists with its belief the compatibility of Islam, democracy and human rights. Although the Salafists, bankrolled by Saudi Arabia, had sided with the Tamarod movement, they, according to El Fadl, 'do not believe in democracy . . . and . . . in civil and human rights', for 'they are the Islamists who will continue to work to root a Saudi style theocracy in Egypt', a far cry from democracy (ibid.).

There seems once again in Egypt to be a re-establishment of the Mubarak-era hierarchies of emphasising stability. In reprioritising stability, those elements of the authoritarian state – the plutocrats, the security and the military – have, according to Jack Shenker of the *Guardian*, who was stationed in Cairo, 'worked hard to shield Egypt's status quo from the full brunt of revolutionary unrest'. Shenker draws attention to his belief that

> there is another, more critical, struggle unfolding too. This is between those fighting to destroy the old authoritarian system –which for decades has denied them political and economic agency and which plunders Egypt's public wealth in the name of private profiteers, and arrests, tortures and kills those daring to defy it – and those seeking to protect it. (Shenker 2013: 2)

Is what is taking place in Egypt a classic case of the restoration of the *ancien régime*, a counter-revolution? We have witnessed the resignations of some of the liberals, like el-Baradei, from the new interim government in protest over the killings of over 600 MB members on 14 August 2013 during the military regime's dispersal of sit-in protests, along with the glee of the *fulul* over the announcement on 19 August 2013 of the release from prison (albeit under house arrest) of Hosni Mubarak, while the democratically elected President, Mohamed Morsi, languished in a detention location. Is the Arab Spring over?

The transition towards revolution in Egypt: viability of the HD hypothesis and Pendulum Model in the Egyptian case

My HD hypothesis is viable in explaining the Egyptian case of transition towards revolution starting in January 2011, and the counter-revolution which seemed to be taking place in Egypt in the summer of 2013. It was the dissonance in values between those of the ruler, who emphasised stability, and those of the ruled, who prioritised economic and social justice to be arrived at democratically, that led to the attempt at revolution in 2011. However, at present there is a reprioritising of stability by the authoritarian rule of the military in the name of national security, and economic justice has not been arrived at yet. Therefore, it may be concluded that the Arab Spring has not been realised as of the summer of 2013. The old regime seems to be coming back. But for how long? Will Egyptians, who prioritised democracy (55 per cent) over a strong leader (36 per cent) as recently as April 2013 (Pew Research Center 2013c: 60), resort to people power and attempt yet another transition to revolution and democracy should another hierarchical dissonance in priorities develop, especially if the economy is not ameliorated?

PART II

The transition towards reform

The transition towards reform

CHAPTER 4

Reforming the Moroccan monarchy

The descendant of the Prophet, Muhammad VI of Morocco, relied on religion, along with co-optation, repression and political liberalisation, all imbued with his version of Islam, since he tried to build on the 38-year stable rule of his father, King Hassan II, while introducing reforms that he considered vital and necessary for his own survival and legitimacy in the twenty-first century, most especially in 2011 when the winds of change blew in the Middle East. His actions in 2011, and the reactions of the ruled, can be explained by the Pendulum Model that I devised in my 2007 book *Middle Eastern Leaders and Islam: A Precarious Equilibrium* and applied to other states: Iraq, Egypt, Syria, Saudi Arabia and Jordan (Alianak 2007). In 2011, the hierarchies of the monarch (stability) and the ruled (economic opportunities through democracy) did not reach the dissonance level, unlike in Egypt and Tunisia, since the King responded to the ruled and instituted reforms which were perceived to be sincere given his powerful religious credentials. A similar pattern can be discerned in Jordan, where the monarch, Abdullah II, also traces his descent from the Prophet. Both monarchs weathered the crises afflicting rulers and ruled in the Middle East in 2011.

This study analyses how the Moroccan monarch tried to push the pendulum back as far as he could towards equilibrium in order to re-establish stability, mainly through religion, but also through co-optation and/or repression, and/or democratic experiments, which themselves were imbued with religion.

Co-optation as a method of regime stabilisation

Muhammad VI, following his father Hassan II, is a master of co-optation. While this has served the monarchy very well in the past, it is being challenged right now, since the co-optation of the privileged few, the elite, has led to serious charges of corruption, to the detriment of the population at large, all of which intensified during the 2011 crisis in the Middle East as a whole.

Traditionally, the Moroccan monarchs relied on the *Makhzen*, or palace elite, composed of wealthy landowners, businessmen, tribal leaders, civil servants and top-ranking military personnel (Lopez 2011). The kings allowed them to control the nation's wealth and hence to pull the political strings of the kingdom (Abend 2011: 2). In return, the palace elite supported the ruler. But when fabulous wealth enjoyed by a few exists alongside the poverty of the multitudes in cities, it spawns feelings of relative deprivation and resentment, which were exhibited during the Moroccan demonstrations of 20 February 2011 (Erlanger 2011: 2). Perhaps a WikiLeaks disclosure of a US diplomatic cable from Morocco, which revealed the vast commercial interests of some of the King's advisers in 'every' real estate project, and hence their 'appalling greed', helped fan the discontent of the young people involved in protests (*Financial Times* 2011: 2).

These demonstrations, however, were not very severe, perhaps because Muhammad VI, unlike his father, had already earned the title 'King [Champion] of the Poor' after he assumed the throne in 1999 (Waraich 2011: 2). As a populist, he embarked then on what he called his first priority, stamping out poverty. This attempt at co-opting the masses was to pay dividends in 2011, twelve years later. His economic reform measures resulted initially in improving the living conditions of the people, reducing poverty and fighting unemployment (*Agence Maghreb Arabe Presse* 2011a). Better basic services were provided in many rural areas and shanty towns. But in urban areas, the rising expectations of the residents exceeded the actual pace of anticipated economic improvements. Poverty remained widespread and unemployment soared to 9–10 per cent in 2010, especially among the numerous young in Morocco, where the median age was 26.5 and where around 20 per cent of the population lived below the poverty line (Erlanger 2011: 2). This was in spite of the positive inroads made by the monarch's National Initiative for Human Development (INDH), which gave top priority to improving the living conditions of the young and of women (*Agence Maghreb Arab Presse* 2011b: 1). But the INDH had raised awareness of the plight of most marginalised rural and urban people and of the need for sustainable development involving local participation, which was only partially achieved (Ben-Meir 2011: 3). Thus, the expectations of the ruled were raised, but not fully met. One protester lamented that he no longer wanted to pay bribes in order to get a job, illustrating the extent of corruption in the system.

To pre-empt the severity of the anticipated demonstrations of 20 February 2011, Muhammad VI resorted once again to co-optation. He promised subsidies, amounting to 1.4 billion euros, ahead of the protests, so as to soften price hikes for staples such as food and cooking oil ('Thousands demand change in Morocco', 2011). Further, after the protests, the King, who realised that he needed to speed up reforms, said that he wanted to continue the 'pursuit of reforms' and 'consolidate [the Moroccan model of state] by way of new reforms ('Big Moroccan political party calls for reforms' 2011). Perhaps he was spurred to do so by a statement by his rival and third in line to the throne, Moulay Hicham, also known as the 'Red Prince' for his leftist views, that demonstrations would occur in Morocco because 'the abyss between the social classes undermines the legitimacy of the political and economic system' ('Morocco will not be spared from unrest' 2011: 1).

Following the demonstrations of 20 February 2011 the King, in his 9 March 2011 speech to the Moroccan nation, emphasised further reforms, including promising government jobs for recent university graduates. For many Moroccans the monarch's promises were sufficient, but for some they did not go far enough. One typical 22-year-old student, Rachid, stated: 'I think he did not mention concrete reforms like the fight against corruption in the circles of power, social injustices, and the unfairness of the access to administrative jobs, which are monopolised by certain families' ('Moroccans welcome king's reform promises' 2011: 2).

Repression as a method of regime stabilisation

Repression and coercion are well-known methods used by rulers in the Middle East, including Morocco. They involve persecution, courts martial, house arrests, imprisonment, fragmentation and segmentation of opposing groups, evacuations, deportations, 'disappearances', and exile. However, repression and coercion are not sufficient to ensure compliance and cooperation in the country. They are usually accompanied by the soft power of religion (Alianak 2007: 7–8).

Although in Morocco there is more freedom of the press than in other Middle Eastern countries, journalists and bloggers face fines and even imprisonment for crossing the Red Lines imposed by the King. According to Reporters Without Borders, concerning these Red Lines, 'religion, the king and the monarchy in general, the country and territorial integrity cannot be questioned' ('Morocco country profile' 2011: 2). Criticism of the monarchy remains taboo. Those expressing 'offensive' views regarding the King and the royal family are prosecuted. The Press Law provides prison terms for recalcitrant journalists. Also, press freedom has recently dwindled (Goldstein 2009: 2). Amnesty International, in its 2009 Report, documents several cases of arrests where journalists were accused of lack of respect for the monarchy (Amnesty International 2009: 2).

The King justified this policy on Islamic grounds. He based his case on his direct descent from the Prophet Muhammad and the 350-year-old rule of his Alawite dynasty. Further, he considered himself to be the 'Commander of the Faithful', who therefore knew what was best and right in religious terms and who hence was above criticism. In fact, Article 23 of the Moroccan constitution states 'The king is inviolable and sacred'. He therefore exercises absolute spiritual power.

Morocco's human rights record was better than that of other Arab states. Nevertheless, many cases of forcible 'disappearances', arbitrary detentions and torture were documented by human rights NGOs during the reign of the King's father, Hassan II.

Seeking to end the culture of victimisation, impunity and fear and thus to rehabilitate all Moroccan society and especially the victims of oppression, the Moroccan Forum For Truth and Equity was set up, and it approached the Palace (Slyomovics 2010: 4–6). Muhammad VI, having succeeded his father, responded to the growing social pressure for change. He consulted with civil society, which included former political prisoners (Hazan 2006: 3).

In a speech on 7 January 2004 he announced the creation, by royal decree, of a Truth and Reconciliation Commission, Morocco's Equity and Reconciliation Commission (*Instance Équité et Réconciliation*) (IER). The IER Commission was to investigate human rights abuses committed between 1956 (the date of Moroccan independence) and 1999 (the year of Hassan II's death). In this way, the King was hoping to improve his image with his citizens and thus disarm his critics and counter the growing appeal of Islamists. He justified the creation of the IER Commission on Islamic grounds (as opposed to the secular reasons given by the leftist civil society elements with whom he was dealing). Furthermore, he wished his version of Islam to predominate. He therefore excluded religious figures from the membership of the Commission. Another reason for the non-selection of Islamists for the task was perhaps that the monarch wanted to keep his distance from even moderate Islamists following the Casablanca bombings, which had occurred earlier, in 2003. Thus he wanted to present an alternative to the Islamist theocracy advocated by some Islamists (ibid.: 4–5).

In an attempt to stabilise his rule, the monarch used the soft power of religion – notably, his version of Islam. By establishing the IER Commission, Muhammad VI hoped to erase the legacy of Hassan II but not the Islamic foundations of the monarchy. The Commission was not to implicate his father directly, but his father's officials – this in order to appease the Moroccan people, who wanted to know the crimes committed ('Morocco: history will keep its secrets' 2006: 1). Hence the IER Commission asked not the King, but the Prime Minister, to assume responsibility for past human rights violations in the name of the Moroccan state, and also to ask the nation for forgiveness (Hazan 2006: 12).

The IER Commission investigated some 16,861 individual cases and awarded compensation in 9,280 of these ('Morocco: history will keep its secrets' 2006: 1). It promised reparations amounting to a total of 50–70 million dollars (Hazan 2006: 12). The King invoked God to legitimise the lack of punishment in other cases. He 'depoliticised' impunity by justifying it on the grounds of the 'spirituality' of forgiveness; whereas the IER Commissioners were reluctant to justify amnesty on religious or cultural grounds (ibid.: 9).

The favourable effect of the IER Commission on the stability of the monarchy could be detected in the mildness of the 2011 demonstrations, which did not target the King himself. IER's long-term effect will, however, ultimately be predicated on whether or not past crimes will be repeated. The Advisory Council on Human Rights (CCDH) reported in January 2010 that progress had been made in aiding victims of human rights abuses, as recommended by IER (Cherkaoui 2010: 1). However, Amnesty International still reported human rights violations. These have mainly been caused by fears of terrorism and by the secession of the Western Sahara region.

Following the coordinated suicide bombings in Casablanca on 16 May 2003 (Jarrah 2003: 10–11), the regime picked up, arrested and convicted hundreds of suspects in unfair trials. Also, it held many in incommunicado detention and extracted coerced confessions. The Government did not target civil society or mainstream Islamist movements (Goldstein 2009: 1–2). However, Amnesty International expressed 'concern' about 'continuing human rights violations in the name of countering terrorism in Morocco', citing instances of 'secret and incommunicado detention; unexamined claims of torture or other ill-treatment and flawed legal proceedings (Amnesty International 2010b: 1).

Concerning the Western Sahara secessionist movement, the Polisario Front, King Muhammad VI declared in a speech on the 34th anniversary of Morocco's 'Green March' to take control of the former Spanish colony: 'One is either a patriot, or a traitor.' He continued: 'Is there a country which would tolerate a handful of lawless people exploiting democracy and human rights in order to conspire with the enemy against its sovereignty, unity and vital interests?' (Goldstein 2009: 2). This argument of 'territorial integrity' served as a pretext to violate human rights. In April 2010 Amnesty International, citing concrete examples, issued a call that 'Morocco must end harassment of Saharawi activists', who wanted independence (Amnesty International 2010a: 1).

This was in spite of the fact that, on 3 January 2010, the monarch had shown some signs of reform by asking the Advisory Committee on Regionalisation to prepare a model for 'advanced Moroccan regionalisation'. On 9 March 2011 he took the bold step of actually calling for decentralisation to be realised through elected regional councils, whose decisions were to be implemented by their Presidents instead of governors and *walis* (patrons or defenders). This change was to be voted upon by the Moroccan people in a referendum on a new constitution later in the year ('HM the King addresses speech to the nation' 2011: 1).

Repression can also be used against demonstrators – beyond journalists and dissenters whose human rights have been violated, as discussed above. While it is true that the Moroccan Government exercised restraint against the 2011 demonstrators, it has not always done so. Morocco has a long history of demonstrations. That they occur shows that there is some tolerance of expression of dissent. However, they must occur within bounds and not cross the Red Lines mentioned above. They must not target the legitimacy of the monarch, the direct descendant of the Prophet Muhammad. Moreover, they should abide by the state's rules and regulations. According to Moroccan law, prospective demonstrators must provide advance notification to the authorities, who may deny them permits or forbid demonstrations if they deem them to be a threat to public order. In addition, once the demonstrations take place, the response of the security forces has ranged from sometimes allowing protesters to proceed undisturbed to sometimes beating them with batons and assaulting journalists who film or photograph the events. On occasion, spontaneous unauthorised demonstrations did occur. Over the years the regime has charged hundreds of Moroccans with participating in 'illegal' demonstrations, which has resulted in the sentencing by the courts of many protesters to prison terms ranging from one or two to several months ('Morocco: thousands march for reform' 2011: 2). However, the police stayed away from the 2011 demonstrations. They intervened only when thugs looted and burned banks and other facilities after the peaceful demonstrations had ended.

Protesters in large Moroccan cities, the frequent scene of demonstrations, ranged from well-organised groups of unemployed citizens, who demanded jobs, to families with political prisoners. In the past there have also been demonstrations in favour of solidarity with the Palestinians. The biggest took place in Casablanca on 12 March 2000. Some half a million people demonstrated their opposition to plans to reform Morocco's Sharia-based family code (ibid.).

In this 2000 crisis involving confrontation with Islamists, and potential implications for and threats to the stability of his rule, Muhammad VI used his version of Islam. He spoke in favour of the changes to the *mudawana* family code, which made polygamy acceptable only in rare circumstances, raised the legal age for marriage for girls from 15 to 18, and gave wives 'joint responsibility' with their husbands in family matters, and the right of divorce (Ennaji 2004: 1). He based his stance on his interpretation of the Qur'ān. The Family Law was approved in 2004. The King has succeeded in winning over many Moroccan women, earning himself the title 'King [i.e. Champion] of Women'. But the pace of change was slowed, owing to considerations of stability. With the 2011 protests the momentum for change accelerated again (Erlanger 2011: 2), as evidenced by the King's speech on 9 March 2011 ('HM the King addresses speech to the nation' 2011: 1).

Political liberalisation as a method of regime stabilisation

Moroccan kings have used a hybrid of authoritarianism, Islam and democracy to stabilise their rule. Although this hybrid was initiated by Hassan II, it was later elaborated upon by Muhammad VI. However, it was under scrutiny in 2011, given the winds of democratic change in the Middle East. But the mildness of the 2011 demonstrations, and the ready acceptance by the majority of the ruled of the reforms suggested by the monarch on 9 March 2011, show the relative success of the political liberalisation method used by the King.

This hybrid model goes beyond state-centred models such as the Patrimonial Leadership Model of James Bill and Robert Springborg, which emphasises the autocratic nature of Middle Eastern monarchies (Bill and Springborg 1990) on the one hand, and society-centred models such as those presented by Augustus Norton, who is overly optimistic about the rise of civil society and democratisation (Norton 1995), to the neglect of rulers, on the other. In elaborating on the hybrid model, I analyse the relationship of monarch and ruled regarding the measures used by Muhammad VI to: (1) control participation while encouraging it; (2) curtail political parties while promoting them; and (3) limit the rise of nascent civil society while channelling it, and while promising or introducing some degree of liberalisation. These are discussed in turn.

Participation

Beginning in the aftermath of the crisis involving riots induced by suggested IMF austerity measures, in the late 1980s and early 1990s the Moroccan monarch, Hassan II, introduced political liberalisation measures. This was followed by the political liberalisation measures of his son and heir, Muhammad VI. In time, both kings emphasised their brand of Islamic democracy (liberal autocracy), which resulted in the equilibrium of the pendulum and their stability in most cases at times of crisis.

Democracy involves the free participation of citizens in the choice of their governments at constitutionally set times. But monarchs in Morocco placed themselves high above this political process. The kings often postponed elections and thereby controlled them. In Morocco, whenever the monarchy did decide to hold elections, the rulers told the people that non-participation would be taken as a personal affront and an act of defiance.

At times of domestic unrest in Morocco, King Hassan II postponed parliamentary elections for one year, as he did in 1983 and (for three years) in 1990 (Denoeux and Maghraoui 1998: 110). His successor and son, King Muhammad VI, who assumed the throne upon Hassan's death in 1999, postponed elections until 27 September 2002. In all three cases, the monarchs did not give up their brand of Islamic democracy, however illiberal it was. They conceived of themselves as the 'representatives of the Prophet on earth' and accountable only to God. They would control the country via a Moroccan style of liberalised autocracy. Muhammad VI only began to promote more liberalisation following the Arab Spring of 2011.

Like his father before him, Muhammad VI tried to combat public apathy once he had decided to hold parliamentary elections in September 2002 (Byrne 2002a: 19–20). Further, 'democracy' was promoted as a buzz-word among the voters at the time of the election (Byrne 2002b: 18). Actual voter turn-out was around 50 per cent, perhaps encouraged by the King's reform pronouncements. But what was disconcerting was that a reported 17 per cent of voters cast blank ballots to show their dissatisfaction with the electoral laws (Wolfe 2007: 2).

Accordingly, the New Electoral Law of 2005, which took effect in 2007, was designed, it was claimed, to bolster political parties and counter voter apathy. It changed the electoral system from first-past-the-post, with single-member districts, to a system of proportional representation with multi-member districts. Voters were to choose parties, which put forward a list of candidates equal in number to the available seats in the district. This was designed to focus electoral campaigns along party lines rather than encourage individual personalities. The party leaders were to determine from party lists who would actually occupy seats allotted to the party and serve in Parliament (ibid.: 1–2).

In reality, the system was skewed far to the right, in favour of the main parties, because it raised the threshold required to take seats from 3 to 6 per cent. However, it ensured that no single party dominated any districts, necessitating the formation of coalition governments. These democratic reforms, according to Adam Wolfe, resulted in 'widespread voter dissatisfaction with the current system. This ultimately helped fuel the Islamist opposition, a potentially alarming prospect in a country that has seen three suicide bombings carried out by Islamists this year [2007]' (ibid.: 1).

As a result, voter turn-out in the 2007 parliamentary elections was lower than in 2002. In fact, it was one of the lowest on record at 37 per cent, down from 58 per cent ten years earlier (Champion 2011: 3). This signalled deep dissatisfaction with the electoral system as designed and manipulated by the regime. The electorate perceived corruption, especially vote buying. There was also frustration at the slow pace of political reform (ibid.) and at the political parties' loss of touch with the population, especially the young. All these factors combined were ominous precursors of the protests of 2011.

It was notable that, before each election, the Ministry of the Interior used its study of public opinion, gathered by the local public servants of the *Makhzen*, namely the sheikhs and *muqaddam*, to redraw the boundaries of the electoral districts to the disadvantage of its opponents, and to favour pro-regime parties and candidates instead. For example, in 2007 the Government redistricted the cities of Casablanca and Tangier prior to the parliamentary elections intending to limit the Justice and Development Party's (the PJD's) chances of winning seats. The electoral system also encouraged corruption and vote buying, because the parliamentary elections were determined by local elites and personalities rather than by campaign discussions of national issues. As a result, the 'legitimacy of the government' was 'very low', in the opinion of Maâti Monjib of the Saban Center for Middle East Policy at the Brookings Institution (Monjib 2011: 13–14).

The parties were perceived as being unable to alleviate poverty and incapable of providing access to equal opportunities. The party leaderships tended to be ageing, and so were seen as being too old and set in their ways ('Moroccan parties call for political reform' 2011: 1). Perhaps in response to this, Muhammad VI called for the strengthening of political parties and civil society the better to guide citizens in their choices during his call for the revision and reform of the constitution on 9 March 2011 ('HM the King addresses speech to the nation' 2011: 2).

The monarch pre-empted the escalation of the 2011 protests by encouraging Moroccans to participate in the political process, specifically in the referendum of 1 July 2011 about the revised constitution, which encapsulated his reform measure. Despite calls for a boycott by the 20 February Movement, which had originally organised the 2011 protest, Moroccans turned out in very large numbers (70 per cent), and gave an overwhelming stamp of approval, 98 per cent showing their solidarity with the regime ('Morocco elections a foretaste for Egyptians' 2011: 1).

In a further response to the Arab Spring, Muhammad VI, again trying to steal the momentum from those who had called for a boycott while attempting to reinforce the support generated by the overwhelming turn-out for the referendum, brought forward parliamentary elections, originally scheduled for September 2012, to October 2011. The elections were finally held on 25 November 2011. The voting system was also reformed by slightly increasing the number of parliamentary seats decided on a local constituency basis from 295 to 305. A national dimension was also added by reserving on national party lists 60 places for female candidates, and 30 for male candidates, under the age of 40. These electoral reforms followed the same proportional representation system as applied to the local districts, but on the national level ('Moroccan general election, 2011' 2011: 4).

Regime critics, like Zouhair Baghough of *Morocco Board News* in Washington, who have analysed Morocco's proportional ballot with its 6 per cent threshold, contend that the reforms did not go far enough. According to Baghough, 'the present ballot system still handicaps rising challengers'; also, 'We cannot also rule out the need for the Interior Ministry to maintain their grip on various constituencies, and thus predict [if not force some] results fitting their own agenda' (Baghough 2011: 1). On the other hand, a first-past-the-post system, such as operates in the UK, would allow for strong parliamentary majorities and would not reward the 'mediocrity' of second and third slot holders. In such a system, the PJD, which in 2011 had lead candidates in almost half of all the 92 districts (divided into 305 seats), would win more seats than under the present reformed ballot system, which could conceivably lead to one-party control of the parliament (ibid.: 2).

The revised Moroccan constitution, however, provided for the eventuality of one party not winning the majority of seats by requiring the King to nominate the Prime Minister from the leading party, irrespective of the fact that it might not have won a clear majority. Nevertheless, the 2011 ballot system prevented the potential concentration of power in the hands of an opposition party which might pose a serious challenge to the monarch. The 2011 system guaranteed the manoeuvrability of the pro-monarchy parties, with whom the leading party would necessarily need to consult and compromise, preventing an anti-monarchical opposition party from controlling the Government and possibly limiting the power of the King.

The speeches of Muhammad VI just prior to the 25 November 2011 parliamentary elections showed his determination to encourage a large voter turn-out and to guide voters in making responsible choices in favour of 'able' candidates (Villanti 2011: 2). This show of support would counter the efforts of the 20 February Movement and the banned Islamist Al Adl wal Ihsane (Justice and Spirituality Movement) to boycott the parliamentary elections. The 20 February Movement had dismissed the elections as a 'piece of theatre', especially in the face of what it considered to be superficial constitutional changes designed to perpetuate a 'façade of democracy', since the King still retained supreme power over foreign, defence and security matters, and since the *Makhzen*'s behind-the-scenes dominance would not be ended under the reforms ('Q&A: Morocco elects new parliament' 2011: 2). Hence it did not want to legitimise a system that 'falls short of a genuine democracy' (Villanti 2011: 1).

Apart from this threat of boycott, the monarch's main preoccupation was with the possible political apathy of the population (Karam 2011: 1). A high voter turn-out, according to analysts, would give credibility to the reforms embodied in the revised constitution, which was passed overwhelmingly by the referendum of 1 July 2011 ('Morocco counts votes in landmark polls' 2011: 2).

The actual turn-out was considered to be moderate and 'decent' at 45 per cent, with a high degree of transparency. There was 'no indication' of fraud, according to the estimated 4,000 national and international observers (ibid.). But perhaps one-third of the eligible voters had been left off the rolls under the current registration system ('Morocco elections a foretaste for Egyptians' 2011: 1). The number of registered voters had indeed dropped from around 15 million to around 13 million, despite population increases ('Morocco holds first poll after king's reform drive' 2011: 1). Of the 21.5 million eligible Moroccans, only 13.6 million were registered in 2011; of these, only 6.2 million had voted; and of these, only 5 million had cast actual 'healthy ballots', the rest, some 20–25 per cent, being invalid and spoiled ballots. This meant that only 24 per cent of adult Moroccans had voted seriously (Baghough 2011a: 1).

According to the National Democratic Institute, a Washington-based democracy assistance group, this signalled 'citizen interest in further and deeper reform' (Allen 2011: 2). According to the same group's Morocco-based resident director, Jeffrey England, the increase in voter participation in 2011 compared to that of 2007 may not reflect increased voter enthusiasm, given that the voting age was lowered from 21 in 2007 to 18 in 2011 and that the voter rolls were trimmed (ibid.). Other analysts were less sceptical, notable among whom was the BBC's Richard Hamilton, who commented that Moroccans were optimistic about 'genuine change' despite the King retaining a lot of power ('Hopes of "genuine change" as Morocco hold elections' 2011: 2).

Political parties

Unlike the British monarchy, which is a symbolic institution, Moroccan monarchs have real power. They promote the image of standing above electoral and power politics, but in fact they are very much involved in them. Following periods of economic crisis, they have emphasised their brand of Islamic democracy, which is a liberalised autocracy. In this way, they frequently bypass modern, free party politics by adopting various tactics. They control the entry of parties into the political arena. So far as Islamist parties with possible competing values of Islamic democracy are concerned, the monarchs allow only moderate ones, co-opt them, and limit them should they perceive them as potentially offering a challenge to the equilibrium of the pendulum that represents their stability. The monarchs seek to 'depoliticise' the parties' agendas, by promoting economic and technocratic issues over political ones.

Morocco has had a multi-party system since 1962, when the one-party system was abolished (Maghraoui 2003: 70). There were 26 officially recognised parties in the 2002 parliamentary elections, whereas in 2007 the number rose to over 30. King Hassan II authorised some parties, and even promoted pro-monarchy ones, while excluding some and repressing others (Layachi 1999: 76). Parties were allowed, as long as they were supportive of the monarchy (Mednicoff 2002: 97). Here it is pertinent to note that Islamic parties, chiefly the Justice and Development Party (PJD) and the Istiqlal Party, were legalised if they adhered to the principle of the Islamic legitimacy of the monarchy.

The PJD, although calling for reforms, has been supportive of the legitimacy of the monarchy. Its moderation was apparent when, in 2003 following the suicide bombings in Casablanca, it voluntarily scaled back the number of boroughs in which it presented candidates in the local elections of 12 September. In this connection, Saad Eddine Othmani, the leader of the party in practice, stated, 'we did not want to find ourselves in the lead and arouse the fears of certain political leaders who are afraid of seeing in control a party based on Islamic references. It was a question above all of reassuring the public authorities. It is also in the interests of the country' ('Morocco: high ground' 2003: 25). The PJD, the third-largest party, wished to appear a loyal opposition without rocking the boat, fearful of the repression and re-exclusion which characterised the plight of Islamists in neighbouring Algeria. In return, there seemed to be a tacit understanding between the Palace and the PJD that it would be allowed to gain control of some of the smaller towns (ibid.: 26). Wegner summed up the stance of the party thus: 'The PJD obviously has not been an active challenger of the regime for most of its existence, but rather a cautious and compromising force.' She also stressed that the PJD 'has even actively legitimised the regime by hiding the party's political strength [prior to 2011] and by endorsing the king's political agenda' (Wegner 2011: 93). The Istiqlal Party, meanwhile, which advocates a tolerant Islam, had always supported the monarchy, although, in an endeavour to increase its influence, it had on occasion called for a truly consti-tutional monarchy (Layachi 1998: 76–7).

The more extremist Islamic groups have not formed parties. One example here is Al Adl wal Ihsane (Justice and Charity), which has mobilised support for Palestinians, opposed the Persian Gulf War in 1991, and was against women's rights (Maghraoui 2003: 74). When, in 1996, the Islamists dared to publicly demand the right to form a political party and the release of their leader Abdesslam Yacine from house arrest, sentiments which they had expressed during a university strike, the monarchy responded with jail terms and repres-sion (Layachi 1998: 99).

When opposition parties, however moderate, were seen as posing a potential threat to the stability of the monarchy (swinging the pendulum out of equilib-rium), the monarchs have responded with illiberal tactics involving changes in electoral laws. An example is the New Electoral Law of 2005, which limited the chances of winning seats, as discussed below.

A further tactic used in Morocco was 'depoliticisation' – a term coined by Maghraoui to mean 'the marginalisation of questions of legitimacy or sover-eignty and . . . the concomitant political primacy given to economic issues' (Maghraoui 2003: 67). Thus, King Muhammad VI appointed a technocrat, Driss Jettou, rather than a party leader to be Prime Minister and placed empha-sis on economic development rather than on party politics (Byrne 2002d: 66–7). The monarch told Parliament in October 2002, after this announcement: 'Democracy is not an end in itself, but rather an instrument to favour popular participation in public affairs and to mobilize for development.' He further called for 'the rehabilitation of the institution of parliament', where opposition parties would set aside 'puerile counter-arguments and sterile controversies, because these duels are not what will give a job to the unemployed or educa-tion to the illiterate'. To deal with unemployment, what was rather needed was 'investment, yes investment, and again investment' (Byrne 2002c: 28).

However, in the aftermath of the 2007 parliamentary elections, the King conceded, by appointing Abbas El Fassi of the winning Istiqlal Party to be Prime Minister (US Department of State 2010: 4). Perhaps as a counter-move, the monarch attempted to rally his allies and to strengthen his power by encourag-ing the formation of the Authenticity and Modernity Party (PAM) on 10 August 2008. A number of political parties merged into PAM, such as Al Ahd, the Environment and Development Party, the Alliance of Liberties and the Civic Initiative for Development. PAM was founded by the former interior minister Fouad Ali El Himma ('Authenticity and Modernity Party' 2010: 1).

Although, in the 2007 parliamentary elections, the Justice and Development

Party (PJD) came first in terms of the number of popular votes (503,396), it won only 46 seats, as against the 52 seats of the Independence Party (Istiqlal) with 494,256 votes. Third in line was the Popular Movement with 41 seats and 426,849 votes; fourth was the National Rally of Independence with 39 seats and 447,244 votes; and fifth was the USFP (Socialist Union of Popular Forces), which won 38 seats and 408,945 votes ('Elections in Morocco 2009: 1–2). These results reflected the New Electoral Law of 2005, which had taken effect in 2007.

However, the moderate Islamist Party, the PJD, which promoted Islamism and Islamic democracy, had, since the 2003 Casablanca and 2007 suicide bombings, softened its criticism of the westernisation of Moroccan society and adopted a more pragmatic attitude ('Justice and Development Party' 2010: 1). Its spokesman went so far as to accept the Family Law changes proposed by the King, stating, 'We agree to the reform because the foundation of Islam remained unchanged' and 'We accept the new law because it focuses not on women but on the family' (Sabra 2004: 2).

Perhaps this was due to the fact that Muhammad VI wished to be the sole interpreter of political Islam. In his address of July 2004, on 'Throne Day', he had made his views about religion and politics clear: 'It is necessary to guard against the use of religion for political purposes', he stated. He further emphasised:

> Under the Kingdom's constitutional monarchy, religion and politics come together only in the person of the King, Commander of the Faithful. In fulfilling the sacred mission with which I am entrusted, I am determined to ensure that politics is practiced by the relevant institutions and within the bounds set for it.

But he was to promote freedom of worship: 'Similarly, I shall see to it that religious matters are dealt with by the relevant councils and institutions, and that religion is practiced in mosques and other places of worship, in strict compliance with freedom of worship' ('Moroccan government' 2010: 2).

It is significant that the PJD did not officially participate in the constitutional reform demonstrations of 20 February 2011 (Champion 2011: 3), although most of its members were educated young people (Wegner 2011: 51–2), who might have participated unofficially. Also, most political parties boycotted the demonstrations. However, demands for constitutional reform were not new. What was new was that a broad spectrum of Moroccans participated. They included apolitical young persons, leftists, Islamists, and the indigenous Amazigh. They called for a parliamentary democracy, the dismissal of the coalition government and the dissolution of Parliament, although they did not want to topple the King. The organisers of the demonstrations, the Movement for Change, were joined by young people from the banned Islamist Justice and Charity opposition group ('Moroccan parties call for political reform' 2011: 1).

Two prominent government coalition parties also showed support for the demands for change. They were the Socialist Union of Popular Forces (USFP) and the Popular Movement Party. The USFP spokesman was respectful, stating 'Our party should be aligned with the demands of young Moroccans' and 'The [planned] reforms are of a nature to preserve the credibility of our action and political pluralism' ('Big Moroccan political party calls for reforms' 2011: 1). The Popular Movement Party announced that it would soon include demands for reform in a memo to the King. Its spokesman stated: 'We want to pinpoint the reforms that are needed ... The constitutional reform is the biggest of reforms.' But he cautioned: 'There are some aspects of the constitution that need reform but we don't necessarily agree with what's being floated' (Karam 2011: 1).

Muhammad VI had survived the winds of change in the Middle East in 2011. The demonstrators did not call for his ousting. The most they wanted was a British-style monarchy. After all, Muhammad VI was the descendant of the Prophet Muhammad.

Cognisant of this, the King responded to the demonstrators with prom-ises of reforms, which included the separation of powers, with a parliament, elected in 'free' and 'fair elections', possessing new powers that 'enable it to discharge its representative, legislative and regulatory mission', in which the people's house, the House of Representatives, 'plays the prominent role' ('HM the King addresses speech to the nation' 2011: 2). The King further promised 'invigorating the role of political parties within the framework of an effective pluralistic system, and by bolstering the standing of parliamentary opposition' (ibid.). Recalling the parties' anger at his unilateral appointment of a non-party technocrat, Driss Jettou, to be Prime Minister in 2002, which had cast doubt on the democratic nature of the results of the election and offered no compensation for all the trouble the parties had gone through, he confirmed 'the appointment of the Prime Minister from the political party which wins the most seats in the parliamentary election, as attested by election results' (ibid.).

Accordingly, he set up an ad hoc committee for the revision of the constitu-tion, to be headed by the respected constitutional law expert Abdeltif Mennouni. Muhammad VI called upon it to listen to the views of political parties, youth organisations, trade unions, and 'qualified' civil society groups, scholars and intellectuals. Its report was to be ready by the end of June 2011 and later be submitted to a popular referendum (ibid.: 3).

The monarch's supporters called the reforms 'the King's revolution', while sceptics were doubtful about the future actualisation of the promises. The response of most political parties was positive, whereas the radical Islamist group Al Adl wal Ihsane rejected the plan, as it was in favour of overthrowing the monarchy and establishing an Islamist regime in its stead. Some sceptical youth protesters also rejected it (Charai 2011: 1).

The opposition Islamist PJD party leader, Abdelilah Benkirane, welcomed the King's speech. Quick to supplement his initial reaction of 'We are almost surprised', he added: 'The PJD is satisfied. This development looks more like a revolution and the concerned parties are asked to work seriously to make the contents of the speech become a reality' ('Morocco to vote on a new constitution' 2011: 2). Abdelwahad Radi of the Socialist Union of Popular Forces (USFP) hailed the prospects of a new constitution: 'The king has honoured the commitments he made at the start of his reign, when he promised to bring in major reforms. The hour has come for a complete revision of the constitution' (Ali 2011: 2–3). This new constitution was adopted by a referendum on 1 July 2011, with 98.5 per cent of Moroccan voters (73 per cent of those eligible) casting affirmative ballots (Maddy-Weitzman 2012: 87–93).

Civil society

In a democratic constitutional monarchy like Great Britain, civil society organisations are allowed to form and function freely. In a liberalised autocracy like Morocco, they are greatly restricted, if they are even allowed to form.

Following the economic crises at the end of 1989 and the beginning of the 1990s, induced by austerity measures called for by the IMF, there was a proliferation of civil society organisations in Morocco in the face of cutbacks in government subsidies. There were complaints about human rights violations by the state. Salafi reformist purists advocated peaceful change in the monarchy's brand of Islam, but jihadists advocated violent change. The former can be viewed as embryonic civil society.

The liberalisation that came about as a result of these crises was illiberal, as the monarchs perceived the civil society organisations as threatening the equilibrium of the pendulum of their legitimacy. The King remained central in controlling nascent civil society organisations via legal and administrative limitations, among other more drastic measures of the watchful state.

In Morocco, whenever civil society organisations emerged, they were countered by top-down policies by the monarchy, involving in many cases ideological integration (Layachi 1998: 40). For example, in the human rights field, King Hassan II created, in 1990, a Consultative Council on Human Rights (CCDH), an official 37-member council, to counterbalance claims made by independent associations such as the Moroccan League of Human Rights, the Moroccan Organisation for Human Rights and the Moroccan Human Rights Association. These organisations had been subjected to government supervision, indirect threats against their leaders and the influencing of their actions by members of the elite and political parties (ibid.: 55–6). In answer to the human rights lobby's alarm that the security services were given a free hand to arrest, interrogate and hold for weeks or months suspected citizens, in January 2004 King Muhammad VI appointed a new Equity and Reconciliation Commission. Thus he retained monarchical supremacy. It was significant that this was also presumably done to show that the kingdom was making progress towards democratisation in a week when a US delegation was visiting Rabat for talks on a bilateral free trade agreement (Byrne 2004: 24).

Other examples of state and civil society collaboration, albeit under the control of the state, which tried to co-opt and channel it into desirable avenues, are in the areas of women's rights, labour and ethnicity. Apart from creating the IER Commission discussed above, in 2004 Muhammad VI adopted a new family law. But beyond that he sought input from women's rights NGOs, such as the Union of Feminine Action and the Democratic Association of Women, in reforming the nationality code in 2008. This allowed a woman to pass on Moroccan citizenship to children of hers possessing a non-Moroccan father. Also, in response to labour demands, the King developed a new labour code guaranteeing equal rights to workers in both the public and private sectors (Ennaji 2010: 1).

Further, responding to pressure from the Amazigh, or Berber, organisations, in 2001 he created the Royal Institute of Amazigh Culture, with a mission to recognise and revive the Amazigh language by introducing it into schools and universities (ibid.). Also, in response to the participation of Amazigh in the demonstrations of 20 February 2011, Muhammad VI called for 'Enshrin[ing] in the Constitution . . . the rich, variegated yet unified character of the Moroccan identity, including the Amazigh component as a core element and common asset belonging to all Moroccans' ('HM the King addresses speech to the nation' 2011: 2). Indeed, the new constitution made the Amazigh language, Tamazight, an official language of Morocco alongside Arabic (*Texte intégral du projet de nouvelle Constitution* 2011: Article 5).

Another organisation created by Muhammad VI, this time aimed at targeting poverty, was the National Initiative for Human Development (INDH). However, poverty remained rampant in Morocco. In 2011 unemployment officially stood at 9–10 per cent, but actually the figure was much higher. Youth unemployment was officially estimated to be around 20 per cent (Lopez 2011: 2). The resultant dissatisfaction was reflected in the demands of the young (and other) demonstrators on 20 February 2011. These included economic demands such as for lower food prices, better access to healthcare and the creation of jobs (Erlanger 2011: 1).

Muhammad VI, contrary to rumours swirling about on Twitter that he would use an investiture speech the next day to acknowledge the protesters' demands, made reference to the events, noting that he 'would not cede to demagoguery and improvisation' (Abend 2011: 2). But he did say that he wanted to promote the 'pursuit of reforms' and was ready to 'consolidate [the Moroccan model of state] by way of new reforms'. His government's spokesman and Communications Minister, Khalid Naciri, declared also that the Government had 'got the message . . . Now we have to speed up [the reform process]' ('Big Moroccan political party calls for reforms' 2011: 1).

Accordingly, the King, on 3 March 2011, announced the creation of the National Human Rights Council to replace the Consultative Human Rights Council, which had been established in 1990 by his father. The new council was to be made up of representatives of public authorities, political parties and independents, and NGOs. It was set up to defend human rights, replacing the existing organisation, which had a purely consultative role ('Morocco creates rights council' 2011: 1). How effective would it really be? Some, for example Khadija Ryadi, President of the Moroccan Association of Human Rights, preferred to wait before passing judgement (Brouksy 2011: 3).

It can be seen that whenever Muhammad VI sensed the demands of civil society he formed his own version of state organisations, thus preventing any truly independent centres of competing power. When he allowed them to exist, he subjected them to legal and administrative limitations. Extensive red tape along with measures designed to prevent some organisations from acquiring legal status prevailed since Hassan II's time. Applications for legal status could be delayed indefinitely. There were strong financial incentives, encouraging only activities considered appropriate (Layachi 1998: 43). Once the organisation was formed its activities could be controlled. Press rules applied to these organisations. These involved prohibitions against criticism of the monarch, attacks on Islam and any questioning of Morocco's claim to Western Sahara. The state could arbitrarily charge the association and its leaders of violations of these rules and give it severe sanctions. The association could be suspended or dissolved and its executive officers could be held personally responsible, fined and imprisoned for a maximum sentence of two years (ibid.: 43–4).

An example of restrictive action by the state at a time of crisis was when it asked the Al Adl wal Ihsane (Justice and Charity) association, a charitable Islamist association, not to participate in the 'march against terrorism', which was held in Casablanca on 25 May 2003 against the Casablanca suicide bombings. Even though the Islamist association wanted to show that it was not an extremist Islamist terrorist group by participating in the march, it was not trusted by the regime, which believed that the association was not sincere. Accordingly, supporters of the association were turned back by the police ('Morocco: darkening skies' 2003: 25). In this connection, although the Islamic Affairs Ministry had kept a watchful eye on the goings-on in the country's mosques, it was, on the one hand, at times accused of being lenient towards Salafi reformists ('Morocco: aftershock' 2003: 19–20). On the other hand, the regime was thought to have gone too far in punitive measures at other times. Human rights organisations complained about unsatisfactory trials and long prison sentences handed down against imams, who were accused of inspiring with their preaching the Casablanca bombings by Salafi *jihadis* (Byrne 2004: 25).

The direction given to civil society by the monarch can be discerned by his speech on 9 March 2011, in which, in an attempt to 'shore up constitutional mechanisms for providing guidance to citizens', he called for 'bolstering up . . . the role of civil society' ('HM the King addresses speech to the nation' 2011: 2). He further urged its participation in an advisory role to the Advisory Committee for the Revision of the Constitution. Here, during the ceremony setting up the Committee, he emphasised specifically the role of leaders of trade unions ('HM the King gives speech' 2011: 1).

In 2011, a new phenomenon had emerged in the organisation of civil society – namely social networking, which bypassed the state. The '20 February Movement', which organised the demonstrations, made extensive use of Facebook and Twitter ('Thousands demand change in Morocco' 2011: 1) and cellphone communications. The state's response was to allow the protesters to proceed without police harassment so long as they were peaceful – although the secret police was active at the gatherings.

On the whole, whenever the Moroccan king perceived a potential threat to the equilibrium of the pendulum of his stability, he set limits on independent associative life, controlled it, and directed it, channelling it towards reform rather than revolutionary demands. Perhaps the existence of civil society organisations spared Morocco from the unrest spreading all over the region (Tuysuz 2011: 3).

The transition towards reform: has the Arab Spring been realised?

Morocco chose evolution rather than revolution in attempting to transition to democracy. According to the amended Moroccan constitution, the King's prerogative to appoint the Prime Minister was curtailed. The monarch was henceforth obliged to choose the Prime Minister from the party that had won the most seats, but not necessarily a majority, in the parliamentary elections since the voting system did not allow any political party to garner an absolute majority ('Elections in Morocco' 2011: 1).

In the parliamentary elections of November 2011, the Islamist PJD won 107 seats in the 395-seat Parliament, short of the 198 seats it needed to form a government by itself ('Benkirane starts talks to form new government' 2011: 1). True to the amended constitution, the King chose Abdelilah Benkirane, the leader of the PJD, which was the leading party, to be Prime Minister and form a coalition government. This was a first, since previously the Islamist Party had not participated in government. Benkirane is from the more conciliatory pro-monarchy faction of the party and is a strong supporter of the monarch, while other party members would perhaps prefer a less powerful king. Accordingly, Benkirane declared: 'The head of the state is the king and no one can govern without him' ('Faith meet Morocco's new Islamist Prime Minister' 2011: 3). Indeed, the monarch still retained the final say on issues of religion, defence, security and justice ('Moroccans vote in first legislative elections under new constitution' 2011: 1).

Under the new constitution, Muhammad VI remained *Amir al Mouminine* (Commander of the Faithful) and presided over the Higher Council of the Ulema, which was charged with issuing all *fatwā* (religious rulings) (Article 41). The person of the King was inviolable and respect was due to him from all subjects (Article 46). Also, he had the right to dismiss government ministers (Article 47). He was chairman of the Supreme Judicial Council (Article 115) and president of the new National Security Council. He remained the symbol of unity of the country, and supreme arbiter between institutions (Article 42) (*Texte intégral du projet de nouvelle Constitution* 2011).

The priorities of the King and Benkirane were similar, and thus no dissonance was experienced. They both emphasised stability. Benkirane stated: 'The interests of the country and the preservation of stability . . . will always be my priority' ('Benkirane: our government will be guided by competence, integrity and credibility' 2011: 1). He emphasised: 'Morocco chose to do its own revolution, while preserving the monarchy and its stability and bring about real change' (Bennis 2011: 1).

Part of this change, according to Benkirane, was aimed at dealing with and overcoming relative economic deprivation, a major demand of the protesters. According to him, the *Makhzen* must realise that its old games (of corruption, etc.) must cease in the face of the new political environment. He declared: 'The *Makhzen* will have to become a bit reasonable. It must understand that it can sacrifice the political parties and the PJD, but that will not resolve the problem' ('Faith meet Morocco's new Islamist Prime Minister' 2011: 5).

But were the economic demands of the protesters met by the summer of 2013? Would the Islamist-led coalition government lead to the realisation of this aspect of the Arab Spring too? An assessment of the Moroccan economy around two years after the 20 February 2011 protests, after the PJD's coalition government had been in power for around a year and a half, shows that the demands of the Arab Spring protesters have not been met yet, although attempts have been made in that direction. For one thing, corruption levels have improved somewhat, from 3.4 in 2010 to 3.7 at the end of 2012 on the Corruption Perception Index (10 being 'very clean'), but corruption was still rampant (Transparency International 2012: 5). But at the macro-economic level, the deficit had widened to 7.5 per cent in 2012, with public debt exceeding 59 per cent, whereas it had been only 48 per cent in 2008 (Belghiti 2013: 1). The budget deficit reached 2.2 per cent of GDP in the first quarter of 2013 ('Subsidy reform dispute imperils Morocco's ruling coalition' 2013: 2). Also, the regime's targets on reducing unemployment were not met. On the contrary, unemployment increased, from 9.1 in 2011 to 9.2 per cent in 2012, according to the Ombudsman for Democracy and Human Rights (MDDH). Moreover, commenting on the Benkirane Government's performance in its first year in power, the Ombudsman was critical so far as the social sectors were concerned. He lamented 'the Executive lack of visibility for the sectors of Health, Education, Housing and Employment' (Boudarham 2013a).

In addition, the economic outlook of the country did not seem very bright. The Government's efforts to avoid a drop in living standards were marred by the Eurozone debt crisis, which hit Morocco's main source of trade, investment and tourism hard, and by the upheavals across the Arab world (El Yaakoubi 2013: 1). Morocco's trade deficit rose to a record $23.6 billion ('Subsidy reform dispute imperils Morocco's ruling coalition' 2013: 2). Benkirane's administration did attempt to diversify by seeking financial aid from and increasing bilateral trade with Ankara (Kozlowski 2013: 1).

At the same time, the Prime Minister sought a bail-out from the IMF by trying to meet its hard bargaining positions. For example, the IMF wanted the PJD Government to cut substantially government subsidies of the food and fuel of all Moroccans. It did, however, negotiate a compromise with Benkirane, favouring direct aid to the poorest Moroccans while reducing subsidies on food and energy for the general public. Indeed, state subsidies had shot up to 57 billion dirhams ($6.6 billion) in 2012, from 48.8 billion in 2011 and 29.8 billion in 2010, which amounted to 15 per cent of total public spending ('Subsidy reform dispute imperils Morocco's ruling coalition' 2013: 1).

Then, in July 2013, there came a major political crisis in Morocco. The projected agreement with the IMF caused the Istiqlal Party, a partner in the governing coalition, to withdraw its ministers. The Istiqlal Party felt discomfort with the political power sharing formula whereby it was a junior partner in the Benkirane Government (Boudarham 2013c). The main motivation behind this defection was, however, fear that the reduction of subsidies would re-ignite street protests. According to Omar Bendorou of the University of Rabat, 'The Istiqlal [move] is not independent from the palace, which retains real power . . . Maybe the palace wants to control the structural reforms and put the PJD under pressure' ('Subsidy reform dispute imperils Morocco's ruling coalition' 2013: 2).

The Istiqlal did, in fact, appeal to royal arbitration by the monarch under Article 42 of the new constitution ratified in 2011. This elevated the King to the role of saviour, a starring role, rather than subtracting from his powers. It raised the spectre of the time when Muhammad VI had appointed Driss Jettou, a technocrat, Prime Minister in 2002 to deal with the economy (Iraqi 2013b: 1–2). Perhaps a divide-and-rule tactic on the monarch's part would be counterproductive after the Arab Spring, for what is really needed may be more fundamental changes such as the overhauling of the electoral system and political parties – for example, changing the electoral system by introducing a threshold deterring national representation for small groups and forcing pre-electoral alliances, which would probably lead to the emergence of three or four homogeneous power blocs, resulting in a majority consisting of one or two major parties only (Iraqi 2013c: 2) and hence avoid unstable coalition governments.

Although the economy may affect the plight of Moroccan governments, it does not tend to have an adverse effect on the monarchy itself. A survey conducted by Mohamed Daadaoui between December 2006 and January 2007 shows that 'Moroccans view government separately from the king, who is practically immune from criticism in areas of socioeconomic performance' (Daadaoui 2011: 95). Seventy-five per cent of the survey respondents were dissatisfied with the performance of their government. But they were very favourably disposed towards Muhammad VI. Daadaoui attributes this to the monarchy's 'invoking culturally and historically resonant symbols' to engender 'legitimacy and submission, without the costly use of violence' (ibid.: 94). These symbols depict the monarch's prophetic lineage, his being Commander of the Faithful, his having *baraka* (spiritual power which is only endowed to the descendants of the Prophet), and his having a *bai'ah* with the people, and elicit legitimacy for the monarchy. The symbols combine the religious, which are derived from religious texts and practices, and the traditional, which are purely customary or tribal. Seventy-seven per cent of the survey respondents viewed favourably the symbol of the King's prophetic lineage as the thirty-fourth direct descendant of the Prophet; 74 per cent believed in his being 'Commander of the Faithful'; 72 per cent expressed approval of his *Baraka*; and 56 per cent would abide by the *bai'ah* (ibid.: 82, 91–2). The *bai'ah* is the contractual covenant between the monarch, as the descendant of the Prophet, and the ruled, which was renewed during a ceremony entitled *tajdid al wala'* (renewal of allegiance) every year in Morocco – a ritual to reinforce support for the monarchy (Daadaoui 2011: 83). Moreover, the interviewees expressed trust in the King, with 42.9 per cent trusting him 'a lot' and 22.6 per cent trusting him 'somewhat' (ibid.: 91).

My study confirms Daadaoui's findings about the importance of religion, and especially religious symbols, plus feelings of trust in the ruler in eliciting the support of the people for the King during the Arab Spring, as depicted by my Pendulum Model. Faced with economic crises, the Moroccan monarch attempted to swing the pendulum of his stability towards equilibrium, by not losing sight of his religious credentials. This led to a liberalised autocracy, a hybrid of autocracy, Islam and democracy.

Liberalisation involves participation, freely competitive political parties, and an active civil society. In all these respects Morocco tends to be illiberal, however liberalised the monarch depicted the country as being prior to 2011. However, the speech of Muhammad VI after the 20 February 2011 demonstrations showed the monarch's inclinations towards reform.

So far as participation is concerned, the monarch placed himself above the political process – at times postponing elections. When he did decide to hold elections, he campaigned for participation, taking non-participation as an act of defiance. He emphasised to an apathetic citizen body a duty, which he depicted as Islamic, to participate in his attempt to swing the pendulum of his stability towards equilibrium, especially at the time of the Constitutional Referendum and the following parliamentary elections in 2011.

As we have seen, in Morocco, the monarch derived his legitimacy by appealing to his direct descent from the Prophet Muhammad. He emphasised his right to a *bai'ah* (an Islamic oath of allegiance between the rulers and the ruled) with the people. While calling for a 'new charter between the Throne and the People' on 9 March 2011, following the pro-democracy demonstrations of 20 February 2011, Muhammad VI reiterated the 'sacred character of our immutable values, which are unanimously supported by the nation – namely Islam as the religion of a state which guarantees freedom of worship' and the monarch's role as '*Imarat al-Muminin* (Commandership of the faithful)' ('HM the King addresses speech to the nation' 2011: 2).

So far as political parties are concerned, the King promoted an image of standing above them. Following periods of crisis, the monarch emphasised his brand of Islam, a liberalised autocracy. The tactics involved here were control of entry of parties into the political arena, the promoting of only moderate Islamist parties supportive of the monarchy, and the 'depoliticising' of the parties' agendas by promoting economic and technocratic issues over political ones. However, in his 9 March 2011 speech the King called for 'invigorating the role of political parties' (ibid.). After the parliamentary elections of November 2011, he appointed the leader of the PJD to head the Government, although it had never been part of the Government in the past.

So far as civil society is concerned, the monarch retained supremacy. When he perceived a potential threat to the equilibrium of the pendulum of his stability, he set limits on independent associative life, controlled it and directed it. In Morocco, a liberalised autocracy involved illiberal tactics such as the requirement of government permission to form an association, harassment by the secret police, legal and administrative limitations, and control over freedom of expression and action, among other more drastic measures of the watchful state. However, this was not allowed to lead to demands for revolution, because the monarch invoked his sacred role as a reformer. King Muhammad VI concluded his speech of 9 March 2011 on this note: 'I only desire [your] betterment to the best of my power; and my success [in my task] can only come from Allah. In Him I trust, and unto Him I look. True is the word of God' (ibid.: 3).

Will the Moroccan monarchy move more in the direction of political liberalisation and democracy – perhaps even to the extent of emulating the British monarchy as a last resort? Certainly the calls for democracy sweeping Middle Eastern countries in 2011 would predispose one to think that political change in

Morocco is inevitable. The monarch himself believed that the time for change had come, as his speech on 9 March 2011 indicated. Muhammad VI's past image as 'King [Champion] of the Poor', and his reform efforts in relation to his father's regime's repressive measures and human rights abuses, will certainly serve as a positive legacy of his rule. He has accepted also a parliamentary government reducing his powers somewhat. Further, the monarch's religious credentials as a direct descendant of the Prophet Muhammad rule out drastic change, as the ruled tend to trust him enough, in his carrying out of his reform promises, not to experience a dissonance of hierarchies, as explained by my HD hypothesis and Pendulum Model.

The evolutionary transition to democracy tends to be accepted by most political parties. But were the demands of the Arab Spring protesters realised in the implementation of the new constitution, as of summer 2013? Now that two years have passed since the adoption of the new Moroccan constitution, the euphoria has given way to the realisation that at best it resulted in 'reform by procrastination', and at worst in many of its articles being left unimplemented. It was generally understood that the new constitution was supposed to be specified by a series of organic laws. However, only four of the nineteen projected laws have been passed. Most notable here is the making of Tamazight the co-official language with Arabic (Article 5).

But the promised human rights reforms, where the new constitution broke new ground in promoting judicial independence and the rights of persons before the courts (Articles 19–40), have not yet been achieved. Indeed, Human Rights Watch reported in 2013 that torture and mistreatment of prisoners continued. It documented many cases where convictions were based largely on contested confessions and where there was denial of timely access to justice. These involved the 20 February Youth Movement protesters and Saharawi activists (Human Rights Watch 2013). Also, as of July 2013, 60 activists from the 20 February Movement remained behind bars. Attempts to demonstrate against their incarceration were met by police efforts to disperse the protesters (Bencheikh 2013).

The record of the new constitution on freedom of the press is better. It guarantees this by Article 28, which reads 'The freedom of the press is guaranteed and may not be limited in any form of prior censure' (*Texte intégral du projet de nouvelle Constitution* 2011). Reporters Without Borders acknowledged some improvement regarding this freedom in moving Morocco up to 136th place (from 138th) on a scale of 1 to 179, where 1 represents maximum freedom and 179 the worst case. But Morocco is still very limiting of the press compared to other countries worldwide (Boudarham 2013b: 1).

So far as freedom of speech goes, that was promised by Articles 10 and 25 of the new constitution of 2011, but it was 'sidelined' in practice. Article 25 stipulated: 'The freedoms of thought, of opinion and of expression under all their forms are guaranteed' (*Texte intégral du projet de nouvelle Constitution* 2011). According to Samia Errazzouki, the proposed changes were 'just window dressing' and 'the government's repression of freedom of expression has remained steadfast even after the new constitution'. She cited examples of incarceration of dissidents – for example, Mouad Belghouat for his anti-regime lyrics, Wahid Bahomane for posting a caricature of Muhammad VI on Facebook, and Abdessamad Hidour, an activist belonging to the 20 February Movement, for uploading on YouTube a video railing against the King's corrupt practices (Errazzouki 2013: 1).

The thorny issue of Islamist prisoners has also preoccupied Muhammad VI. As of April 2013 some 500 Salafists were still in jail. Here, the King was sole master of the game. He alone could give a royal pardon, which he timed according to circumstances to guarantee the stability of his rule. For example, when, just three days before the 20 February 2011 protests, the Salafist prisoners staged a noisy sit-in at Sale prison, the King took notice of it and acted promptly, as it coincided with the Arab Spring. Thus, not long afterwards, on 25 March, he promised to pardon 196 Salafist prisoners, who were promptly released from jail on 14 April 2011 (Eddahbi 2013: 1–2).

Faced with cleavages in Moroccan society between secular and extremist Islamist groups and between the very traditional *Makhzen* and the too progressive forces, Muhammad VI adopted a cautious wait-and-see attitude. This would allow him the luxury of choosing the policy and timing necessary to collect dividends (Bencheikh 2013: 2; Iraqi 2013a: 1). By means of this gradualism, he stood above the different groups as 'Commander of the Faithful', the final arbiter, the descendant of the Prophet Muhammad, and guaranteed the stability of the rule of the monarchy following the Arab Spring.

Viability of the HD hypothesis and Pendulum Model in the Moroccan case

The Pendulum Model can be applied very well to the Moroccan case of transition towards reform. There was very little dissonance in the hierarchies of Muhammad VI and Moroccans during the Arab Spring. The people trusted the King almost completely, because he had been a genuine reformer well before the Arab Spring of 2011, being known as 'King [i.e. Champion] of the Poor' and 'King [Champion] of Women', in stark contrast to Mubarak of Egypt and Ben Ali of Tunisia, who favoured the rich at the expense of the poor. So Muhammad VI rose above everyday politics as the final arbiter and guardian of the country through his distinguished lineage. He could afford to make some concessions to popular demands for political reform, as he was perceived to be the 'Commander of the Faithful'. His family had enjoyed unbroken successful rule for almost the past 350 years. This was a period of rule more than three times longer than that of the Jordanian Hashemite monarchy, which was the creation of the British after World War I. Perhaps this explains why Abdullah II of Jordan chose a more limited and slower timetable for reform, as will be seen in the next chapter.

CHAPTER 5

Reforming the Jordanian monarchy

How did the forty-third direct descendant of the Prophet Muhammad, King Abdullah ibn Al Hussein (King Abdullah II) of Jordan, weather the 2011 Arab Spring, stabilise his rule and attempt to transition towards reform rather than succumb to revolution? I attempt here to explain Abdullah II's actions as a ruler who has survived up until now using my Pendulum Model. The explanatory value of this dynamic, interactive model of the relationship between rulers and ruled at times of crisis is assessed, as Abdullah II (unlike the secular leaders of the Middle East, who were toppled) resorted to religion, which permeated his other methods of co-optation, repression and, especially, political liberalisation, and which lessened the severity of the hierarchical dissonance in values experienced at the crisis-point in the 2011 Arab Spring between rulers and ruled, and hence contributed to the survival of the regime by making accommodation and reform more tenable.

The King was always aware of the significance of his lineage and emphasised it on every occasion, but he was also realistic enough to recognise the dangers he faced. In his most recent book, entitled *Our Last Best Chance*, he wrote: 'The Hashemite lineage has always commanded respect across the Arab and Muslim world, but our traditional moderation, coupled with our openness to the West, has often made us a target of extremists' (King Abdullah II of Jordan 2011: 245). Specifically, he always emphasised his piety. For example, in the chapter entitled 'My Islam' he wrote: 'As the head of a country, I pray for my people, for improvement in their standard of living and health. Sometimes I pray for specific things like creating more jobs for young people' (King Abdullah II of Jordan 2011: 240). He wrote this out of an awareness of the demands of young unemployed protesters.

Indeed, according to a Pew Study, Jordanians preferred a strong economy (61 per cent) to a good democracy (33 per cent). Jordanians were not as enthusiastic for democracy as Tunisians and Egyptians. Further, Jordanians responded that they would prefer a larger role for Islam in the politics of the country (Pew Study 2012: 2, 3). In line with this, they supported King Abdullah II's leadership 'as a point of consensus' for the country, for after all he is a Hashemite and a descendant of the Prophet Muhammad. In fact, the Secretary-General, Hamza Monsour, of the leading opposition party the Islamic Action Front (IAF), had declared, as far back as 31 January 2011, 'We recognise and acknowledge the legitimacy of the Hashemites' ('Islamists: Jordan is not Egypt' 1 February 2011:

1). Also, the priorities of Jordanians were not far removed from the King's – that is, valuing stability – even though for them the economy was the first priority. Even the IAF, the political arm of the Muslim Brotherhood, which decided to boycott the parliamentary elections scheduled for 23 January 2013, opted for stability, the IAF spokesperson, Murad Adayleh, stating to the *Jordan Times* in December 2012 'What we want is to reform the regime, as the country's stability is of the utmost importance to all opposition groups, particularly since we live in a turbulent region' (Omari 2012b), in reference perhaps to the raging civil war in neighbouring Syria. But were Jordanians co-opted, so far as their first priority of the economy was concerned?

Co-optation as a method of regime stabilisation

Conditions for a hierarchical dissonance of values of rulers and ruled were ripe by December 2010. Jordanians had their hopes for political and economic reforms raised in 2002 with the King's launching of the Jordan First concept, and again in 2005 with the monarch's holistic initiative, the Jordanian National Agenda, which was to serve as a blueprint for political, economic and social reforms, only to be dashed again and again.

The 2002 Jordan First concept was later seen as more of an attempt to deflect Jordanian public attention away from divisive regional issues and towards domestic priorities such as national unity and economic development than an attempt at genuine political reform. For example, in December 2002, the Planning Minister, Bassam Awadallah, urged voters and candidates for the 2003 parliamentary elections to concentrate on the Jordan First motto – that is, on the 'doable and practical platforms for domestic change' – rather than to focus on 'the Palestinian–Israeli conflict and the Iraq crisis'. The latter were represented as being inconsistent with the 'national interest' – on the basis, mainly, of the fear that they could help the Islamist political opposition win seats in Parliament (Greenwood 2003: 101–2). Indeed, of the five themes discussed by the committee set up for the task, only one was realised, namely the six-seat parliamentary quota for women (Dimou 2011: 3).

Later, in 2005, a Jordanian National Agenda committee once again came up with recommendations for reform. It focused on three areas: basic rights and freedoms, economic and social policies and state infrastructure. Building on these, the then Prime Minister, Marouf al-Bakhit, called for a meeting of 700 participants over a two-day period in 2006, which developed a document entitled 'We Are All Jordan', covering fifteen priorities set to be achieved over the next ten years. It emphasised the sovereignty of the state, national security, and loyalty and nationalism (ibid.) – all pertaining to national security. Indeed, in the wake of the November 2005 suicide bombings at three hotels by a wing of al-Qaeda, the top priority in the hierarchy of values of the King had shifted towards security and stability. Abdullah II had called then for a new strategy to deal with the 'changed circumstances' ('Country profile: Jordan' 2011: 2).

Further, there was in Jordan a fear on the part of many, especially the East Bank minority of original Jordanians, that political reforms would lead to 'Palestinisation' of the country (Dimou 2011: 2). Therefore, 'little or nothing was done' in the realm of the National Agenda of reforms (Sweis 2011b: 1). According to Mohammed Sweidan, assistant managing editor of the Amman independent daily newspaper *Al Ghad*, 'There was not enough internal or external pressure like there is now [2011] to move forward and apply reform' (ibid.).

Co-optation as a method of appeasing the elite had been practised by King Hussein, and continued under Abdullah II. However, the unusual events of the Arab Spring, with the ensuing demonstrations, called for unusual, much broader and deeper methods of co-optation. New groups, such as the unemployed but educated youth, including the Jordanian street, had to be appealed to. Abdullah II resorted to co-optation in the economic realm.

The economic co-optation package that Abdullah II put together must be viewed within the context of the realities of the Jordanian economy as a whole and the demands of the 2011 protesters in particular. The economy had been improving since 2000. Annual growth of the GDP had averaged 6.7 per cent between 2000 and 2010 (World Bank 2012: 215). At the beginning this had raised Jordanians' expectations, only for them to be dashed by the worldwide economic downturn of 2008–11, a precondition of revolution according to the J-Curve theory of Davies (Davies 1962: 5–19).

Moreover, Jordan, as a small developing country with no oil wealth, had great disparities of income, which contributed to perceptions of relative deprivation resulting in instability. In 2010, the poorest 10 per cent of Jordanians and the poorest 20 per cent of the population had incomes of 3.4 and 7.7 per cent respectively of the total national income. At the other end of the income scale, the highest-earning 10 per cent and the next-highest 20 per cent received 28.7 and 43.6 per cent of the national income respectively (World Bank 2012: 75). The poverty rate (those on the national poverty line) was 13.0 per cent of the population in 2010 (ibid.: 66). Youth unemployment (i.e. unemployment among 15- to 24-year-olds) ranged from 23 per cent for males to 46 per cent for females (ibid.: 79). The Jordanian Government faced challenges in alleviating the economic situation owing to an increase in the deficit, which had risen from -2.0 per cent of GDP in 2000 to -5.4 per cent in 2010. In addition, total Jordanian debt amounted to 59 per cent of the GDP in 2010 (ibid.: 259). However, Jordan continued to rely heavily on grants and other revenues from rich Gulf States, the EU and the USA (among others), up to 36 per cent of its revenue (ibid.: 267), to help alleviate the overall economy.

Many of the protesters blamed the neoliberal economic policies of the Government, involving the privatisation of state enterprises, and the corruption that, it was believed, this had caused. On 5 February 2011, a group of 36 tribal figures went so far as to publish an accusation that the public coffers had been 'looted' by unbridled individuals with criminal intent and called for action against the pervasive corruption of 'power centers [an oblique reference to the Queen and to other Palestinians] [who] are plundering the country' (Susser 2011: 4–5). Queen Rania, herself born of Palestinian parents in Kuwait, was accused of using her office to help some 78,000 Palestinians, between 2005 and 2010, to obtain Jordanian nationality, adding to the fear of East Bank Jordanians that the addition of more Palestinians could burden Jordan politically by facilitating Israel's goal of turning it into a substitute homeland for the Palestinians. Further, Queen Rania was likened to Leila Trabelsi, the wife of the ousted Tunisian President, Ben Ali, who had led a lavish lifestyle and sought to benefit her family. Specifically, the Jordanian tribesmen accused Rania of extravagant celebration of her 40th birthday in September 2010, and called on the King to return to the Treasury the farms and land that they alleged he had given to the Queen's Yassin family (Habib 2011: 1–2; Sandels 2011: 1). These allegations were subsequently denied by the royal court ('Royal court denies Jordan tribes targeting queen' 2011: 1).

It was obvious that government retrenchment had hurt the original Jordanians, who relied more on government programmes than private-sector businessmen, most of whom tended to be Palestinians. All this resulted in counter-demonstrations by pro-Government individuals (Susser 2011: 2). However, there were other complaints, at demonstrations organised by the National Campaign for Defending Jordanian Workers on the occasion of Labour Day, about the adoption of a free-market economy, which had adversely affected workers and small business owners (Kheetan 2011e: 2).

The King, after meeting with Jordanian citizens, stated on 10 May 2011 that he was aware of the fear generated among citizens and officials and in the private sector by the dire economic situation, which, he believed, had been exacerbated by the global financial crisis. His priority was to attract Arab and foreign investment so as to provide jobs, since there was an annual need for 60,000 jobs while 'the private sector cannot provide more than 10,000' ('Political reform to meet aspirations of Jordanian people – Monarch' 2011: 1).

Indeed, his immediate response to the demonstrations in January 2011 had been the designation of a $169 million plan towards the reduction of price increases and unemployment (Dimou 2011: 2). Also, on 11 January 2011, the Government had announced an aid package for raising subsidies on basic foodstuffs and for reducing taxes on fuel. When the protests continued, the monarch called for an aid plan which included a cost-of-living allowance for members of the military, pensioners and civil servants (Susser 2011: 4). Furthermore, later, in May 2011, pay rises and improvements in living conditions were proposed for public-sector and for 3,500 municipal employees respectively (Omari 2011a: 1; 2011b: 1).

However, as the protests continued, the King did not have the relatively unlimited funds of Saudi Arabia, which had designated its own $125 billion fund as a palliative for its people. But Jordan's admission by the hereditary rulers of the Gulf to membership of the Gulf Cooperation Council as a gesture towards a fraternal Arab monarchy generated regional economic aid for the monarchy and represented a mitigating shot in the arm (Dimou 2011: 4). Also, the newly discovered rich uranium mines in Jordan (the eleventh-largest deposits in the world) could potentially generate additional revenues for the state to be used in the long run (Obeidat 2011: 1).

In response to the extended demonstrations of June, Abdullah II reiterated, in a televised speech on 12 June 2011, 'the importance of economic reform . . . foremost of which are tax reforms to achieve social justice' and 'secure work opportunities for youth' ('Full text of His Majesty King Abdullah's speech' 2011: 3). The monarch had reached out to the disadvantaged and was trying to appease them.

But the protesters also called for battling corruption more effectively. Jordan possessed an Anti-Corruption Commission that had been established in November 2006 to deal with cases of *wasta* (nepotism) (Dimou 2011: 3). In 2010, Transparency International, in its Corruption Perception Index for that year, gave Jordan a score of 4.7 on a scale of 10 (where 10 was least corrupt and 0 most corrupt). It ranked the monarchy sixth in the region, ahead even of Morocco, which it ranked tenth with a score of 3.4 (Transparency International 2010: 12). The 2011 Corruption Perception Index ranked Jordan 56th out of 183 countries worldwide (Freedom House 2012: 2).

The Anti-Corruption Commission reported in April 2011 that it had investigated 399 suspected cases of corruption during the first quarter of 2011, compared with 1,890 cases in 2010 and 1,758 in 2009. Around 41 per cent of cases centred on the exploitation of government posts (Hazaimeh 2011a: 1). As it tried to increase its transparency and accessibility, the Commission even created a Facebook page in April and promised to issue monthly reports about its efforts (Sweis 2011a: 3).

But the demonstrations against corruption continued into late May and early June ('Jordanians slam corruption, demand elected government' 2011: 1; Kheetan 2011g: 1–2). They mainly centred on three high-profile cases, the Shahin case, the housing project case and the casino case. In the first case, the Commission's investigation led to the resignation of two ministers over the fact that they had mistakenly given permission to Khalid Shahin, a convicted tycoon who was serving a jail sentence for bribery, to travel abroad for medical treatment when he was later seen at a London café and was obviously well (Hazaimeh 2011e: 1–2). The second case related to a nationwide housing project involving kickbacks received by former ministers and senior officials for corruption as adduced by the Anti-Corruption Commission. Since the sole party entrusted by the constitution to impeach ministers, either incumbent or former, was the Lower House of Parliament, the case was referred to it by the Prime Minister, much to the consternation of the protesters ('Former ministers implicated in housing "corruption" case' 2011: 1). The third case even involved the sitting Prime Minister, Marouf al-Bakhit, who was later exonerated from the charges of granting a casino licence to British investors back in 2007 under his prime ministerial watch. The deal with the British firm was signed, but never materialised, owing to reneging on the part of the Jordanian officials. When the investors sued for damages of $1.4 billion they were bought off with strategic parcels of Jordanian land (Hazaimeh 2011e: 1–2). In the Lower House of Parliament, 53 deputies voted against the Prime Minister, but the motion was defeated even though a parliamentary report had previously implicated him (Al-Sharif 2011c: 1).

In an endeavour to reach out to the protesters, Abdullah II, in his political concession speech on 12 June 2011, also dealt with his 'firm' belief in the Anti-Corruption Commission's role 'in our fight against corruption in all its forms', and he 'welcome[d] all ideas of how best to institutionalise the role of the Anti-Corruption Commission, empower it to take swift action', and 'encourage it to open channels of communication so as to receive complaints'; but he cautioned that 'Dealing with corruption on the basis of rumors and gossip . . . at the expense of countering it through the judicial system . . . mars Jordan's reputation . . . and negatively affects any endeavor to attract investment' ('Full text of His Majesty King Abdullah's speech' 2011: 2).

Amid public criticisms about the misuse of public funds, some progress was made. For example, in a high-profile case, the anti-corruption crackdown driven by popular protests resulted in the trying and jailing of a member of the political elite. The retired general Muhammad al-Dahabi, the ex-spy chief, was found guilty by a civilian court in November 2012 of money laundering, embezzlement and abuse of power and ordered to return $30 million to the Treasury (Al-Khalidi 2012b: 1). Further, in December 2012 a National Integrity Commission was created by means of a holistic, preventative approach to rooting out corruption and instilling greater transparency and oversight. The Commission was also to expedite investigations and prosecutions of offenders and to provide concrete recommendations to the monarch ('Key facts on elections and Jordan's political reform' 2013: 6). In spite of these anti-corruption measures, there were sporadic demonstrations demanding more results, such as those planned by the Muslim Brotherhood and leftists in late June 2013, which led the Jordanian Prime Minister, Abdullah Ensour, to announce the launch of a 2013–17 national anti-corruption campaign (JT 2013: 1; Petra 2013: 1).

Another step against corruption, especially pertaining to Members of Parliament, was taken by the Royal Committee on Constitutional Review on 14 August 2011. It added two sections to Article 75 of the constitution. One dealt with a possible conflict of interest and said, 'Each member of the Senate and Chamber of Deputies should refrain during his/her membership from contracting with the government, public legal persons, public companies, state-owned enterprises or other legal persons'; whereas the other provided for the revocation of the membership of deputies of the Senate or Lower House by a two-thirds resolution of each chamber, 'provided that such a resolution, if passed by the Senate, is submitted to the King for ratification' ('Recommendations made by the Royal Committee on Constitutional Review' 2011).

Abdullah II, however, reneged on the economic co-optation promises to Jordanians owing to the financial constraints faced by the Treasury in 2012. In order to address the budget deficit and secure a two-billion-dollar loan from the IMF, he announced that he would cut subsidies on fuel and food. It was estimated that such cuts would increase the cost of cooking gas by 50 per cent, of heating gas by 33 per cent, and of low-grade car gasoline by 14 per cent. Protests immediately followed in the streets across several cities in Jordan, such as Salt City and Amman, the capital city, on 13 November 2012. Thereupon, the Prime Minister defended the cuts, but failed to provide any convincing economic arguments, although he claimed that there would be *da'm* (support) for the poor, which seemed unlikely (Abu-Rish 2012: 1).

But the demonstrations continued well into March 2013, when protesters urged the newly elected parliament to reject the decision to cut fuel prices, noting that the parliamentary deputies would lose public trust (Neimat 2013: 1). Jordanian citizens demanded that their government keep its side of the bargain, especially *vis-à-vis* the increasing numbers of the disadvantaged. According to a Gallup Poll taken in the spring of 2012, 79 per cent of Jordanian respondents put the onus to help the poor on the Government (Gallup 2012: 1). Moreover, a later Gallup poll, taken in December 2012, showed that Jordanians were expressing pessimism about their economic well-being. Of the respondents, 73 per cent reported that they were 'struggling', 16 per cent that they were 'suffering', and only 11 per cent that they were 'thriving' (down from 28 per cent in 2011) (Gallup 2013: 1). Indeed, a year after the Arab Spring, seven in ten respondents to a Pew Research Poll released in July 2012 stated that the Jordanian economy was performing poorly (Pew Research 2012: 1). This indicated that the demands of the Arab Spring protesters had not yet been met – heralding a period of low-key instability with continued street protests, albeit without threatening the throne seriously.

Repression as a method of regime stabilisation

The ruler's priority of security, as a result of the November 2005 suicide bombings by al-Qaeda, was reinforced by regional developments such as the ongoing Iraq War, to which many Jordanians were opposed, and the 2006 victory of

Hamas in elections in the West Bank and Gaza, which were followed in 2007 by the Hamas takeover of the Gaza strip. Hence the monarch resorted to increased repression, only to be challenged by the 2011 Arab Spring protests.

Although he granted some freedom to the press, Abdullah II nevertheless curtailed it. He used state media to project his own version of Islamic religious mythology concerning Hashemite rule (Alianak 2007: 17). However, in these times of new communications and information technology, he was less able to control political images, which often came from rival regional networks such as Al Jazeera and other international foreign media, and especially from the Internet, namely via Facebook and Twitter. This was most significant at the time of the Arab demonstrations of 2011, which led the monarch ultimately to introduce reforms so as to swing the pendulum of his rule towards equilibrium and hence ensure the stability of his regime.

Restrictions on the press operated in the areas of licensing, access of journalists to information, and publication Red Lines, concerning sensitive subjects such as the monarchy, the security apparatus and the armed forces, violations of which often led to State Security Court charges and sentencing. According to a January 2011 poll of 505 journalists conducted just prior to the protests by the Center for Defending the Freedom of Journalists (CDFJ) and reported in a survey entitled 'Media Freedom on the Edge', government interference with the media increased by 23 per cent between 2004 and 2010. Of the polled journalists, 40.1 per cent believed that the level of freedom had declined, 41.1 per cent stated that it remained the same, and only 18.4 per cent said that freedoms were increasing (Malkawi 2011a: 1).

For one thing, the government licensing system had been very restrictive and often non-transparent, and hence needed reforming according to media experts (Dalgamouni 2011: 1). In 1999, a new draft law introduced some liberal elements by halving the capitalisation requirement for weekly publications from the steep JD 300,000 (approximately $440,000) which the monarch's father, King Hussein, had instituted just prior to the 1997 parliamentary elections (Moaddel 2002: 129, 198). The law had also transferred the power to revoke a publication's licence from the Minister of Information to the courts and had reduced fines (Kassay 2002: 58). Further, reforms included the dissolution of the Ministry of Information, a symbol of government monopoly, and the establishment of the Audio-Visual Commission in 2005, which made it possible to establish private sector radio and TV stations with relative freedom from government interference. However, the regime used many 'tricks and tactics' to postpone the King's 2003 announced reforms, entitled 'Royal vision for the Media' (Al Sharif 2011b: 1). Still, more than 75 TV satellite stations and several radio stations, newspapers and news websites were established during the next few years (Hazaimeh 2011b: 1).

The next step for the media was access to information in order for it to function well. The existing law, the Access to Information Law, although it was the first of its kind in the Arab world, still needed improvement (Al Sharif 2011b: 1). The Minister of State for Media Affairs and Communications and government spokesman Taher Odwan acknowledged as much in May 2011. He pointed out that there were still many obstacles that restricted freedom of the press so far as freedom of information was concerned, but, he said, 'currently, there is a movement towards reform', which involved his recent directives to all ministries to classify their documents in terms of their fitness for public and media availability in accordance with the Access to Information Law (Malkawi 2011b: 1).

The actual publication of news was limited, too, by the Press and Publication Law, whose violators were often referred to the military-dominated State Security Court instead of to civil courts. For example, one day before the start of the Iraq War in March 2003, the Government amended the Press and Publication Law of 1998 to permit the speedier prosecution of journalists who transgressed the law. Immediately after the start of the war, King Abdullah II stated that he wanted to guarantee that local coverage of the war would be 'responsible' and would 'protect our national unity', and he warned against 'fallacious or inaccurate news' (Greenwood 2003: 105). However, in 2007, the Government eliminated the criminal sanctions from the Press and Publication Law. But prosecutors still routinely relied on provisions of the Penal Code to prosecute regime critics or even to settle personal scores, according to Christoph Wilcke of Human Rights Watch (Wilcke 2011: 1–2).

One of the many cases referred to the military-dominated State Security Courts featured a *cause célèbre* involving the arrest of a website editor who had allegedly endangered national security. According to the CDFJ, under the amendments introduced to Article 42 of the 2010 Press and Publication Law, this case should have been referred to the Amman Court of First Instance instead of to criminal courts. Upon protests and appeals by journalists, the King intervened and ordered the editor's release on bail (Numan 2011: 1).

An earlier, more lenient decision by a judge in another case indicated a general change of attitude by the Government in response to the 2011 protests. Judge Salamat ruled that Article 118 of the Penal Code, which stipulated punishment for writings and speeches that harm the country's relations with other countries, in this case involving two commentators' political remarks regarding Jordan's involvement in Afghanistan specifically, was 'unconstitutional' (Husseini 2011: 1).

Indeed, earlier, in 2011, the King had responded to the appeals for reform and had set up a committee charged with formulating a strategy for the media to make it freer and more independent (Hazaimeh 2011d: 1). In his remarks to the nation on 12 June 2011, Abdullah II restated his resolve: 'Recent regional developments and transformations have confirmed the importance of the media in maintaining the relationship between the state's institutions and society through openness to all views and positions'. But he warned against 'the deterioration of political and media discourse into one that aims to trigger hatred', and he admonished the media: 'I will not accept any infringement on the freedom of Jordanians, their dignity or national unity, and I emphasise my opposition to chaos that leads to destruction' ('Full text of His Majesty King Abdullah's speech' 2011: 2). Indeed, in September 2011 a law was passed which issued fines to journalists of up to approximately $85,000 for reporting on corruption without 'solid facts' (Freedom House 2012: 3).

On 14 August 2011, the Royal Commission on Constitutional Review set up during the Arab Spring proposed to revise Article 15 of the constitution to prohibit the suspension of newspapers from publication, or revocation of their permits, by adding to the article the provision 'except by judicial order' ('Recommendations made by the Royal Committee on Constitutional Review' 2011). Thereupon, the amendment came into effect on 1 October 2011 and is still in force ('The Constitution of Jordan with all the amendments thereto' 2011: 13). However, to be on the safe side, the press exercised self-censorship because it was afraid of threats of fines and detentions (Human Rights Watch 2012: 1). The regime regularly received tips concerning potentially offensive articles by informers and urged the press to remove such materials. The Government regularly gave both warnings and bribes to journalists to keep them from crossing Red Lines. Similar restrictions applied to websites, where the police had considerable discretion in sanctioning and even monitoring online content. There were also some assaults on journalists by the police – for example in July 2011, when the press was covering the protests in Amman (Freedom House 2012: 3).

Online media outlets were targeted by a draconian press and publication law, as they were increasing in number and demanding reforms. They had to be registered with the Government, and they were required to fork out a hefty registration fee of JD 1000 (around $1,400). The websites were to be held responsible for the remarks made in their comments sections. Further, they were required to keep records of all electronic data relating to comments for six months so that intelligence services could locate and prosecute individual commentators (Fox and Sammour 2012: 2).

An individual's freedom of expression was guaranteed under Article 15 of the constitution, 'provided that he does not go beyond the limits of the law' ('The Constitution of Jordan with all the amendments thereto' 2011: 12). In practice, the regime interpreted the law very broadly – for example, against protesters who were detained for allegedly chanting 'illegal slogans' at rallies in the autumn of 2012 (Freij 2012: 1). According to Sarah Leah Whitson, the Middle East director at Human Rights Watch, 'Jordan's claim to be making democratic reforms rings hollow while prosecutors hunt down public figures simply for criticising the government's foreign policy' (Human Rights Watch 2013: 1).

The 'chaos' that Abdullah II had alluded to in his June speech indeed prevailed in many an Arab country in 2011. Although the King had to confront demonstrations and protests in Jordan too, they were mainly more peaceful, smaller, and more limited in scope. For one thing, they did not call for the toppling of the Hashemite monarchy. After all, the monarchs were the descendants of the Prophet Muhammad. As one demonstrator aptly put it, 'We are satisfied with the regime, we just want to reform it' (Kheetan 2011g: 1). The protester appealed to the King to do this, only at a faster pace. As a 24 March Youth Movement member put it, 'From now on, we will address neither the government nor the Parliament, only the King' (ibid.). And even when they were attacked by pro-Government supporters, the pro-reform protesters appealed to the monarch and did not turn against him. Trying to dodge the stones hurled at them, the protesters called on 'His Majesty the King and the police to protect us from the thugs' (Kheetan 2011c: 1).

Jordan had a history of demonstrations, but they had been sporadic and were skilfully contained by the monarchs. According to Jillian Schwedler, 'Jordan's mainstream Islamists have long been at the forefront of the political demonstrations' (Schwedler 2003: 22). However, the monarchs contained those demonstrations they deemed outside the boundaries of formal politics. The coercive tactics adopted by the regime included giving or denying permits, not allowing demonstrations to proceed even if they were legal, and using force against demonstrators (Wiktorowicz 1999: 614). Parliament itself had passed a law in 2003 which required Jordanians not only to inform the Government of a planned gathering but also to get permission for the protest, and which held the organisers personally responsible for any damage that might ensue during the event. The regime used the law to channel, structure, deflate, encourage or suppress certain kinds of protests (Schwedler 2012a: 3–4). The Government had in the past prosecuted peaceful dissidents, who were routinely made to sign confessions by the General Intelligence Department and were often tortured in the process, according to a 2010 report by Amnesty International ('Human rights in Hashemite Kingdom of Jordan 2009' 2010).

Islamic Action Front leaders had often consulted with government officials about organising political demonstrations (Schwedler 2003: 22) and they were usually advised against doing so. According to the former Speaker Abdul Latif Arabiyyat, they were routinely told they could not demonstrate, because 'the situation [was] too dangerous' and national security and national unity were threatened – especially in cases involving the peace treaty with Israel (Wiktorowicz 1999: 612–14).

But the situation was very different in 2011. Emboldened by the success of the Tunisian street protests, the Muslim Brotherhood, on 26 January 2011, called upon Jordanians to demonstrate in the streets against Prime Minister Samir Rifai's economic policies and to demand his dismissal. The police did not confront the ensuing peaceful demonstrators on 28 January following Friday prayers ('Thousands protest in Jordan' 2011). What was new about the subsequent wave of Friday demonstrations, which ebbed and flowed, were the additional new media methods used in organising them, the extent and variety of the cascades of participants, the nature of the demands of the protesters, and the King's response to them, which ultimately resulted in his reluctant promise of some limitations to his powers.

Apart from the traditional methods of street demonstrations called by the political parties and professional organisations, the 2011 demonstrators used the Internet, namely Facebook, to connect with one another virtually. A June 2010 estimate put the number of Jordanians who had Internet access at 1.7 million out of a total population of 6.5 million ('Country profile: Jordan' 2011: 2–3). Many members of the Jordanian Youth Movement who had participated in the protests stated that they had met for the first time through Facebook in February 2011 ('Protest camp set up in Jordan capital' 2011: 1). This method was used not only in Amman but also in other Jordanian cities. For example, over 1,100 people in the southern towns announced on Facebook their intention to take part in the demonstrations scheduled for Friday 3 June 2011 (Kheetan 2011h: 1). This happened in spite of the regulations which the Government had instituted in its August 2010 Amendment to the Law of Information Systems Crimes, which had extended the law to the Internet ('2011 Jordanian protests' 2011: 1).

The venue for the demonstrations was also important. The protests focused on major government landmarks in the cities, and especially the Interior Ministry Circle at Amman, where a sit-in by the Youth Movement over 24–5 March 2011 had lasted for 30 hours. Although the requirement to get a permit for the demonstrations was lifted on 15 February 2011, the Government, following the attack on pro-reform protesters by pro-Government groups and their subsequent confrontations (which resulted in one death and over 150 people injured at a sit-in on 25 March 2011 at the Interior Ministry Circle in Amman), announced that it would henceforth designate special areas for protests to ensure the safety of the peaceful demonstrators ('Government vows to protect peaceful demonstrators' 2011: 1).

The cascading wave of protesters also exhibited a coordination of unprecedented variety and quantity in terms of individuals and groups. The specific composition of the demonstrators changed during the four months from 28 January to 10 June 2011, the Friday before the King's major concessionary speech on 12 June. The protesters ranged from 6,000 to 10,000 individuals demanding reforms in Amman on 25 February to an estimated 30,000 expressing their 'support and loyalty' to the King and his process of 'national reform, in accordance with legitimate and constitutional channels' on Friday 25 March 2011, also in Amman (*BBC News* 2011a; Kheetan 2011a: 1).

Generally, on Fridays after noon prayers, many individuals and groups congregated in the streets flowing in and out of the pro-reform protests at different times. They included Islamists, the Muslim Brotherhood and IAF members, up to nineteen smaller parties, trade unions, communists, leftist organisations, youth movements such as the 24 March Youth Movement, the *Jayeen* (We Are Coming), the youth branch of the Jordanian Democratic Popular Unity Party (*Wihda*) and other young people, and even tribal members (Al-Khalidi 2011b: 1; Keetan 2011b: 1). There were periods of intense activity and periods of wait-and-see. For example, there was a lull for around a month, from mid-April to mid-May, when the activists and the protesters said they wanted to 'reorganise' themselves and give the Government a chance to meet their reform demands (Keetan 2011b: 1; 2011g: 1). But they resumed their activities with gusto on the Fridays of 20 May, 3 June and, especially, 10 June 2011, when they urged the King to speed up the reforms ('Jordanians slam corruption, demand elected government' 2011: 1; Kheetan 2011h: 1).

What were the major reform demands of the protesters so far as repression is concerned, and how did the King respond to them? Firstly, amendments were introduced to the Public Assemblies Law in May 2011. Henceforth, any public meeting or demonstration would not require the approval of administrative directors, but only a 48-hour period of notice from the organisers. However, freedom of assembly was 'generally restricted', as seen later, in March and July 2012, when security forces reportedly used wooden clubs and water hoses to disperse protests in Amman, which resulted in injuries to a number of demonstrators (Freedom House 2012: 3).

Secondly, Abdullah II pardoned some prisoners. On 9 June 2011, he declared a general amnesty pardoning around 4,000 prisoners ('MB in Jordan embarks on fresh protests' 2011: 1). Just the week before, he had directed the Government to draft a general pardon law 'in line with the observed legal channels', thus easing the suffering of wrongdoers 'from harsh economic conditions prevailing in the world today, affecting our social situation and aggravating the social impact of penalties' ('King decrees general pardon on Independence Day' 2011: 1). However, demonstrations continued on 10 June 2011, two days prior to the King's major political concessions speech. Previously, the Salafis of the city of Zarqa had been engaged in a showdown with police during their protest against the non-inclusion of their detained relatives in the Royal Pardon, and they kept up demands for their freedom as well (Al-Sharif 2011c: 2).

Thirdly, other demands by the opposition included the removal of the Intelligence Department from politics and even the dismantling of it in its present form, and the abolition of the military tribunal, the State Security Court, which many demonstrators believed had passed sentences against hundreds of innocent Jordanians and even protected the corrupt ('Jordanians slam corruption, demand elected government' 2011: 1; 'MB in Jordan embarks on fresh protests' 2011: 1). Anti-corruption measures were indeed called for persistently by the protesters, which the King believed should be dealt with by the Anti-corruption Commission that he had created previously.

Fourth, Abdullah II's attempts at serious reform efforts were shown by his initiative to create committees such as the National Dialogue Commission (on 14 March 2011), a Royal Panel of ten statesmen, the Royal Commission on the Constitution (on 26 April 2011) tasked with discussing possible amendments to the Jordanian constitution, and a committee to examine economic development opportunities, among others (Kheetan 2011f: 2). Fifth, Abdullah II dissolved the unpopular parliament.

The Royal Commission on Constitutional Review presented its report to the King on 14 August 2011. Notable here were its recommendations to advance human rights. For example, the revised Article 8 prohibited the torture and detention of citizens in undisclosed locations rather than in prisons. An accused person was to be considered innocent until proven guilty in the revisions of Article 101, which included the provision that 'A civilian may not be tried in a criminal case before a court where all judges are not civilians, with the exception of crimes of high treason, espionage and terrorism', and the verdict had to be pronounced in a public session ('Recommendations made by the Royal Committee on Constitutional Review' 2011). There were further provisions to guarantee the independence of judicial power (in the revised Article 27) and the limiting of the jurisdiction of the State Security Court to sensitive cases of high treason, espionage and terrorism. In addition, all postal, telegraphic and telephonic conversations of Jordanians were guaranteed secrecy except under judicial order in the revisions of Article 18 (ibid.).

But what was actually achieved? Articles 8, 18, 27 and 101 were amended on 1 October 2011 ('The Constitution of Jordan with all the amendments thereto' 2011: 9, 15, 19, 79); while the restrictions on the State Security Court (SSC) still needed specific legislation, as of late 2012, to institutionalise the change, which led groups like the IAF to continue to call for the dissolution of the SSC (Freedom House 2012: 3). A National Human Rights Centre, which had been created in 2002, was revamped as an independent body responsible for conducting visits to detention centres and reform institutions in order to check up on the well-being of prisoners and receive complaints about human rights violations ('Key facts on elections and Jordan's political reform' 2013: 15). However, according to Freedom House (2012), prison conditions remained poor and inmates were reportedly abused by the guards. According to Human Rights Watch (2012), this notice of mistreatment and allegations of torture by government and security officials were met with impunity, as the regime did not really take positive steps to prosecute or punish the abusers (Human Rights Watch 2012: 1).

Further, arbitrary arrests and denial of due process through indefinite administrative detentions, which were ordered by provincial governors, continued, resulting in a fifth of all Jordanian prisoners being held under this provision and the adding of 10,000 new such cases each year (Freedom House 2012: 4). Moreover, there were allegations of nepotism and influence of special interests on the judiciary (Human Rights Watch 2012: 1). The judiciary is 'subject to executive influence' by the Justice Ministry and the Higher Judiciary Council, most of whose members are appointed by the King (Freedom House 2012: 3).

Sixth, the monarch also embarked on a public relations spree. He gave several Royal Court auditions to and engaged with people in all walks of life. He also travelled to the governorates, outside Amman proper, to listen to the views of the inhabitants of even the tiniest of villages, it was reported (Al Sharif 2011a: 1). However, that some discontent perhaps still existed was shown on 13 June 2011 in Tafila, 125 miles south of Amman and home to earlier anti-Government protests, where the King had gone to inspect several development projects. While there, just a day after he had addressed the controversial issue of an 'elected' Prime Minister, he was confronted by a crowd of youths, who flung stones and empty bottles at his motorcade. The monarch was unharmed. Government spokesmen tried to put a positive spin on the incident by stating that the attack involved a quarrel with the police, not an attempted assault on the King ('Jordanian King unharmed in motorcade incident' 2011: 1).

Political liberalisation as a method of regime stabilisation

Although he had increasingly prioritised repression after the terrorist attacks of 2005, political liberalisation was the option that Abdullah II promised to pursue in response to the peaceful protests of 2011. Historically the Jordanian monarchs had used a hybrid of authoritarianism, Islam and democracy to stabilise their rule. Although this hybrid, initiated by King Abdullah's father King Hussein and later continued by him, had proved adequate, the protests of the spring of 2011 showed the hybrid regime to be weak because of its emphasis on the authoritarian component. Indeed, the Economist Intelligence Unit's democratic index for 2010 had ranked Jordan 117th out of 167 countries and thereby had labelled it 'authoritarian' (Shaikh 2012: 2). Accordingly, the Jordanian monarch, following the example of the Moroccan monarch, Muhammad VI, opted to introduce further liberalisation and to promise to enhance the democratic ingredients of the hybrid, in an attempt to reform the political system by tailoring it to specific Jordanian conditions in order to avert the crisis and hence guarantee the stability of the kingdom.

Abdullah II showed a preference for formal politics over street politics, and accordingly initiated reforms to stem the tide of the protests. For him, political liberalisation as a method of regime stabilisation entailed, ideally, promises/ efforts to address low participation levels, electoral inequalities, political parties' ineffectiveness, the choosing of Prime Ministers by the Palace, and civil society restrictions, all of which had been common practices previously. Were these promises for reform actually realised?

Participation

Abdullah II preferred citizen participation via the ballot box rather than via street politics. Here, he followed the example of his father, King Hussein, who had encouraged voter turn-out by even prodding Shaikh Saad Hijjawi, the acting Jordanian Mufti, to issue a *fatwā* (religious ruling) in 1997, prior to the parliamentary elections of that year, when the IAF, the political arm of the Muslim Brotherhood, had decided to boycott the elections. Indeed, since 1993, when the King had changed the election law from block voting to a one-person-one-vote system and had allocated districts on a pro-regime basis rather than on population size, the Islamists had been dissatisfied. They even called for a 'true *fatwa*' for 'putting an end to the government's disregard of the people's will' to vote (*Jordan Times* 1997: 3).

Like his father, King Abdullah II encouraged participation, around four years after his accession to the throne, in his first parliamentary elections, to be held on 17 June 2003. It was a triumph for him that the moderates within the Islamic Action Front gained the upper hand and the party decided to take part in the elections – however dissatisfied and critical they were subsequently. Voter turn-out was 58.8 per cent of eligible voters, with 70–84 per cent of rural voters hailing from the districts which favoured the King. According to analysts, urban areas like Amman and Zarqa exhibited lower voter turn-out (43 and 48 per cent respectively) than the national average, which reflected a lack of confidence that their participation would change matters, and hence a general sense of apathy prevailed in the cities (Abdullah 2003a: 13).

Promising democratic reforms, Abdullah II's new election law in May 2010 boosted the quota for women (18 seats out of 120-member parliament). The law also allotted new seats to some districts which had been under-represented. But it still over-represented rural areas, and certainly it did not favour the bigger cities like Amman where votes cast carried only a quarter of the weight of votes cast in provincial towns such as Ma'an. The electoral system discriminated against the larger cities, where most people were of Palestinian descent and less loyal to the monarchy. It favoured instead the hinterlands, where the strong tribal ties of the inhabitants of the east side of the Jordan River strongly favoured the Hashemites ('Elections in Jordan' 2010: 1). Indeed, almost half (47 per cent) of voting respondents stated that they had cast their ballots according to tribal affiliations rather than on the basis of the policies and qualifications of the candidates, according to a survey conducted by the Al Quds Centre for Political Studies in 2011 (Hazaimeh 2012a: 1).

Voter turn-out was 53 per cent according to official sources, but was estimated as much lower, namely 30 per cent, by the Islamic Action Front, which had boycotted the election in protest over constituency boundaries set by the May Election Law (Habib 2010: 1). Turn-out in Amman was only 34 per cent. Accompanying the favouring of and hence the victory of loyalists, there were 'signs of growing unrest on the streets', especially over such issues as increased poverty and the Government's failure to pressure Israel more force-fully over the stalled peace talks ('Jordan loyalists sweep election' 2010: 2).

Responding to the low-key yet persistent discontent of Jordanians during the Arab Spring of 2011, the King, as mentioned above, set up a National Dialogue Committee, and stated in a letter to the committee's head, Taher al-Masri, 'We call on you to reach a draft democratic election law that would bring a parlia-ment that represents all Jordanians and plays a leading role in enhancing justice and rule of law' (Al-Khalidi 2011a: 1). Planning for a fair and equal representa-tion of voters where all citizens had an equal political voice, the Committee called for proportional representation at both the national and governorate levels to replace the disputed one-man-one-vote principle, the creation of an independent monitoring agency in response to international rights bodies to verify the fairness of elections, and the granting of a final say on the legality and fairness of future elections to the judicial system instead of to Parliament. It concluded, on 26 May 2011, that it 'hoped that the country will witness a more vibrant, more participatory political life, one in which citizens will have a say in the way their future is shaped' ('Encouraging development' 2011: 1). Earlier, it had also discussed the need to redraw the electoral districts seat map (Neimat 2011a: 1).

What effect could the National Dialogue Committee have on voter apathy or on the trust accorded to the monarch in terms of future turn-out? A poll conducted in June 2011 by the Al Quds Centre for Political Studies showed that 54.5 per cent of the sample were not even aware of the existence of the committee or its outcomes, whereas 32 per cent had no idea of its composition (Hazaimeh 2012a: 1). A more specific and detailed poll, conducted later by the University of Jordan's Centre for Strategic Studies (CSS) concerning the pro-posed Constitutional Amendments, showed that only 38 per cent of the national sample, and 88 per cent of opinion leaders, were aware of them. However, there was a general feeling of satisfaction, as seen by the fact that 72 per cent of the national sample and 82 per cent of 'opinion leaders' expressed satisfaction with the amendments, with 74 per cent of both groups being optimistic that the changes would 'push political life in Jordan forward' (Neimat 2012d: 1). This optimism was also reflected even in the previous (June) study of the Al Quds Centre of Political Studies, which showed that 70 per cent of the respondents were willing to participate in any future upcoming elections compared to 21.4 who stated that they would not do so with 8 per cent undecided (Hazaimeh 2012a: 1). Thus there was a general trust in the leadership of the King even as there was no widespread or detailed knowledge about the specifics of the actions of his committee.

On 12 June 2011, on the occasion of Coronation Day and Army Day, Abdullah II appealed to this trust by addressing the nation on his reform measures, calling for a 'modern elections law that leads to the election of a Lower House representative of all Jordanians, able to earn their trust by safeguarding their rights and achieving their aspirations' ('Full text of His Majesty King Abdullah's speech' 2011: 2). Concerning these proposed changes in the electoral system, 75 per cent of Jordanians surveyed in June showed that they were in favour of changing the Elections Law by annulling the virtual districts, and 50 per cent showed support for a mixed electoral system (Hazaimeh 2012a: 1).

On 22 June 2012, the new Electoral Law was approved by royal decree. Each voter was given two votes, one for a candidate at the district level and the other for the closed proportional list. Each voter would be able to pick a list of five candidates in his or her constituency (European Forum for Democracy and Solidarity 2013: 3). A total of 108 deputies out of a total of 150 representatives would be directly elected in 45 'local' electoral districts (International Foundation for Electoral Systems 2013: 3). The number of seats in the House of Deputies was increased from 120 to 150, of which 27 were to be chosen nationally by way of lists and 15 allocated to a women's quota. The electoral system thus favoured local tribal chiefs rather than national political leaders based on parties, which elicited protests, among the protesting parties being the IAF, which complained that the electoral law would not bring substantial change from the past (Kuttab 2013: 1).

Accordingly, the IAF, leftist parties and some youth groups decided to boycott the elections of 23 January 2013 in protest against the new electoral law that did not favour parties but rural and tribal regions, the backbones of Hashemite rule. The resulting new parliament, they believed, would not be representative enough to institute the needed reforms. According to the IAF the new election law, which was very similar to the unacceptable 2010 law, would once again lead to political weakness and social instability, and therefore elections should be held instead on the basis of an even newer revised electoral law favouring political parties. Thus the 2012 electoral law, which provided only a 27-seat list (increased from 17, but not up to the 50 demanded by the IAF) of parties' candidates, would not fulfil the promised pledges for a parliamentary government, as these seats would be rivalled by the remaining 123 seats to be occupied by candidates from rural tribal areas and independents, and would under-represent urban and Palestinian areas.

Indeed, the National Democratic Institute concluded: 'systemic distortions remain. The unequal size of districts [between rural and urban areas] and an electoral system that amplifies family, tribal and national cleavages limit the development of a truly national legislative body and challenge King Abdullah's stated aim of encouraging full parliamentary government' (Sharp 2013: 5). An analysis of the parliamentary elections of 23 January 2013 by Ziad Abu-Rish confirmed this assessment. Abu-Rish wrote that 'there is a structural limit to how much opposition participation can alter the outcome', thus justifying contentious politics rather than formal politics (Abu-Rish 2013: 4). Also, Fahed Kheitan, a political analyst, commented, concerning the remarks he had heard of prospective voters, that 'the public was right to believe that the candidates most likely to win are either former MPs or influential businesspeople who cannot bring the real reforms the country needs' (Obeidat 2013: 3). Thereupon, King Abdullah II, aware of this criticism, did not cancel the scheduled elections, but called upon the newly elected parliament to amend the Electoral Law (Sharp 2013: 5).

Some democratic electoral improvements were proposed by the Royal Committee on Constitutional Review on 14 August 2011. The Committee revised Article 67 by calling for the establishment of an independent commission to oversee elections in order to guarantee the 'integrity of elections at all stages'; also, it referred the decision about the determination of the validity of the election of members of the Lower House of Parliament to the Judiciary instead of to the Chamber itself in the revised Article 71, which was incorporated in the constitution effective as of 1 October 2011 ('Recommendations made by the Royal Committee on Constitutional Review' 2011; 'The Constitution of Jordan with all the amendments thereto' 2011: 48–9, 51).

Leading up to the 23 January 2013 elections, Abdullah II urged citizen participation as a 'constitutional right' and a 'national duty' in his first of a series of discussion papers issued in December 2012 (Hazaimeh 2012b: 1). Before that, in an important speech given to over 3,000 public figures at the Royal Court on 23 October 2012, he had declared: 'It is citizens' vote in this election that will determine the make-up of the next Parliament and the next Parliamentary government, thus determining the policies and decisions that will affect the life of every citizen.' He had added emphatically: 'Therefore, citizens must not allow anyone to deprive them of their right to vote and effect change' (King Abdullah of Jordan 2012b: 2). Moreover, he had emphasised the importance of the ballot box and the elected parliament, which would be the 'true representative of the will of the people', and through which any additional reforms or changes to the Electoral Law could be effected. This statement to the notables was aimed at countering the announced boycott of the 23 January 2013 elections by the IAF.

Thus, voters were presented with two narratives: one championing the elections as an opportunity for change, development and reform, and the other calling for the boycotting of the elections because of a perception that the regime was not serious about reforming itself and that its real intent was to reproduce its centralisation of power via the electoral rules it had set up (Abu-Rish 2013: 1). Voter turn-out was 56.6 per cent of registered voters, or 40 per cent of eligible voters (both registered and unregistered) (Sharp 2013: 5). When consideration is given to the fact that around 70 per cent of Jordan's 3 million eligible voters country-wide had registered, according to the Government, a turn-out of 70 per cent of eligible voters would have endorsed the status quo and rejected the Brotherhood's tactics (Luck 2013: 2). But voter turn-out in the different geographic areas of the country varied. In the major cities (strongholds of the Muslim Brotherhood) and Amman, average voter turn-out was 40 per cent of both registered and unregistered voters; whereas in the sparsely populated rural and Bedouin areas, it averaged at more than 70 per cent (European Forum for Democracy and Solidarity 2013: 4). Perhaps this was because the urban areas, which contained two-thirds of the population, were allocated less than one-third of the seats in the House of Representatives ('Jordanian general election' 2013: 1), and hence their inhabitants were not as motivated to participate.

Abdullah II, intent upon encouraging greater participation in future elections, covered the topic in his fourth discussion paper entitled 'Towards Democratic Empowerment and "Active Citizenship"', issued on 1 June 2013. He wrote: 'But politics only works if we all embrace the principle of "active citizenship", which is based on three pillars: the right to participate; the duty to participate; and the responsibility to participate peacefully and respectfully' (King Abdullah II of Jordan 2013: 5).

Political parties

The Jordanian electoral system had led to weak political parties in the past. Other reasons for this weakness of parties included the dispute over the number of parties, the self-limitation of the largest opposition party, the Islamic Action Front, the King's powers of dismissing Parliament at will and ruling by decree, and also of postponing general elections at will, and the monarch's appointment of the Prime Minister and his cabinet regardless of the relative strength of political parties in Parliament. Following the protests of the Arab Spring of 2011, Abdullah II and the commissions which he had set up initiated reforms. They tended to lean towards more vibrant political parties so that politics would be channelled in an orderly way through parliaments rather than through the amorphous people power of the streets. Were they successful?

The electoral system's over-representation of rural areas, which make up only 30 per cent of the country, and under-representation of urban areas, which represent 70 per cent (US Department of State 2010: 2), were two of the reasons for the low opinion Jordanians had of the resulting parliament, as polls conducted in the aftermath of the 2007 elections indicated. A survey conducted by the state-funded Center for Strategic Studies (CSS) showed that 56 per cent of respondents were not satisfied with the Members of Parliament representing them. The deputies, it was believed, had failed to address such problems as unemployment, economic woes, corruption and restricted freedoms (Mustafa

2009: 1). This perceived unwillingness by legislators to pass significant reforms was compounded by the elimination in the 2007 elections of several strong popular personalities who were bidding to win a seat, and the manipulation of the results to cut the representation of the main opposition party, the IAF, from 17 to 6 seats. The ordinary citizen felt marginalised and left out of the political arena, where national leaders in Parliament were perceived to be corrupt to boot (Lynch 2009: 1 and 3).

The November 2010 election results were no improvement. Only seventeen out of a total of 120 elected members were from opposition political parties (not including the IAF, which had boycotted the election), and more than half of the elected legislators, a total of 78 MPs to be exact, were newcomers. Many of these were from rural Bedouin tribes, the monarch's loyalists ('Jordan loyalists sweep election' 2010: 1, 2). This repeated the results of Abdullah II's first parliamentary elections in 2003, when independent candidates loyal to the King won two-thirds of the seats, to the detriment of the parties (*BBC News* 2011b). After the Arab Spring of 2011, the 23 January 2013 elections did not bring about the desired changes in the elected parliament.

The number of parties was also a matter of contention. Whereas Jordan had 37 political parties in the 2007 elections, their number was reduced to fourteen under a new Political Parties Law which became effective in April 2008. The new law, unlike the old law which had not set a minimum number of original members required, stipulated that any political party, to be licensed, had to have at least 500 members in five governorates. According to critics, the new law would impede the development of Jordanian political life; whereas the Government's position was that fewer political parties would result in stronger parties (Mustafa 2008: 1).

In line with this, in April 2011 Abdullah II expressed the hope that the number of political parties would be fewer in the future, representing the rightist, leftist and centrist currents or blocs which would facilitate the formation of cabinets (Gavlak 2011: 1; 'Jordan working to achieve comprehensive reform in all fields' 2011: 1). However, the National Dialogue Committee, bowing to critics, proposed otherwise. It called for a draft law making it easier to form political parties. It would halve the minimum number of members required to form a party from 500 original members to 250, 25 of whom had to be women (Sweis 2011b: 1, 3). But it was ultimately to settle for larger parties.

Another reason, apart from the electoral system, why the parties were weak was that the largest opposition party, the IAF, exercised self-limitation in the elections in which it decided to participate. For example, in the parliamentary election of 2003, the party negotiated with the palace the manner of its participation by fielding only 30 candidates, excluding the candidacy of controversial IAF figures like Abd al-Mun'im Abu Zant and deciding that the Secretary-General, Hamza Mansour, and the president of the party's Shura

Council, Arabiyyat, would not run themselves ('Islamic Action Front' n.d.: 1). This trend was confirmed by Ibrahim Gharaibeh, who wrote: 'As in all previous elections, the movement will deliberately calibrate the number of its candidates to ensure that it does not win a parliamentary majority' (Gharaibeh 2010: 2). Also, preceding the 2007 elections, IAF doves reached an understanding with the monarchy that the IAF would limit the number of seats its candidates would run for, and also that it would avoid fielding explicitly pro-Hamas candidates (Project on Middle East Democracy 2008: 2).

Thus, although it was an opposition party, the IAF backed the royal family and did not wish to undermine it. In an interview in 1999, Abd al-Latif Arabiyyat, then head of the IAF, expounded the basis for the party's support for the regime: 'The monarchy is Islamically legitimate, and has the same Arab and Islamic goals as the Muslim Brotherhood. It would never take measures against Islam' (Singh 2002: 87). However, following the Arab Spring, the IAF boycotted the 23 January 2013 elections, citing structural deficiencies in the new electoral law, which it believed was rigged against national political parties and especially against them, because it marginalised the urban areas, which were their strongholds.

A further reason for the weakness of political parties was that they knew that, if they did manage to get into Parliament, they were liable to the whims of the King, who could dissolve the legislature at any time and delay elections. The monarch could then rule by decree, as Abdullah II had done from 2001 to 2003. He had also dissolved Parliament in November 2009, halfway through its four-year term. This decision happened to be popular: a poll conducted earlier, in May 2009, had indicated that a quarter of Jordanians would support the dissolution of the chamber (Mustafa 2009: 1). However, hopes were raised that the subsequent elections of 2010 would result in a more inclusive parliament to follow the previous parliament, only to be dashed, as described above.

Indeed, a major demand of the protesters focused on the composition of the Lower House of Parliament. The demonstrators called for the dismissal of the existing unpopular parliament and for new elections based on a more equitable election law and a revised political party law. Although again he initially resisted, the King gave way around two months into the protests, on 14 March 2011, and in a bid to calm the protesters and show the seriousness of his resolve he appointed a 52-member National Dialogue Commission (NDC) to study and make recommendations about revising both of these laws. The members were drawn from former ministers, trade unionists, writers and members of political parties ('Jordan creates commission to examine reform' 2011: 1). However, the Muslim Brotherhood refused to join this commission, because, it said, the NDC was to deal only with electoral and political party laws and not constitutional changes which could result in a curbing of the monarch's powers (Al-Khalidi 2011b: 1). There was also criticism of the composition of this commission involving the under-representation of Palestinians and members of the opposition, which could jeopardise true reform efforts (Susser 2011: 6). Later, the King acquiesced and in 2012 he dismissed the unpopular parliament.

Many of the protesters also wanted at least a return to the 1952 version of the Jordanian constitution, stating that some 29 amendments passed since then had adversely affected the balance between the three branches of government. For example, a controversial amendment to Article 57 passed in 1958 had made the appointed Senate President also the chief of the Higher Council for the Interpretation of the Constitution, which looked into the laws passed by Parliament. Prior to that, a judge had headed the Council. Hence the importance of establishing a constitutional court to review parliamentary laws was understood. Other examples were a 1960 amendment that gives the monarch power to prolong the term of the Chamber of Deputies for a period ranging from one to two years; also, since 1976 the king has been able to postpone the holding of a general election owing to an emergency, which the appointed Council of Ministers would always deem necessary.

These and other constitutional amendments, including a parliamentary government, were on the list of demands of several political parties, civil society organisations, new opposition groups, and several thousand Jordanians who had taken to the streets. Some demands dated as far back as December 2010, and certainly from January 2011. Abdullah II responded by creating the Royal Commission on the Constitution on 26 April 2011. Despite being given carte blanche by the King, the Commission's mandate was confined to the issues discussed and debated by the NDC, namely the elections law and political party legislation (Kheetan 2011d: 1; 'King tasks panel to review the Constitution' 2011: 1; Sadi 2011: 1).

The ensuing Draft Political Parties Law was debated in the Jordanian Lower House of Parliament in early 2012. It reflected the ambivalence on the part of the reformers intent on political liberalisation. On the one hand, it complied with the King's encouragement of young people to be active in public life and hence it encouraged the formation of political parties; but on the other hand, it ran contrary to the King's preference for a limited number of parties. Indeed, the Draft law made licensing more democratic and much easier. The Interior Ministry was no longer to be the sole licensing authority, as the task was also to be the responsibility of a committee which was to include the president of the Legislative and Opinion Bureau, the Secretary-General of the Ministry of Justice, the Secretary-General of any other ministry named by the premier, two commissioners from the planned independent elections commission, and the commissioner-general of the National Centre for Human Rights. Therefore, NGOs and other organisations apart from the Interior Ministry had a say in the matter (JT 2012: 1). The main provision was that a party should not be founded on a 'sectarian, ethnic or factional basis' (Neimat 2012b: 2).

Parties were to be guaranteed a measure of security, which also made them more attractive because once vetted they were to be protected against arbitrary dissolution, which was to be the prerogative only of the judiciary and no other executive agency. Also, parties were to be protected further from the authorities. For example, they were to enjoy guaranteed privacy against confiscation of their documents and their headquarters could not be searched except under judicial orders. In addition, individual party members were not to be subjected to any harassment by any agency (ibid.: 1–2).

The monarch was, however, cautious at best. He wanted 'mature political parties', albeit parties limited in number before the ultimate goal of 'parliamentary government' was achieved. In October 2011, at the opening of the 16th Parliament's second ordinary session, he stated:

> All these steps will bring us closer to the ultimate goal of parliamentary government. Until the political party system matures and can play its rightful role in Parliament, we need to adopt an inclusive consultative approach to government formation, so that citizens can trust that through their elected representatives, they are truly participating in the process of forming governments, monitoring them, and holding them accountable. We are fully committed to pressing ahead with an evolutionary and incremental process towards parliamentary pluralism and political diversity. And this evolutionary and incremental approach should not be interpreted as procrastination. ('Our priority today is political reform – King' 2011: 2)

He declared that creating 'governments formed by political parties' is 'very much conditional [on] the ability of political parties to freely compete' (ibid.). This process of evolution could, he said, conceivably take several years, although later he pledged a parliamentary government soon.

While it is true that the King had lost his prerogative to postpone elections indefinitely, he was still appointing the Upper House of Parliament and the Prime Minister (Ottaway and Muasher 2011: 11–12). Indeed, the Royal Committee on Constitutional Review deleted from Article 73 the provision enabling the King to postpone the general elections from its revised version of the article on 14 August 2011 ('Recommendations made by the Royal Committee on Constitutional Review' 2011). The constitution of 2011 included amendments to Article 73, which stipulated that, after the dissolution of Parliament, the King could not postpone for more than four months the holding of general elections (revised Article 73). A further check on the king's powers was provided by Article 74, which did not allow the monarch to dissolve the new House, for the same reason (revised Article 74) ('The Constitution of Jordan with all the amendments thereto' 2011: 53–5).

The Islamists were dissatisfied. They called for an elected senate, and suggested that the King call the leader of the parliamentary majority to form the government as Prime Minister (Neimat 2012c: 1). The displeased IAF even threatened to boycott the upcoming elections to the Lower House of Parliament in 2013 unless its demands were met. The King did not comply with the elected senate, but introduced cosmetic changes in his designation of the Prime Minister.

Among the reforms introduced by the new 2011 constitution was the establishment of the Constitutional Court. It was to be 'an independent and separate judicial body' to be appointed by the king (Article 58) with 'the competence of oversight on the constitutionality of applicable laws and regulations' (Article 59). Also, according to the revisions to Article 71, 'The Judiciary shall have the competence to determine the validity of the election of the members of the House of Representatives' ('The Constitution of Jordan with all the amendments thereto' 2011: 40–1, 51). These amendments were hailed by the protesters.

However, the new Political Parties Law enacted in 2012 was very controversial. It provided for each party to have at least 500 founding members from a minimum of five different governorates with equal representation. This was aimed at having larger and more consolidated parties and at paving the way for official funding, according to the Government. The opposition feared that most existing parties would not be able to reregister. Also, as surveys showed that there was an increase in political apathy among Jordanians, the new regulations, it was feared, would further hinder the ability of parties to lure new members, while parties attempted to comply with the new law. Despite these fears, the number of registered political parties in 2013 was 30, 22 of them being represented by at least one seat in the newly elected Jordanian Parliament of 2013 (European Forum for Democracy and Solidarity 2013: 3–4).

Most parties presented narrow parochial interests centred on prominent individuals from tribes or particular wealthy families (Sharp 2013: 5). Also, the new law did not restrict lists to political parties, which meant that individuals could get together at the last minute before the deadline and set up a list and potentially gain membership using the nationwide second ballot, thus limiting political parties (Kuttab 2013: 3).

However, Abdullah II perceived that 'the real challenge facing the opposition today is voters' reluctance to join political parties'. He cited polls reporting that 90 per cent of Jordanians 'are averse to joining political parties, a matter that requires serious efforts on the part of the next parliament and government as well as the opposition, to develop platforms that encourage citizens to become members of political parties and that respond to the interests of voters and encourage them to make voting decisions based on party platforms'. He urged political parties to develop with the aim of establishing larger units of the right, the left and the centre. He stated: 'As political parties evolve over parliamentary cycles, the parliamentary blocs will be based on political parties.' Abdullah II made this conditional on his new designation powers over the Prime Minister, that were to change following the 23 January 2013 elections ('Full text of His Majesty King Abdullah's interview with *Le Nouvel Observateur*' 2013: 7).

Choice of Prime Ministers

Prior to the protests of 2011, parties did not have the possibility of selecting the Prime Minister. This was the prerogative of the monarch. For example, Jordanians had to depend on the King to sack his Prime Minister, whom they accused in 2011 of being insensitive to their economic hardships. Yet this favourable outcome would not always be guaranteed. In spite of this, most Jordanians did not want the other extreme option, whereby the king would become just a figurehead ruler like the Queen of England (Gavlak 2011: 1).

Indeed, upon ascending to the throne in 1999 Abdullah II had floated the idea of a constitutional monarchy, but he did not follow up on it (Halaby 2011: 1). Around ten years later, in 2009, he was reminded of this when Richeil Gharibeh, a leading IAF figure, had suggested that limitations be put on the authority of the king by calling for a move towards a constitutional monarchy akin to the British system (Barari 2009: 1–2).

Following the protests of 2011, Abdullah II called for reforms in the direction of parliamentary monarchy during a televised address to the nation on 12 June 2011, a day after he had celebrated the 90th anniversary of the Kingdom's establishment amid cheering crowds ('King to address nation today' 2011: 1). He called for 'the formation of governments based on parliamentary majority and political party manifestos in the future', to 'enable members of Parliament to participate in the government based on their party programmes and the proportion of their representation in the House of Representatives' in the name of 'faith in parliamentary democracy' ('Full text of His Majesty King Abdullah's speech' 2011: 2). Having chosen to speak on the occasion of Coronation Day, he emphasised his belief in a future with a 'firmly established parliamentary monarchy, based on the separation of powers that shall be accountable to the nation' ('King outlines vision for Jordan's future' 2011: 1).

During his first thirteen years in power, Abdullah II had gone through ten cabinets. Following the Arab Spring, he had had at least five Prime Ministers by October 2012. According to analysts, Abdullah II replaced Prime Ministers whenever there was discontent. He would blame them for policy lapses by himself rising above them and not taking any blame. They served as a 'shock-absorbing tactic – to blame his government and sack his prime ministers' (*The Economist* 2012: 2). This enabled him 'to buy off demands for real change' (Riedel 2012). Further, this provided him with the opportunity to reward and co-opt an ever widening retinue of individuals.

Among the demands of the demonstrators in 2011 were those pertaining to Prime Ministers. There was a general dissatisfaction with the King's choice of Prime Ministers. The protesters called for the dismissal of two successive Prime Ministers. Following the protests of 28 January 2011, Abdullah II met their demands and dismissed his unpopular Prime Minister, Samir Rifai, on 1 February 2011. He then appointed Marouf al-Bakhit, a former military intelligence major-general, who was charged with a mandate to introduce reforms. However, the IAF and many of the protesters were dissatisfied with this choice, since al-Bakhit had previously, as Prime Minister, supervised the 2007 parliamentary elections, which were tainted by irregularities. So the protests continued on 2 February 2011, calling for the dismissal of the new Prime Minister. The monarch tried to co-opt the opposition. This involved trying to include the opposition groups, both Islamist and leftist, in the new government of Prime Minister al-Bakhit (on the initiative of the latter). But the IAF refused to join, because it perceived the Prime Minister to be insincere in pursuing 'real reform'. But despite these calls to stay away, some IAF members, and five leftists, were represented in the new government, which was sworn in on 10 February 2011 ('2011 Jordanian protests' 2011).

However, the IAF persisted in its opposition. According to Hamza Mansour, a leader of the Muslim Brotherhood, al-Bakhit 'doesn't believe in democracy' (ibid.). Instead, Mansour demanded elections to choose another Prime Minister. Indeed, the massive demonstrations on Friday 10 June 2011 had repeated this demand emphatically ('Jordanians slam corruption, demand elected government' 2011: 1). The Prime Minister was accused of failing to meet the growing demands for reform of the economy, politics and corruption (Nimah 2011: 1). To regain the trust of the street and the discontented parliamentarians the King accepted his resignation, and did not take any royal blame for this lack of progress and 'procrastination'. He stated: 'We have accepted the resignation of the Prime Minister Marouf al-Bakhit, taking into consideration the views of the various sectors of society as well as a letter we have received from the parliamentary majority' ('Jordan King names PM, security chief to push reform' 2011: 1). And he appointed, in October 2011, International Court of Justice judge Awn Khasawneh as Prime Minister with specific instructions and a mandate for a faster pace of reform. Thereupon, Khasawneh proceeded to engage the Islamists by explicitly stating that his new government would be 'open to everyone and we welcome the participation of Islamists and other groups in Parliament. We actually hope they would take part' ('Jordan's new PM urged to rebuild trust with people' 2011: 1). In spite of this the Islamists were dissatisfied. So on 2 May 2012, the monarch appointed Fayez Tarawneh as Prime Minister to replace Khasawneh. But later, in October 2012, Tarawneh had to resign, as mandated by para. 2 of Article 74 of the constitution of 2011, which stipulated that within a week of the dissolving of Parliament by the King (which the monarch had done on 4 October 2012) the government in office must resign ('The Constitution of Jordan with all the amendments thereto' 2011: 55). Thereupon, the King appointed Abdullah Ensour, who had backed the opposition calls for wider reforms, as interim Prime Minister until the 23 January 2013 elections (Al-Khalidi 2012a: 1). Despite the appointed Prime Minister's moderation, demonstrations occurred, because activists doubted his sincerity in saying he would abide by his 'reformist ways' since he had refused to call for the amending of the controversial new Election Law (Luck 2012: 1).

According to Abdullah II, referring to what the 23 January 2013 elections entailed regarding the Prime Minister, 'the designation of the new Prime Minister will be based on consultation with the majority coalition of parliamentary blocs emerging from the new parliament or the overall parliamentary blocs if no clear majority emerges'. Then, the Prime Minister designate will 'consult with the parliamentary blocs to form the new parliamentary government, which will still have to obtain and maintain parliament's vote of confidence' ('Full text of His Majesty King Abdullah's interview with *Le Nouvel Observateur*' 2013: 7). The monarch did abide by these statements. Following consultations, he happened to choose Ensour again as Prime Minister.

Civil society

For political liberalisation to develop and result in more permanent stability, there is a need for a vibrant civil society with its many components, such as charitable organisations, trade unions, university students' organisations, youth movements, professional organisations, and many others. In Jordan these organisations were limited by administrative and legal restrictions. The protests of 2011 sought to reform these too. In response, the King opted for a balanced 'managed reform' (Sweis 2011a: 1).

The Public Gatherings Law hampered the formation of civil society organisations, since it required prior permission from the governor for a gathering to take place. Governors in the past often turned down these requests. For example, Christoph Wilcke of Human Rights Watch cites a case where the governor refused to grant permission to a coalition of local organisations to meet in a rented hotel room to coordinate independent monitoring ahead of the 2007 parliamentary elections (Wilcke 2011: 1). However, as a result of the protests an amendment to the Public Gatherings Law was approved by the Lower House of Parliament, whereby the requirement of prior permission was replaced by a simple requirement of advance notification, thus guaranteeing freedom of assembly (Sweis 2011a: 3; Wilcke 2011: 1).

Administrative and legal restrictions of NGOs by the Government still prevailed, however, even though a new law was passed in 2008 and amended in 2009. These restrictions on the formation of civil society organisations included denying registration, delaying the issuance of licences, government interference through rules about membership and leadership, denying permission to seek foreign funding, harassing of applicants by the *Mukhabarat* (Intelligence Services or Secret Police), and even the shutting down of NGOs (Wiktorowicz 2001: 129–31; Wilcke 2011: 2). An example occurred when the *Mukhabarat* forced a cultural organisation to exclude certain individuals from membership because they had criticised the regime. This was a precondition for the registration of the organisation in order for it to engage in cultural activities. Also, the *Mukhabarat* demanded that a member of its administrative committee resign from his position of leadership (Wiktorowicz 2002: 121–2).

Limitations were also placed on the kind of topics the civil society associations could deal with. The NGOs were, in general, denied permission to discuss such sensitive issues as the monarchy, the security apparatus and the armed forces (Greenwood 2003: 105). Further, Islamist cultural and charitable organisations were not permitted to engage in political activities. There was a clash between these organisations and the Government over the meaning of 'political'. According to the Director of Charitable Organisations at the Ministry of Social Development, politics and culture were separate. But the Islamist cultural organisation argued otherwise – that Islam applies to all aspects of social existence. As a result the charity stated that it was difficult for it to render activities completely separate from political import. In this way it actively challenged the boundaries of the political realm as directed by the state (Wiktorowicz 1999: 609–11, 620).

Tensions escalated when, in 2005, the Government took over the board of the charitable arm of the Muslim Brotherhood, the Islamic Centre Society, under the pretext that it was suspected of corruption. However, the Islamists cited the usual charge that this move was 'purely political' as the several schools and the hospital concerned had helped the Islamists gain popularity, especially among the urban poor. After the protests of 2011, there was an attempt at reconciliation when a deal was negotiated between the Government and the Muslim Brotherhood to return the administration of the charity society to the Islamists. However, according to Bani Rasheid, head of the Islamic Action Front politburo, the agreement seemed to have been scuttled because of the intervention of the General Intelligence Department (Neimat 2011b: 1; 2012a: 1).

In dealing with professional associations, King Abdullah II alternated tough action with measures of liberalisation. For example, he dissolved the councils of fourteen syndicates, giving as his reason the illegality of their political activities, which opposed the normalisation of relations with Israel. However, a year later, in November 2003, his new Prime Minister, Abu al-Ragheb, made gestures of reconciliation by addressing them (Abdullah 2003b: 20). After the Arab Spring, the Lower House of Parliament attempted to 'restore public confidence' in its performance by resorting to a dialogue and partnership with civil society. The need for it to go further, to include the popular protest movements beyond the established political powers in this effort, was emphasised by several associations, notable among which was the Jordan Medical Association (Neimat 2012e: 1). Indeed, 'associations' had gained prominence through the Constitutional Amendment to Article 16, which made special provision for them and which was endorsed by Parliament (Omari 2012a: 2). However, they were to be strictly controlled. Article 16 still provided for the law to regulate their 'manner of establishment' and to control their resources ('The Constitution of Jordan with all the amendments thereto' 2011: 14).

Realising that the groundwork for effective liberalisation went beyond Article 16, Abdullah II sought to build 'a democratic culture that guarantees a tangible bottom-up change' through the 'vital role that civil society plays in enhancing our democratic model' (King Abdullah II of Jordan 2013: 4). He planned to go to the grass roots, which were to be energised by civil society across Jordan, by creating the King Abdullah II Fund for Development in order to establish a Democracy Empowerment Programme (*Demoqrati*) on 10 December 2012, on the occasion of the University of Jordan's 50th anniversary and reconfirmed on 1 June 2013. *Demoqrati* would monitor, provide selective support for, and enhance the political performance of existing civil society organisations and encourage the formation of new creative associations and their participation in community activities (ibid.: 6).

Moreover, starting in 2011, following the protests, Abdullah II was especially active in seeking out the different sectors of the Jordanian community by travelling around the country and engaging them in talks about how to tackle the challenges facing Jordan. Notable here are his engagement of tribes, who see him in a favourable light (Hazaimeh 2011c: 11), and his reaching out to young people, who are often critical of his regime. One example of his success occurred when he met with representatives of tribes that came originally from the West Bank city of Hebron, and the tribal leaders reasserted their allegiance to the Hashemite monarchy and voiced their support for the King's reform plans (Ghazal 2012: 1). In return, Abdullah II showed his strong appreciation of the tribes when on 16 June 2013, in response to the outbreak of demonstrations across Jordan, he stated at Mutah University in Karak:

> Our culture and authentic tribal structure do not accept violence. We are all sons and daughters of tribes from various backgrounds and origins, whether the badia, villages, cities or refugee camps ... This is the most important source of our strength, national unity, and our society's security and stability. (Ghazal 2013: 3)

He added that the tribes were a symbol of valour and of authentic peaceful values, which contributed to the stability of the country, his highest priority.

Abdullah II, in his appeal to young people, encouraged them especially to participate in public service and in political parties, which he believed should henceforward make an effort to include the young. At the Jordan Youth Forum on 14 June 2011, the monarch specifically urged young people to form political parties but cautioned that it would take 'at least two or three years to render these parties mature and well enough established to make gains in legislative elections', and therefore they 'should start now for there is no time to waste'

(Ghazal 2011: 1). Moreover, on 10 October 2012, the King, in his letter of designation to the new interim Prime Minister, Abdullah Ensour, tasked him with responsibility for young people via implementation of the National Employment Strategy, 'which attaches great importance to youth in order to empower them to build their future and find suitable jobs' (King Abdullah II of Jordan 2012a: 4).

The transition towards reform: has the Arab Spring been realised?

The Arab Spring touched Jordan as it did the other Arab countries. But the Jordanian Spring was 'civilised', according to Abdullah II, who wrote in October 2012, 'History and national memory will record that the Jordanian Spring was civilised, characterised by a high sense of responsibility and awareness, and a model for peacefulness' (ibid.: 3). Jordanians settled for reform instead of revolution, unlike Tunisians and Egyptians. The ruled in Jordan opted for stability, albeit tempered with limited liberty, to be achieved through evolution rather than revolution. Jordan therefore presents a reform model which is still evolving. Many Jordanians do not seem to be impatient.

The King tends to believe that reform is a 'process' to be continued in the newly elected parliament of 2013. He has stated: 'there is no final destination on the reform path. Reform is a process' (Omari 2012b). This means, according to the Government, 'reform through parliament, not via street protests' (Nicky 2012: 2).

The conditions for a hierarchical dissonance in values existed in Jordan as they did in other Arab countries, with Abdullah II prioritising stability, especially after the extremist Islamist attacks in Amman in 2005, to the detriment of his previously promised economic reforms, while the ruled emphasised employment and better standards of living. Again in the autumn of 2012 the regime foiled an al-Qaeda plan to attack multiple sites in Jordan, which refocused the attention of Jordanians on domestic security, the highest priority of the King, and away from real political reform and the unpopular presence of US troops in the country (Schwedler 2012b: 1). But this did not supersede the protesters' demands for economic justice, their highest priority, especially as a result of the cut in fuel subsidies by the regime. However, the dissonance between these two hierarchies or priorities – stability (the priority of the ruler) and economic justice (the priority of the ruled) – was rendered less acute at this time of regional crisis, starting in 2011, because of the perceived legitimacy of the Hashemite monarch as a direct descendant of the Prophet Muhammad, as suggested by my Pendulum Model. The clever use of religion by the King, along with his stated intentions of reform, though not yet completely actualised, contributed to the stability of his rule, even though the Islamist opposition continued to demonstrate often and push for more reforms, urging no procrastination. The opposition thus did not call for the overthrow (*iskat*) of the monarch, but for reform (*islah*) of the regime.

When faced with protests, the King emphasised his lineage, achieving positive results. For example, on 23 October 2012 he declared that he did not seek power, but had to shoulder responsibilities: 'As for me personally, Abdullah ibn Al Hussein, I will continue true to this path. Being King to me is not a gain I seek, it is a responsibility, "for only to Allah belongs all dominion".' He continued, referring to his lineage:

> What I cherish the most is the honour of being a descendant of our forefather Prophet Mohammad (PBUH). After this honourable lineage and what it entails in terms of commitments, I am honoured to be a Jordanian and to share with this noble and genuine people their stances and great sacrifices. (King Abdullah of Jordan 2012b: 5)

He then referred to his father, King Hussein:

> After this, comes my duty to shoulder my responsibilities and foster the interests of my people and my beloved country. Al Hussein, may God bless his soul, taught me and taught us all that pleasing God and serving this country are our sole purpose in this life. (ibid.)

All three forces active in Jordan at the time of the Arab Spring of 2011 concurred in considering the monarch legitimate, although they differed regarding specific solutions to the crisis of 2011. The first group was composed of the conservative security apparatus backed by the old-guard politicians, the majority of tribal members, and the military officers. The leaders of more than 75 tribes had, earlier in the year, signed Islamic pledges of allegiance (*bai'ah*) and loyalty (*wila'*) to the Hashemite monarchy and had rallied round (*iltifaf*) Abdullah II (Susser 2011). This first group was against major political reforms, lest they should turn out to benefit the Islamists (Al-Sharif 2011c: 2).

The second group was made up of the Islamists, led by the Muslim Brotherhood, and other opposition groups, who favoured political reforms that would limit the powers of the king and would result in newer elections than those of 2013 that they had boycotted, ultimately leading to a new more representative parliament. The third group was the young people, who appealed to the street and who had a social media following. Many of them distinguished themselves from the Islamists. They called for constitutional and other reforms (ibid.).

Despite his status as descendant of the Prophet Muhammad, Abdullah II opted for concessions involving a modest accession of managed reforms and liberalisation measures. He appointed several commissions to study and make recommendations for reform. Notable here were the recommendations of the Royal Committee on Constitutional Review. According to Abdullah II, much has been achieved, such as 'unprecedented political reform process with wide-ranging amendments to one-third of the constitution, new democratic institutions such as the Independent Elections Commission and Constitutional Court, stronger checks-and-balances mechanisms, enhanced separation of powers . . . and new limitations to the king's constitutional powers' ('Full text of His Majesty King Abdullah's interview with *Le Nouvel Observateur*' 2013: 6). But were the demands of the protesters for reform realised after two years?

The economic demands of the protesters, their first priority, had not been met by the summer of 2013. The economy did not improve – in fact it deteriorated somewhat. Unemployment was still rife, even though the Government took measures to improve the situation. This was worsened by the huge influx of Syrian refugees (Susser 2013b: 4). According to the King, 'refugees are competing for jobs with Jordanians, not to mention impact on education and healthcare' ('Full text of His Majesty King Abdullah's interview with London-based *Asharq Alawsat*' 2013: 5). Jordanians believed that the economy had deteriorated since 2011, according to a poll conducted by the Pew Research Center in the spring of 2013. Whereas, in 2011, 33 per cent of Jordanian respondents believed that the economic situation of the country was 'good', in 2012 the figure had declined to 27 per cent. When asked about their personal economic situation, 30 per cent believed it was 'good' compared to 37 per cent in 2009 (Pew Research Center 2013a). Further, corruption did not improve. The Corruption Perceptions Index was virtually unchanged, at 4.8 at the end of 2012 compared to 4.7 in 2010 (Transparency International 2012: 5).

Moreover, Jordanians suffered from the decision of the Government to lift the fuel subsidies, as required by the austerity measures called for by the IMF. This led to protests in November 2012. The monarch called the decision 'painful, but at the same time necessary'. He justified his action by citing the 'unprecedented fiscal pressure due to the global financial crisis on the one hand, and the disruption of [the] Egyptian gas supply, which doubled our energy bill'. But he did mention the measures he planned to take to improve the Jordanian economy, stating that a 'compensation mechanism was also rolled out at the same time, providing direct cash assistance to more than 70 per cent Jordanians' ('Full text of His Majesty King Abdullah's interview with *Le Nouvel Observateur*' 2013: 6). This was a necessary step in meeting the protesters' demands for social and economic justice and averting further demonstrations. It remains to be seen whether the King will be able to make good on his latest economic commitments to the people given the financial constraints the country is under and the demands of the IMF. This would in the end depend on the generosity of the EU, the USA, Japan, and the Gulf States (notably Saudi Arabia), many of whom are not as wealthy as they used to be. According to Asher Susser, ultimately, the meeting of economic demands will trump the importance of the pace of political reforms so far as the stability of the regime is concerned (Susser 2013a: 3).

Were the political promises of a transition to democracy made at the time of the Arab Spring realised in practice by the summer of 2013? Perhaps a Pew Research Center Poll released on 30 April 2013 offers a glimpse of what Jordanians thought two years after the Arab Spring of 2011. When asked whether 'people like me don't have any say about what the government does', Jordanians did not feel empowered: 42 per cent 'strongly agreed' and 21 per cent 'mostly agreed' with the statement. By contrast, 25 per cent 'mostly disagreed' and 11 per cent 'completely disagreed' with the statement (Pew Research Center 2013b: 174). Jordanians were, however, about evenly divided on how best to solve the country's problems – that is, whether through democracy or through a strong leader. Only slightly more leaned towards democracy (49 per cent) than leaned towards a powerful leader (41 per cent) to solve the problems of the country (ibid.: 60). Perhaps this is due to the fact that most Jordanians trusted Abdullah II to do what was best for the country in his judgement, for he was after all the direct descendant of the Prophet Muhammad.

In June 2013, Abdullah II reasserted his belief in democracy and commented on a conditional date for its achievement: 'I see no alternative to democracy . . . The date of achieving reform is linked to the accomplishment of democratic milestones and requirements I just mentioned.' These milestones were general, such as 'constitutional institutions that guarantee the political process and pluralism, progressive and fair legislation, checks and balances, separation of powers, a vibrant civil society and real, platform-based parties that make it to Parliament and form governments on the basis of a parliamentary majority and a constructive opposition', and the 'need [for] a majority of society to believe in them so that we can embark on translating them into facts on the ground' ('Full text of His Majesty King Abdullah's interview with London-based *Asharq Alawsat*' 2013: 7). This was quite an undertaking, which would take some time to accomplish.

All parties in Jordan, however, tended to uphold the stability provided by Abdullah II, who for them acts as a rallying 'point of consensus' in the country. As Laith Shubeilat, a former Islamist politician and later a public intellectual, put it in 2011, 'Jordan needs the throne. Without the throne there will be civil war. The people of Jordan are tribal . . . [but] . . . nobody would dare say "Our family is nobler than the Hashemites" . . . they are a point of meeting for us all' (Nicholson 2013: 1). The Hashemites are thus perceived to be the first tribe (with genuine Islamic credentials, of which King Abdullah II boasts) among tribes, and hence the great unifiers and guarantors of stability.

Viability of the HD hypothesis and Pendulum Model in the Jordanian case

The Pendulum Model depicting the dynamic interactions between Abdullah II and Jordanians is viable in the case of Jordan. The hierarchical dissonance at the time of the Arab Spring was indeed less acute, because Jordanians tended to believe in the monarch's judgement and trusted that he was basically well-disposed as the direct descendant of the Prophet. In this capacity, the King rose above everyday politics as a final just arbiter, even though he did not actually make good on all of his promises. He was given almost complete carte blanche time-wise too by his people. Although he met with opposition, it was from fellow Islamists, that is from the IAF, the political arm of the Muslim Brotherhood. The King's version of Islam tended to be more trusted than theirs. This Islamist opposition, however, did not demand his ousting, but rather called for a faster pace of reform, which Abdullah II has resisted so far even during the crises engulfing the region in the summer of 2013. Compared to the Moroccan dynasty, the Hashemite dynasty settled for a slower pace of change, perhaps because it did not feel as secure.

CHAPTER 6

Conclusion

Iskat (overthrowing) or *islah* (reforming)? That was the question faced by Middle Eastern protesters during the Arab Spring of 2011. Moroccans and Jordanians opted for transitioning towards reform by calling for a mere change of government (*hukuma*), whereas Tunisians and Egyptians resorted towards transitioning to revolution by demanding the changing of the entire regime (*nizam*). Why was this so? Were the transitions realised, and to what extent had they been realised by the summer of 2013?

My study of these four cases has shown that the conditions for hierarchical dissonance in values between the priorities of the rulers for stability and of the ruled for economic justice and democracy were rife across the region during the Arab Spring of 2011. But they were rendered less acute in Morocco and Jordan as the kings in these countries resorted to religion as a palliative, because they genuinely believed in it and because they imbued their other diversionary methods of co-optation, repression and illiberal democracy in it. On the other hand, in the more secular republics of Tunisia and Egypt, the rulers made short shrift of religion, resulting in an intolerable dissonance between the hierarchies of the rulers and the ruled. Their diversionary tactics of co-optation, repression and illiberal democracy were hence perceived as insincere, opportunistic and, most of all, unjust. The only way left for the protesters was to overthrow these secular rulers and attempt to take matters into their own hands by attempting to transition towards democracy.

Moreover, the role of the military is important in all four cases. I suggested that, as descendants of the Prophet Muhammad and hence as legitimate 'Commanders of the Faithful', the Moroccan and Jordanian monarchs retained and commanded the support of their militaries. In Tunisia and in Egypt, by contrast, the military proved to be fickle, changing sides and abandoning the rulers, especially since these rulers, unlike the kings, decided to use excessive force against their own people, from which the military conscripts and officers emanated. While it is true that both Ben Ali and Mubarak were military generals, they had alienated their base. Ben Ali had demoted his military to second-class positions, and emphasised and rewarded instead his security and intelligence services. Mubarak had angered his military by emphasising neoliberal economic policies involving privatisation efforts and crony capitalism on a large scale, carried out by his son Gamal Mubarak, which ended up competing with the military's own business enterprises, and instilled in the officers the fear of losing their privileges if privatisation went too far.

Contribution of this study

Contribution to the Arab Spring literature

While the literature on the events of 2011 is replete with excellent one-country monographs, a more comprehensive comparative analysis of the Arab Spring is necessary in order to generate a better understanding of the phenomenon. Important contributions here are to be found in Haas and Lesch (2013), Habeeb (2012), Gelvin (2012, 2013), Goldstone (2011) and Lynch (2012). However, the latest of these studies stops in the summer of 2012, whereas my study extends to the summer of 2013.

Some authors, such as Habeeb (2012), who dwells on the historical reasons for authoritarianism, emphasise 'ruler-oriented' reasons for the Arab Spring. Others, such as Haas and Lesch (2013), concentrate on 'ruled-oriented' reasons for discontent. Both approaches fall short of offering a more complete picture of the events of the Arab Spring, a deficiency which my study endeavours to overcome by presenting the dynamic interaction of rulers and ruled via the HD hypothesis.

Lynch (2012) places rulers and ruled on a more equal footing, but his study is more journalistic and descriptive than analytical in explaining why some countries underwent revolutions and others reform. Gelvin (2013) and Goldstone (2011) attempt to eliminate this shortcoming by presenting a more theoretical comparative analysis region-wide.

Gelvin (2013) groups countries into four clusters: (1) Tunisia and Egypt, where revolutions occurred; (2) Yemen and Libya, where the elite was splintered; (3) Syria and Bahrain, where the elite maintained cohesion against the uprisings and where sectarian divisions were exploited; and (4) the monarchies, like Morocco, Jordan, Saudi Arabia, Kuwait and Oman, where protests occurred on a limited scale but no uprising resulted. Gelvin's (2013) analysis achieves further sophistication by subdividing the monarchies into four groups, giving different reasons for their survival, such as their being oil-rich and-oil poor kingdoms, minority and majority community states, extended family-rule monarchies and those ceding partial control to allies, and those with high or low percentages of non-citizens. However, he does not consider the effect of religion, which my Pendulum Model suggests.

While Goldstone (2011) surpasses also merely journalistic accounts of the Arab Spring by presenting a theoretical explanation of events as being motivated against 'sultanistic' dictatorships, his study exhibits some shortcomings that my study attempts to overcome. His theory tends to be mainly oriented towards rulers, and as such it does not tend to include ruled-oriented aspects, a deficiency which my HD hypothesis attempts to overcome by presenting the dynamic interaction between rulers and ruled. Also, in his explanation of why monarchies have survived, Goldstone dwells on the monarchs' shifting of the blame onto their parliaments, which is true as regards Morocco and Jordan, but is not true in the case of Saudi Arabia, where no parliament exists. Certainly there must be an intervening variable which Goldstone does not consider and which my study attempts to present: namely the use of religion by the monarchies, which my Pendulum Model depicts. While it is true that, in the cases of Morocco and Jordan, the kings deflected blame onto their Prime Ministers and parliaments, the fact remains that this was accepted by the people, mainly because the monarchs were seen to be 'Commanders of the Faithful', as direct descendants of the Prophet Muhammad, and therefore above reproach, and above the give-and-take of daily politics. In the case of Saudi Arabia, the attachment of the ruling family and the monarch to the Wahhabi branch of Islam, and their active promotion of this together with their financial compensating of the people, saved the day.

Contribution to fourth generation theory

My HD hypothesis, in combination with the Pendulum Model, attempts to meet the requirements of a fourth generation theory as called for by Goldstone (2001), as mentioned in my introductory chapter. To repeat: the HD hypothesis treats stability as problematic, with the pendulum swinging from the area representing the increased stability of the ruler to the area representing the increased vulnerability of the leader as a result of crises, as the extent of stability is constantly negotiated and renegotiated between ruler and ruled. Thus the HD hypothesis includes the time factor, since it deals with conditions of regime sustainability, which are changeable over time. My case studies cover the years which preceded the transitions to revolution and reform in 2011, and show that the transitions are still evolving.

Rulers and ruled have been depicted as involved in a dynamic interaction provided for by the Pendulum Model. In accordance with Goldstone's (2001) suggestion, my model depicts the interplay of multiple actors. The rulers tended to be supported by the elites, who acted in both formal and informal behind-the-scenes ways in the cases studied. Thus the rulers were not monolithic: on the contrary, they included crony capitalists, ruling party members, important families, prestigious religious institutions such as al-Azhar (in Egypt), security and intelligence officials and the military (unless they abandoned the rulers, as for example in Tunisia and Egypt). Poor circulation into the elite ranks was found in all four countries studied, but it was especially significant in those transitioning towards revolution, such as Tunisia and Egypt.

Where the rulers resorted to religion, such as calling for unity under a common unifying majority faith (Islam) and asking for endorsements from religious institutions or seeking legitimacy through descent from the Prophet, hierarchical dissonance in values was mitigated and transitioning towards reform was preferred, as in Morocco and Jordan. Where religion tended not to be resorted to, transitions towards revolution occurred, as in the cases of Ben Ali in Tunisia and Hosni Mubarak in Egypt.

My HD hypothesis also covers possible conditions for the sustainability of the regimes, as Goldstone (2001) calls for. More specifically, it embraces the diversionary methods used by the ruling groups to avert revolutions and stay in power. My hypothesis pits these methods used by rulers, which include the co-opting of the elite, the power of repression and the installing of illiberal democracy, interactively against the demands of the ruled for economic and social justice, people power and populist democracy (in the cases of Tunisia and Egypt), and constitutional monarchy (in the cases of Morocco and Egypt). My study shows that extreme repression tended to be counterproductive; co-optation without elite circulation tended to lead to feelings of relative deprivation and, when coupled with the realisation that this injustice was not inevitable, led to protests; also, reforms initiated at the last minute at times of regime weakness tended to be ineffective (as in Tunisia and Egypt), but to be effective when initiated at times of regime strength (as in Morocco and Jordan). Illiberal democracy tended to raise the expectations of the people only for them to be dashed as the regime resorted to rigged elections, leading to demonstrations.

I borrow from third generation theories the idea of the malfunctioning of governmental structures, but I modify these theories in explaining that the structures need to be addressed in an interactive manner, from the angle of how they are perceived by the ruled (that is, when the existing structures are perceived to be ineffective in solving the economic priorities of the ruled). These perceptions were especially acute among the bulging numbers of young people with university degrees, who could not find jobs and who believed that their governments were not serious about addressing this problem. The perceptions of the ruled are analysed, in my case studies, through the use of reliable public opinion polls (notably those of the Pew Research Center and the Abu Dhabi Gallup Center among others), and of the chants and statements of the protesters.

Moreover, my HD hypothesis accords a prominent role to the networks of the ruled, as both Goldstone (2001) and the newer rational choice models call for. My study analyses group and mass mobilisation networking efforts that generated people power through the use of social media (Facebook, Twitter, YouTube), mobile phones and satellite TV. As such, it attempts to excavate the rational choices of the protesters, as depicted by their pronouncements. In this way it attempts to unify the case studies with the new rational choice models as perceived by the demonstrators. Here, the role of nearness to the goal of ousting Mubarak was important in Egypt, as the protesters glimpsed the possibility of quick success seeing that the Tunisians had, just recently in January 2011, ousted Ben Ali.

However, the need, suggested by Goldstone (2001), to address the role of the single (or double) leadership of the revolutionaries, although provided for by my HD hypothesis, has not proven to be pertinent as regards the initial transitions to revolution or reform studied here. The protesters tended to be amorphous masses and somewhat leaderless (that is, without a discernible unified leadership). Also, Goldstone (ibid.) suggests that outcomes need to be addressed. But outcomes tend to be fluid and not settled quickly, if ever. My study, in dealing with the process of transitions, attempts to address outcomes in asking the question 'Is the Arab Spring realised?'. But it concludes that, as of summer 2013, the transitions are still evolving in the four case study countries covered.

Case studies

Monarchies transitioning towards reform

In the case of Morocco, King Muhammad VI was trusted to institute reforms not only because he was a descendant of the Prophet but also because he had acted on his pedigree in attempting to bring about economic justice by helping both the poor and women, and by being known as 'King [Champion] of the Poor' and 'King [Champion] of Women' long before the Arab Spring. In the case of Jordan, King Abdullah II was also trusted, as the descendant of the Prophet, to institute reforms. He had embarked on the Jordan First concept before the Arab Spring, but had not achieved the same economic results as his Moroccan counterpart since he had reverted to prioritising stability owing to an al-Qaeda threat in 2005, and also because Jordan was considerably poorer economically.

After the Arab Spring, both countries sought economic relief by appealing to the IMF, only to be told to cut subsidies to fuel and food, which did not sit well with economic justice, the highest demand of their peoples. In addition, Jordan, a country with a small population, faced further economic problems owing to the influx of Syrian refugees. In the political realm, both countries attempted reforms, with the Moroccan king relinquishing more of his powers (for example, in his choosing the Prime Minister from the party with the largest percentage of parliamentary seats) since he felt more secure than the Jordanian king, for the simple reason that the Moroccan dynasty was around three hundred and fifty years old whereas the Jordanian was less than one hundred years old. Also, Jordan faced greater instability owing to Palestinian and Islamist opposition to the country's signing a peace treaty with Israel. The Jordanian king was hence more cautious, and put off any full-scale transition to democracy. Abdullah II stated that this would ultimately depend on the population developing a democratic culture – quite an open-ended proposition, which nevertheless tended to be accepted by the majority of Jordanians, who believed that the monarch's Hashemite tribe was the first among all the tribes, and hence that they had to obey the monarchy.

Republics transitioning towards revolution

The HD hypothesis and the Pendulum Model proved to be viable in explaining the toppling of Ben Ali and Mubarak. Certainly, conditions embodying a hierarchical dissonance of values, where the ruler prioritised stability and the ruled emphasised economic justice to be arrived at by transitioning towards democracy, prevailed in Tunisia and Egypt during 2010 and 2011. The dissonance became intolerable, as Ben Ali and Mubarak were perceived to be unjust and hence not be trusted in remedying the problems of the country, especially since they did not resort to the palliative of religion. Ben Ali did not learn from his successful use of religion at the beginning of his rule in order to achieve stability. In fact, he clamped down on religion.

This study has concentrated on the dynamic, interactive relationship between rulers and ruled, where the rulers had used in the past effectively tactics such as co-optation, repression and illiberal democracy to ensure the longevity of their power, and where the ruled had, albeit grudgingly, acquiesced to this. These methods proved to be relatively ineffective in 2011. What was different?

Co-optation had, with time, increasingly benefited only the few, who had become more greedy and corrupt, which led to perceptions of relative deprivation on the part of the increasing numbers of young university graduates, who had no prospects of finding jobs without bribes but who were educated enough to be savvy with social media mobilisation and the use of cellphones inspired by the 'Twitter Revolution' in Iran, even at a time when the macro-economy as a whole was improving prior to the world economic downturn, which affected Tunisia and Egypt.

Repression, which had been used selectively against extremist Islamists in the past to please the USA in its 'war on terror', was extended to the moderate dissident population at large in the name of Ben Ali's and Mubarak's highest priority of stability. Repression became more and more severe, to such an extent that it elicited Western public condemnation, as evidenced by the Cairo speech on 4 June 2009 by the newly elected US President Barack Obama, and subsequently repeated in his numerous other speeches prior to 2011, which addressed the dictators as being on 'the wrong side of history' (Alianak 2012: 7).

Political liberalisation efforts, urged by the Bush and Obama administrations, were at best half-hearted, and resulted in the expectations of the populations of Tunisia and Egypt being raised, only to be dashed over and over again by rigged, tampered-with and otherwise controlled elections. This led to frustration, anger, and feelings of lack of trust and hopelessness as regards gaining redress given existing governmental structures, and to a determination on the part of the protesters to transition towards democracy.

Further, both Ben Ali and Mubarak were ageing and hence facing a succession problem. Ben Ali was 74 and did not have a clear successor, eliciting fears that a corrupt member of his despised family might take over in the unlikely event of his deciding not to run again because of the constitutional age limit. The hopes of the people for a populist democracy – their priority – were thus dashed as well. The hierarchical dissonance between the values of ruler and ruled became intolerable, and Ben Ali was toppled.

In the case of Egypt, people also resented the fact that there was to be no clear democratically elected successor to the ageing Mubarak, who was in his eighties and in ill health. He was perceived to be grooming his unpopular son Gamal for the post. Gamal's neoliberal economic policies had alienated Egyptians, who resented the shrinking number of 'crony capitalists', who were perceived to have illegally and unjustly amassed great wealth and were corrupt to boot.

Heuristic value of the HD hypothesis and Pendulum Model in analysing the region-wide impact of the Arab Spring

My HD hypothesis and Pendulum Model have heuristic value in explaining the impact of the Arab Spring region-wide in terms of the toppling of some regimes and the survival of others in the Arab Middle East. The monarchies and hereditary rulers of the Gulf States survived because the diversionary method of co-optation, coupled with the use of religion, prevailed, as explained by the Pendulum Model. There was hardly any dissonance between the values of the Saudi royal family and Saudi citizens, since the economic needs of the people were more than adequately met by the massive infusion of subsidies from the coffers of a regime that enjoyed immense wealth generated by oil revenues. Also, co-optation was backed up by the Wahhabi Islamic ties of the kingdom.

The case of Bahrain was unique. It is an emirate (resembling a monarchy). Hierarchical dissonance in values occurred with the Sunni emir emphasising stability and the majority Shi'ite population prioritising the closing of the gap between the rich minority Sunnis and the impoverished majority Shi'ites and demanding democracy. But the uprising of this majority was thwarted by the outside intervention by the Saudi military. Thus the emir precariously survived.

Libya, Yemen and Syria are republics, which were secular and where the palliative of religion, as depicted by the Pendulum Model, was not used. Hence, in all three cases violence occurred with the dissonance in values between the rulers' emphasis on stability and the prioritising by the ruled of economic justice and democracy, but here outside forces intervened decisively. In Libya the role of NATO was significant in the toppling of Qaddafi, as the Libyan military had sided with the ruler in the ensuing civil war. In Yemen, the role of US drones and of Saudi influence was paramount. While it is true that the ruler was ousted in a deal, no revolution occurred since the rest of his regime continued to remain in full force, with the backing of the USA and Saudi Arabia.

In Syria, a dissonance in the hierarchy of values between Bashar al-Assad and the ruled grew to intolerable levels, accompanied by large-scale violence, with a death toll that had reached well over 100,000 by the summer of 2013. The ruler prioritised stability, while a number of the ruled emphasised economic justice and democracy. The ruling Ba'ath party was secular, with followers among the Alawites, Christians and some Sunnis. However, the uprising had religious undertones, and with the military siding with al-Assad a vicious civil war was fought, where no possibility of compromise occurred. Thus the Arab Spring led to a major humanitarian disaster. Moreover, it degenerated into a region-wide proxy war. Saudi Arabia, the Gulf States and members of the Iraq-based al-Qaeda and foreign fighters supported the Syrian, mostly Sunni, insurgents. Shi'ite Iran, on the other hand, supported al-Assad and his mostly Alawite and Christian backers. An international dimension was added when Russia and China backed al-Assad in the UN Security Council, blocking any UN-authorised military intervention, as had been the case previously in Libya with the UN's decision to involve NATO. The USA has since sided with the insurgents through its decision to provide armaments to the rebels, claiming, as a reason for doing so more actively, that the Syrian regime had used chemical weapons in a limited way.

The Arab Spring realised?

Had the demands of the Arab Spring protesters for economic justice, for doing away with corruption and for instituting democracy been met in the countries studied by the summer of 2013? Had economic justice, the priority of protesters in 2011, been realised by then? Unemployment, that had plagued young university graduates and other citizens, had worsened in all four countries studied relative to 2010. The reasons for this were the world economic downturn and the Eurozone debt crisis, both of which had shut off tourism and foreign investment. The situation was aggravated by the instability that prevailed in the case-study countries in question. Further, the influx of massive Syrian refugees into Jordan was a drain on the Jordanian economy and worsened an already bad economy – by far the weakest of the four states studied here. A bail-out given by the IMF to these countries carried with it what were perceived to be unfair conditions, stipulating a cut in fuel and other subsidies, which led to further outrage on the part of the young Arab Spring protesters, as witnessed, especially, in Morocco, Jordan and Tunisia. (Egyptian–IMF negotiations went nowhere.) This dissatisfaction on the part of the young, the middle class and the poor could have further destabilising effects in the future.

How did the declared efforts of the post-Arab-Spring governments to reduce corruption actually fare by the summer of 2013? Here too the demands of the Arab Spring protesters were not met. According to Transparency International in its survey released in July 2013, corruption had worsened in the Arab countries, in spite of the fact that anger against corrupt officials had been a major fuel of the uprisings of 2011. According to Christoph Wilcke of Transparency International, 'There is a contradiction between policy and rhetoric' (Torchia 2013: 1). He blamed this on the social and economic turmoil that followed the Arab Spring, allowing the governments little time to push for reforms. Also, in order to attract foreign investment, the governments at times colluded with former regime members convicted of corruption – for example in Egypt (ibid.). The Arab public's frustration with the lack of progress over the corruption question could therefore undermine stability, which could in turn hinder foreign investment and ultimately economic growth – all this in a vicious cycle.

Was the Arab Spring realised, in the countries studied here, in terms of their transitioning towards democracy? None of the countries covered achieved a full transition to democracy. But there were degrees of transition, such as could be represented by a continuum with democracy at one end and authoritarianism at the other. Polls conducted by the Pew Research Center which were released on 30 April 2013 confirmed my findings that Tunisians, more than Egyptians and more again than Jordanians, preferred democracy to a strong leader as a means of solving their countries' problems. Seventy-five per cent of Tunisians preferred democracy as against 22 per cent who preferred a strong leader, while the figures for Egyptians were 55 per cent for democracy and 36 per cent for a strong leader; whereas Jordanians were more evenly divided, 49 per cent being for democracy and 41 per cent for a strong leader (Pew Research Center 2013: 60). Thus Jordanians settled for partial reforms and Tunisians desired more democracy, whereas Egyptians periodically veered between democracy and authoritarianism. Although Moroccans were not polled, my study shows that they can be placed nearer to the democracy end of the continuum than Jordanians.

But what were the perceptions of Tunisians, Egyptians and Jordanians as regards their actual empowerment as of 30 April 2013? These also differed. Jordanians felt least empowered, with 63 per cent saying that they did not have any say in their government; Tunisians were next, with 61 per cent saying this; and Egyptians were last, with 49 per cent (ibid.: 174). The polls supported my findings that Jordanians, although not feeling as empowered as Tunisians and Egyptians, trusted their king because of his lineage, and hence opted for reform. Egyptians felt more empowered than Jordanians or Tunisians, and yet they were more dissatisfied. Perhaps the even division of Egyptian respondents concerning empowerment could be taken as a harbinger of the inception of competing 'people powers' in the summer of 2013, as Egyptians were more emboldened and demanded even more empowerment, resulting in Egypt becoming more turbulent than the other two countries, as my case studies show. In so doing, Egyptians unwittingly flirted with the authoritarianism of the Egyptian military. Moreover, since Tunisians felt less empowered than Egyptians but according to the polls desired more democracy, this could be a warning sign of instability, unless the situation should be mitigated by corrective economic measures undertaken by the al-Nahda-led coalition government, and by the weakness of the Tunisian military and the fact that very few Tunisians (22 per cent) have indicated belief in the need for a strong leader to solve the country's problems. Moroccans, although they were not polled, were the least prone to demonstrations against their ruler, since he had limited his powers and the people tended to trust him because of his lineage, as my case study shows.

The future of the Arab Spring in the four countries studied

Given that, as we have seen in this study, the demands of the Arab Spring protesters have not been realised as of summer 2013, the prospects for the newly elected regimes of achieving stability seem remote. The Islamists initially won elections in Morocco, Tunisia and Egypt, but they faced strong challenges from the secularist liberals. Perhaps there is a threshold at which the Pendulum Model could operate in terms of the palliative of religion, and could be effective in bridging the hierarchical dissonance of values between the Islamist rulers and the ruled and be effective in producing stability; but beyond that point, we need to look at the prolonged duration of dissonance in terms of the patience of the people and the degree of malfunctioning of the economy. At such a time, the need arises for alternative, secular solutions, such as a return to socialism or a restoration of 'crony capitalism', although both solutions have been tried in the past and have proven inadequate, as coverage of the historical backgrounds in my case studies has demonstrated. For example, Egypt is reverting to the restoration of the secular elite through the toppling the Islamist Mohamed Morsi and his Brotherhood by the military. Western-style liberal democracy has tended to be sidelined, replaced to a large extent by a preference for direct people power expressed through demonstrations. The ultimate aim, in all four countries, has seemed to be a return to the prioritising of stability in the quest for ever-elusive economic prosperity.

Bibliography

Chapter 1: Introduction

Alianak, Sonia (1987) *Hierarchical Dissonance in Values and the Iranian Revolution*, Ph.D. dissertation, University of Texas at Austin.

Alianak, Sonia (2007) *Middle Eastern Leaders and Islam: A Precarious Equilibrium*, New York: Peter Lang.

Alianak, Sonia (2012) 'Obamapower: the rhetoric, response, and reality', *Southwestern Journal of International Studies*, 5(1), 1–39.

Arendt, Hannah (1963) *On Revolution*, New York: Viking Press.

Berkowitz, L. (1968) 'The concept of aggressive behavior', in L. Berkowitz (ed.), *The Roots of Aggression: A Re-examination of Frustration-Aggression Hypothesis*, New York: Atherton Press.

Bill, James Alban (1972) *The Politics of Iran: Groups, Classes and Modernization*, Columbus, OH: Merrill.

Brinton, Crane (1965) *The Anatomy of Revolution*, New York: Prentice-Hall.

Davies, James C. (1962) 'Toward a theory of revolution', *American Sociological Review*, 27, 5–19.

Eckstein, Harry (1965) 'On the etiology of internal wars', *History and Theory*, 4(2), 133–63.

Edwards, Lyford P. (1970) *The Natural History of Revolution*, Chicago, IL and London: University of Chicago Press.

Eisenstadt, S. N. (1978) *Revolution and the Transformation of Societies: A Comparative Study of Civilizations*, New York: Free Press.

Eisenstadt, S. N. (1999) *Fundamentalism, Sectarianism, and Revolution: The Jacobin Dimension of Modernity*, New York: Cambridge University Press.

Erdle, Steffen (2010) *Ben Ali's 'New Tunisia' (1987–2009): A Case Study of Authoritarian Modernization in the Arab World*, Berlin: Klaus Schwarz Verlag.

Feierabend, Ivo K. and Rosalind L. Feierabend (1966) 'Aggressive behaviors within politics, 1948–1962: a cross-national study', *Journal of Conflict Resolution*, 10(3), 249–71.

Goldstone, Jack A. (2001) 'Toward a fourth generation of revolutionary theory', *American Review of Political Science*, 4, 139–87.

Green, J. D. (1984) 'Counter mobilization as a revolutionary form', *Comparative Politics*, 16, 153–69.

Groth, A. (1966) *Revolution and Elite Access: Some Hypotheses on Aspects of Political Change*, Davis, CA: University of California Press.

Gurr, Ted R. (1970) *Why Men Rebel*, Princeton, NJ: Princeton University Press.

Hoffer, Eric (1951) *The True Believer: Thoughts on the Nature of Mass Movements*, New York: Harper.

Huntington, Samuel (1968) *Political Order in Changing Societies*, New Haven, CT: Yale University Press.

Ireland, T. (1967) 'The rationale of revolt', *Papers in Non-Market Decision Making*, 1, 49–66.

Johnson, Chalmers (1966) *Revolutionary Change*, Boston, MA: Little, Brown.

Kurzman, C. (1996) 'Structural opportunity and perceived opportunity in social movement theory', *American Sociological Review*, 6, 153–70.

Laqueur, W. (1968) 'Revolution', *International Encyclopedia of Social Sciences*, 10, New York: Macmillan/Free Press.

Lasswell, Harold and A. Kaplan (1950) *Power and Society: A Framework for Political Inquiry*, New Haven, CT: Yale University Press.

Lasswell, Harold, Daniel Lerner and C. E. Rothwell (1952) *The Comparative Study of Elites*, Stanford, CA: Stanford University Press.

Leiden, Carl and Karl M. Schmitt (1968) *The Politics of Violence: Revolution in the Modern World*, Englewood Cliffs, NJ: Prentice Hall.

Lenin, V. I. (1970) *The State and Revolution*, Peking: Foreign Language Press.

Lupsha, Peter (1969) 'On theories of urban violence', *Urban Affairs Quarterly*, 4(3), 273–96.

Luttwak, Edward (1969) *Coup d'Etat*, New York: Knopf.

Marx, Karl and Frederick Engels (1959) *Basic Writings in Politics and Philosophy*, ed. Lewis S. Feuer, New York: Doubleday.

Moore, Barrington (1978) *Injustice: The Social Bases of Obedience and Revolt*, White Plains, NY: Sharpe.

Mosca, Gaetano (1939) *The Ruling Class*, trans. Hannah D. Kahn, New York and London: McGraw-Hill.

Ortega y Gasset, José (1932) *The Revolt of the Masses*, New York: Norton.

Pareto, Vilfredo (1935) *The Mind and Society*, New York: Harcourt, Brace & Co.

Schrecker, P. (1966) 'Revolution as a problem in the Philosophy of History', in Carl J. Friedrick (ed.), *Revolution*, New York: Atherton Press.

Scott, J. C. (1985) *Weapons of the Weak: Everyday Forms of Peasant Resistance*, New Haven, CT: Yale University Press.

Scott, J. C. (1990) *Domination and the Arts of Resistance: Hidden Transcripts*, New Haven, CT: Yale University Press.

Silver, M. (1974) 'Political revolutions and repression: an economic approach', *Public Choice*, 14, 63–71.

Skocpol, Theda (1979) *States and Social Revolutions: A Comparative Analysis of France, Russia and China*, London: Cambridge University Press.

Sorokin, Pitirim A. (1925) *The Sociology of Revolution*, New York: Lippincott.

Tilly, Charles (1978) *From Mobilization to Revolution*, Reading, MA: Addison Wesley.

Tilly, Charles and Sidney Tarrow (2007) *Contentious Politics*, Oxford: Oxford University Press.

Tocqueville, Alexis de (1856) *The Old Regime and the Revolution*, trans. John Bonner, New York: Harper.

Tullock, G. (1971) 'The paradox of revolution', *Public Choice*, 11, 87–100.

Tullock, G. (1974) *The Social Dilemma: The Economics of War and Revolution*, Blacksburg, VA: University Publications.

Weede, E. and E. N. Muller (1997) 'Consequences of revolutions', *Ration. Soc.*, 9, 327–50.

Chapter 2: Tunisia

Achy, Lahcen (2011) 'Tunisia's economic challenges', *The Carnegie Papers, The Carnegie Middle East Center*, December, 1–27.

Ajmi, Sana (2011) 'Tunisian leaders: Tunisian revolution mainly due to youth discontent, not Wikileaks', *Tunisia-live.net*, 21 December, <http://www.tunisia-live.net/2011/12/21/tunisian-leaders-tunisian-revolution-mainly-due-to-youth-discontent-not-wikileaks/> (last accessed 10 July 2012).

Amnesty International (2011) 'Tunisia: human rights agenda for change', 24 January, <http://www.amnestyusa.org/document.php?id=ENGUSA201102110048&lang=e> (last accessed 22 April 2011).

Anderson, Lisa (2011) 'Demystifying the Arab Spring', *Foreign Affairs*, 90(3), 2–7.

Andrew-Gee, Eric (2011) 'Making sense of Tunisia', *The New Republic*, 17 January,<http://www.tnr.com/print/article/world/81611/making-sense-tunisia> (last accessed 10 June 2012).

'Anonymous Operation Tunisia rages, US government grows worried' (2011) *Myce Data*, 8 January, <http://www.myce.com/news/anonymous-operation-tunisia-rages-on-us-govt-grows-concer. . .> (last accessed 22 June 2011).

Arieff, Alexis (2011) 'Political transition in Tunisia', *Congressional Research Service*, 2 February, 7-5700, RS21666, <http://www.fpc.state.gov/documents/organization/156511.pdf> (last accessed 6 February 2014).

Ayari, Sadok (2011) 'The 'big four' new powers in Tunisia', *Tunisia-live.net*, 30 October, <http://www.tunisa-live.net/2011/10/30/the-big-fours-to-govern-tunisa/> (last accessed 31 October 2011).

Brody-Barre, Andrea G. (2012) 'The impact of political parties and coalition building on Tunisia's democratic future', *Journal of North African Studies*, 18(2), 211–30, <http://dx.doi.org/10.1080/13629387.2012.742365> (last accessed 6 February 2014).

Brooks, Risa (2013) 'Abandoned at the palace: why the Tunisian military defected from the Ben Ali regime in January 2011', *Journal of Strategic Studies*, DOI:10.1080/01402390.2012.742011, <http://dx.doi.org/10.1080/0142390.2012.742011> (last accessed 6 April 2013).

Chomiak, Laryssa (2011) 'The making of a revolution in Tunisia', *Middle East Law and Governance*, 3, 68–83.

'Corruption Perception Index 2010 results' (2011) in Clement M. Henry (2011), 'Countries at crossroads 2011: Tunisia', *Freedom House*, 12.

Davies, J. C. (1962) 'Toward a theory of revolution', *American Sociological Review*, 27, 5–19.

Doucet, Lyse (2012) 'Tunisia's frustrations, two years on', *BBC News*, 10 December, <http://www.bbc.co.uk/news/world-20663981?print=true> (last accessed 10 April 2013).

Doucet, Lyse (2013) 'Clouds gather over bellwether Tunisia', *BBC News*, 10 February,

<http://www.bbc.co.uk/news/world-africa-21402778?print=true> (last accessed 10 April 2013).

Dreisbach, Tristan (2013) 'Debate remains over Leagues for the Protection of the Revolution', *Tunisia-live.net*, 21 March, <http://www.tunisia-live.net/2013/03/21/debate-remains-over-leagues-for-the-protection-of-the-revolution/> (last accessed 4 May 2013).

Dunne, Michele (2011) 'What Tunisia proved – and disproved – about political change in the Arab World', *Carnegie Endowment for International Peace*, 19 January, <http://carnegieendowment.org/2011/01/19/what-tunisia-proved-and-disproved-about-political-change-in-arab-world/3wdo> (last accessed 31 July 2012).

El-Issawi, Fatima (2012) 'Tunisian media in transition', *Carnegie Endowment for International Peace*, July (Washington, DC), 1–24.

'Ennahda movement' (2012) *Wikipedia*, 16 December, http://en.wikipedia.org/wiki/Ennahda_Movement> (last accessed 30 December 2012).

'Ennahda says it may leave power in Tunisia' (2013) *Aljazeera*, 13 February, <http://www.aljazeera.com/video/africa/2013/02/2013213193949416377.html> (last accessed 11 April 2013).

Erdle, Steffen (2010) *Ben Ali's 'New Tunisia' (1987–2009): A Case Study of Authoritarian Modernization in the Arab World*, Berlin: Klaus Schwarz Verlag.

Fisher, Max (2011) 'Tunisian election results guide: the fate of a revolution', *The Atlantic*, October, <http://www.theatlantic.com/international/print/2011/10/tunisian-election-results-guide-the. . .> (last accessed 27 October 2011).

Garton Ash, Timothy (2011)',Tunisia's revolution isn't a product of Twitter or WikiLeaks. But they do help', *Guardian*, 19 January, <http://www.guardian.co.uk/commentisfree/2011/jan/19/tunisia-revolution-twitter-facebook/print> (last accessed 10 July 2012).

Goldstone, Jack A. (2011) 'Understanding the revolutions of 2011: weakness and resilience in Middle Eastern autocracies', *Foreign Affairs*, 90(3), 8–16.

Haffar, Racha (2013a) 'Legal confusion over Prime Minister's call for technocratic government', *Tunisia-live.net*, 7 February, <http://www.tunisia-live.net/2013/02/07/constitutional-confusion-reigns-over-pms-push-for-technocratic-government/> (last accessed 4 May 2013).

Haffar, Racha (2013b) 'Coalition formed to continue legacy of former ruling parties', *Tunisia-live.net*, 15 April, <http://www.tunisia-live.net/2013/04/15/coalition-formed-to-continue-legacy-of-former-ruling-parties/> (last accessed 4 May 2013).

Halpern, Micah D. (2007) *Thugs: How Most Notorious Despots Transformed the World Through Terror, Tyranny, and Mass Murder*, Nashville, TN: Thomas Nelson.

Hanafi, Sari (2011) 'Lessons of the Jasmine Revolution', *Aljazeera*, 23 January, <http://english.aljazeera.net/indepth/opinion/2011/01/201111985641326467.html> (last accessed 13 June 2011).

Hanafi, Sari (2012) 'The Arab revolutions: the emergence of a new political subjectivity', *Contemporary Arab Affairs*, 5, 2,198–213, <http://dx.doi.org/10.1080/17550912.2012.668303> (last accessed 9 May 2013).

Henry, Clement M. (2007) 'Tunisia's "sweet little" regime', in Robert I. Rotenberg (ed.), *Worst of the Worst: Dealing with Repressive and Rogue Nations*, Cambridge, MA: World Peace Foundation, 300–23.

Henry, Clement M. (2011) 'Countries at the crossroads 2011: Tunisia', *Freedom House*, 1–18.

'How social media accelerated Tunisia's revolution: an inside view' (2011), *e.politics*, 10 February, <http://www.epolitics.com/2011/02/10/how-social-media-acceler ated-tunisias-revolution-an-inside-view/> (last accessed 10 July 2012).

Human Rights Watch (2010a) *Repression of Former Political Prisoners in Tunisia: 'A Larger Prison'*, March, 1–42.

Human Rights Watch (2010b) *The Price of Independence: Silencing Labor and Student Unions in Tunisia*, October, 1–62, <http://www.hrw.org> ISBN 1-56432-698-5.

Joya, Angela, Patrick Bond, Rami El-Amine, Adam Hanieh and Mostafa Henaway (2011) 'The Arab revolts against neoliberalism', *Centre for Social Justice*, December, 1–67.

Kaboub, Fadhel (2011) 'On the Jasmine revolution: Tunisia's political economy exemplifies a region in transition', *Dollars & Sense*, March/April, 7–8.

Khlifi, Roua (2013) 'Talks to form new government lag', *Tunisia-live.net*, 18 February, <http://www.tunisia-live.net/2013/02/18/talks-to-form-new-government-lag/> (last accessed 4 May 2013).

Kirkpatrick, David D. (2011a) 'Behind Tunisia unrest, rage over wealth of ruling family', *New York Times*, 13 January, <http://www.nytimes.com/2011/01/14/world/ africa/14tunisia.html?_r=1&sq=ben%20ali%2...> (last accessed 31 March 2011).

Kirkpatrick, David D. (2011b) 'Chief of Tunisian army pledges his support for the revolution', *New York Times*, 24 January, <http://www.nytimes.com/2011/01/25/ world/africa/25tunis.html?ref=mohamedghannouchi> (last accessed 31 March 2011).

Knickmeyer, Ellen (2011) 'Just whose side are Arab armies on, anyway?', *Foreign Policy*, 28 January, <http://www.foreignpolicy.com/articles/2011/01/28/just_whose_ side_are_arab_armies_on_anyway> (last accessed 6 February 2014).

Laaribi, Zied (2012) 'Tackling Tunisia's unemployment problem, one job at a time', *Tunisia-live.net*, 23 February, <http://www.tunisia-live.net/2012/02/23/tackling-tunisia%e2%80%99s-unemployment-problem-one-job-at-a-time/> (last accessed 10 July 2012).

Lalami, Laila (2011) 'Tunisia rising', *The Nation*, 7 February, 7–8.

Lawrence, William (2012) 'Tunisia must address economic woes to avoid unrest spilling over', *Guardian*, 7 July, <http://www.guardian.co.uk/commentisfree/2012/jul/ 07/tunisia-arab-spring/print> (last accessed 10 July 2012).

Le Nevez, Adam (2012) 'No quick fix for the Tunisian economy', *Tunisia-live.net*, 4 March, <http://www.tunisia-live.net/2012/03/04/no-quick-fix-for-the-tunisian-economy/> (last accessed 10 July 2012).

Lynch, Marc (2012) *The Arab Uprising: The Unfinished Revolutions of the New Middle East*, New York: Public Affairs.

Masrour, Amira (2013a) 'Opposition parties call for nationwide general strike', *Tunisia-live.net*, 6 February, <http://www.tunisia-live.net/2013/02/06/opposition-parties-calling-for-national-general-strike/> (last accessed 4 May 2013).

Masrour, Amira (2013b) 'Ali Laarayedh's new government loses two potential allies', *Tunisia-live.net*, 7 March, <http://www.tunisia-live-net/2013/03/07/ali-laarayedhs-new-government-loses-two-potential-allies/> (last accessed 4 May 2013).

Masrour, Amira (2013c) 'List of Prime Minister-designate's new government', *Tunisia-live.net*, 11 March, <http://www.tunisia-live.net/2013/03/11/list-of-prime-minis ter-disignates-new-government/> (last accessed 4 May 2013).

Masrour, Amira (2013d) 'Government unsure of responsibility for UGTT attacks', *Tunisia-live.net*, 18 April, <http://www.tunisa-live.net/2013/04/18/government-unsure-of-respnsibility-for-ugtt-attacks/> (last accessed 4 May 2013).

Melki, Wiem (2011) 'Martyrs of revolution seek justice as elections roll on', *Tunisia-live.net*, 26 October, <http://www.tunisia-live.net/2011/10/26/martyrs-of-revolu tion-seek-justice-as-elections-ro. . .> (last accessed 27 October 2011).

Miladi, Noureddine (2011) 'Tunisia: A media led revolution?', *Aljazeera.net*, 17 January, <http://english.aljazeera.net/indepth/opinion/2011/01/2011116142317498666.html> (last accessed 13 June 2011).

Milne, Seumas (2013) 'Tunisia and Egypt need the Arab revolutions to spread', *Guardian*, 2 April.

Ministry of Finance, Republic of Tunisia (2009) *Summary Results of the Budget's Execution*, 17 June, <http://www.portail.finances.gov.tn/en/accueil_en.php> (last accessed 4 January 2011).

'Mohamed Bouazizi' (2011) *Wikipedia*, 31 March, <http://en.wikipedia.org/wiki/Mohamed_Bouazizi> (last accessed 31 March 2011).

Muasher, Marwan (2011) 'Tunisia's lessons for the Arab World', *Carnegie Endowment for International Peace*, 1 November, <http://carnegieendowment.org/2011/11/01/tunisia-s-lessons-for-arab-world/b1b2> (last accessed 31 July 2012).

Mullin, Corinna and Azadeh Shahshahani (2011) 'Western complicity in the crimes of the Ben Ali regime', *Open Democracy*, 24 June, <http://www.opendemocracy.net> 9 (last accessed 25 June 2011).

'Operation Tunisia' (2011) *Wikipedia*, 7 June, <http://en.wikipedia.org/wiki/Operation_Tunisia> (last accessed 22 June 2011).

Paciello, Maria Cristina (2011) *Tunisia: Changes and Challenges of Political Transition*, MEDPRO Technical Report No. 3, May.

Parker, Emily (2011) 'In announcing details of voting procedures, local and International observers announce clear winner elections: "Democracy"', *Tunisia-live.net*, 25 October, <http://www.tunisia-live.net/2011/10/25/in-announcing-details-of-voting-procedures-local-. . .> (last accessed 27 October 2011).

Pew Research Center (2013a) *Global Indicators Database*, Spring Survey, <http://www.pew global.org/database/indicator/5/country/223>; <http://www.pewglobal.org/database/indicator/14/country/223> (last accessed 10 August 2013).

Pew Research Center (2013b) 'The world's Muslims: religion, politics and society', *Pew Forum on Religion and Public Life*, 30 April.

'Pew Study: most Muslims want democracy, personal freedoms and Islam in life' (2012) *Ikhwan Web*, 12 July, <http://www.ikhwanweb.com/article.php?id=30184> (last accessed 16 July 2012).

Pickard, Duncan and Todd Schweitzer (2012) 'Overcoming binding constraint to economic growth in post-revolution Tunisia, *John F. Kennedy School of Government, Harvard University*, March, 1–48.

'Promises and challenges: The Tunisian revolution of 2010-2011' (2011) *Delegation of Attorneys to Tunisia*, June, 129–73, <http://nlginternational.org/report/Tunisia-Report-2011.pdf.> (last accessed 6 February 2014).

Reporters Without Borders (2010) 'Tunisia', 5 January, <http://en.rsf.org/spip.php?page=imprimir_articulo&id_article=35443> (last accessed 22 June 2011).

Rifai, Ryan (2011) 'Timeline: Tunisia's uprising', *Aljazeera.net*, 23 January, <http://english.aljazeera.net/indepth/spotlight/tunisia/2011/01/201114142223827361.html> (last accessed 13 June 2011).

Ryan, Yasmine (2011) 'How Tunisia's revolution began', *Aljazeera.net*, 26 January, <http://english.aljazeera.net/indepth/features/2011/01/2011126121815985483.html> (last accessed 22 June 2011).

Samti, Farah (2013a) 'Former Tunisian PM's stance exposes discord within ruling Islamist party', *Tunisia-live.net*, 23 February, <http://www.tunisia-live.net/2013/02/23/former-tunisian-pms-stance-exposes-discord-within-ruling-Islamist-party/> (last accessed 4 May 2013).

Samti, Farah (2013b) 'Updated: four arrested in connection to assassination of opposition leader', *Tunisia-live.net*, 26 February, <http://www.tunisia-live.net/2013/02/26/media-report-arrest-of-islamist-in-killing-of-opposition-leader/> (last accessed 4 May 2013).

Stepan, Alfred and Juan J. Linz (2013) 'Democratization theory and the "Arab Spring"', *Journal of Democracy*, 24(2), 15–30.

Stevenson, Tom (2013) 'Tunisia: labour and the capital', *Aljazeera.net*, 15 February, <http://www.aljazeera.com/indepth/features/2013/02/201321354659178276.html> (last accessed 11 April 2013).

'Strike called over Tunisia killing' (2013) *Aljazeera.net*, 8 February, <http://www.aljazeera.com/news/africa/2013/02/20132793714745946.html> (last accessed 11 April 2013).

'The Islamist conundrum: Tunisia's election', *The Economist*, 22 October, <http://go.galegroup.com/ps/retrieve.do?sgHitCountType=None&sort=DA-SORT&inPS=t. . .> (last accessed 29 October 2011).

Torchia, Andrew (2013) 'Corruption worsened in Arab countries since uprisings: Poll', *Reuters*, 9 July, <http://www.reuters.com/assets/print?aid=USBRE/96805U20 130709> (last accessed 10 July 2013).

'Tunisia: country profile' (2011) *BBC News*, 2 February, <http://news.bbc.co.uk/2/hi/middle_east/country-profiles/791969.stm> (last accessed 28 February 2011).

'Tunisia: Islamist party sweeps election' (2011) *All Africa*, 28 October, <http://allafrica.com/stories/printable/201110280554.html> (last accessed 28 October 2011).

'Tunisia PM Ali Larayedh unveils new government' (2013) *BBC News*, 8 March, <http://www.bbc.co.uk/news/world-africa-21711345?print=true> (last accessed 10 April 2013).

'Tunisia: protests erupt as Islamist party wins first democratic election' (2011) *Daily*

Telegraph, 28 Oct., <http://www.telegraph.co.uk/news/worldnews/africaandindi anocean/tunisia/8854503/Tuni. . .> (last accessed 31 October 2011).

'Tunisian Constituent Assembly election, 2011' (2012) *Wikipedia*, 6 October, <http:// en.wikipedia.org/wiki/Tunisian_Constituent_Assembly_election,_2011> (last accessed 30 December 2012).

'Tunisians undecided ahead of October vote' (2011) *Aljazeera.net*, 6 July, <http:// english.aljazeera.net/news/africa/2011/07/20117617715460755.html> (last accessed 23 October 2011).

Versi, Anver (2000) 'Tunisia: 44 years of independence', *Middle East*, March, 03050734, Issue 299, 1–9.

Watson, Ivan and Kindah Shair (2011) 'Once-banned party wins in Tunisia elections, early results show', *CNN.com*, 25 October, <http://edition.cnn.com/2011/10/25/ world/africa/tunisia-election-results/> (last accessed 27 October 2011).

WikiLeaks (2010) 'Viewing cable 08TUNIS679, CORRUPTION IN TUNISIA: WHAT'S YOURS IS MINE' [created 23 June 2008, released 7 December 2010], <http://wikileaks.ch/cable/2008/06/08TUNIS679.html> (last accessed 29 March 2011).

Wolf, Anne (2011) 'Tunisians respond to Ennahda's victory', *Tunisia-live.net*, 25 October, <http://www.tunisia-live.net/2011/10/25/tunisians-respond-to-ennah-das-victory/> (last accessed 27 October 2011).

World Bank (2010) *Global Economic Prospects*, Washington, DC: World Bank.

Yaros, Bernard (2013a) 'Ennahdha party rallies supporters in downtown Tunis', *Tunisia-live.net*, 10 February, <http://www.tunisia-live.net/2013/02/10/ennah dha-party-rallies-supporters-in-downtown-tunis/> (last accessed 4 May 2013).

Yaros, Bernard (2013b) 'Survey finds low levels of trust for political leaders', *Tunisia-live. net*, 8 March, <http://www.tunisia-live.net/2013/03/08/survey-finds-low-levels-of-trust-for-political-leaders/> (last accessed 4 May 2013).

Zisenwine, Daniel (2011) 'Ahead of the curve? Tunisia's "Jasmine Revolution"', *Sharqiyya*, The Arab Spring – Special Issue, autumn, 35–40.

Chapter 3: Egypt

'2011 Egyptian revolution' (2011) 2 June, http:/en.wikipedia.org/wiki/2011_Egyptian_ revolution (last accessed 6 February 2011).

'2011 Provisional Constitution of Egypt' (2011) *Wikisource*, <http://en.wikisource.org/ wiki/2011_Provisional_Constitution_of_Egypt> (last accessed 21 July 2011).

'35 Pct voter turn-out in Egyptian election', *Egyptian Gazette*. <http://213.158.162.45/ ~egyptian/index.php?action=news&id=13387&title=35Pctvotertur. . .> (last accessed 18 July 2011).

Abu Dhabi Gallup Center (2011a) *Egypt: The Arithmetic of the Revolution: An Empirical Analysis of Social and Economic Conditions in the Months before the January 25 Uprising*, 25 March.

Abu Dhabi Gallup Center (2011b) *Egypt from Tahrir to Transition*, <http://www.arab newsblog.net/2011/06/08/abu-dhabi-gallup-center-egypt-from. . .> (last accessed 5 February 2014).

Ahmed, Amir (2012) 'Egypt's Morsy taps new military commanders', *CNN.com.*, 14 August, <http://edition.cnn.com/2012/08/14/world/meast/egypt-security/index.html?hpt-hp_t2> (last accessed 6 February 2014).

Ajami, Fouad (2011) 'Fouad Ajami on the road to serfdom and the Arab Revolt', *Wall Street Journal*, 8 July, <https://outlook.utpa.edu/owa/?ae=Item&t-IPM.Note&id=RgAAADLGmtbuiXSRK9fCt7...> (last accessed 17 July 2011).

Ali, Randa and Sara Mourad (2012) 'Morsi's Sunday surprise met with broad support by Egypt political forces', *Ahram Online*, 13 August, <http://english.ahram.org.eg/NewsContentPrint/1/0/50261/Egypt/0/Morsis-Sunday-surprise-met-with-broad-support-by-E.aspx> (last accessed 17 August 2012).

Alianak, Sonia (2007) *Middle Eastern Leaders and Islam: A Precarious Equilibrium*, New York: Peter Lang.

Al Sharekh, Alanoud (2011) 'Reform and rebirth in the Middle East, *Survival*, 53(2), 51 60, 2 April, <http://www.informaworld.com/smpp/section?content=a935792831&fulltext=713240928> (last accessed 7 April 2011).

Amnesty International (2005a) 'Egypt: continuing arrests of critics and opponents' "chill" prospects for reform', 27 May.

Amnesty International (2005b) 'Public. USA/EGYPT. Sami al-Laithi (m), teacher. Fear of torture/ill-treatment/health concern', 3 October.

Amnesty International (2007a) 'Egypt: Amnesty International Report 2007. Human Rights in Arab Republic of Egypt', <http://www.amnesty.org/en/region/egypt/report-2007> (last accessed 19 July 2011).

Amnesty International (2007b) 'Egypt: Proposed constitutional amendments greatest erosion of human rights in 26 years', 18 March.

Amnesty International (2008) 'Egypt: Amnesty International Report 2008. Human Rights in Arab Republic of Egypt', <http://www.amnesty.org/en/region/egypt/report-2008> (last accessed 19 July 2011).

Amnesty International (2009) 'Egypt: Human rights in Arab Republic of Egypt', <http://www.amnesty.org/en/region/egypt/report-2009> (last accessed 19 July 2011).

Amnesty International (2010) 'Egypt: Amnesty International Report 2010. Human rights in Arab Republic of Egypt', <http://www.amnesty.org/en/regioon/egypt/report-2010> (last accessed 19 July 2011).

Amnesty International (2011) 'Annual Report 2011: the state of the world's human rights: Egypt', <http://www.amnesty.org/en/egypt/report-2011> (last accessed 19 July 2011).

Asad, Talal and Ayca Cubukcu (2013) 'Neither heroes, nor villains: a conversation with Talal Asad on Egypt after Morsi', *Jadaliyya*, 23 July, <http://www.jadaliyya.com/pages/index/13129/neither-heroes-nor-villains_a-conversation-with-ta> (last accessed 25 July 2013).

Ashour, Omar (2012) 'Egypt's new old government', *Brookings Institution*, 7 August, <http://www.brookings.edu/research/opinions/2012/08/07-egyptian-cabinet-as hour> (last accessed 17 August 2012).

Attalah, Lina (2013) 'The Brotherhood responds', *Middle East Institute*, 18 July, <http://www.mei.edu/content/brotherhood-responds> (last accessed 25 July 2013).

Baldwin, Leigh (2011) 'Egyptians may move funds to Switzerland, banker says',

Bloomberg, 4 February, <http://www.bloomberg.com/news/print/2011-02-04/egypt-s-rich-ask-about-moving-funds-t. . .> (last accessed 20 July 2011).

Black, Ian (2013) 'Mohamed Morsi: the Egyptian opposition charge sheet', *Guardian*, 3 July, http://www.guardian.co.uk (last accessed 7 July 2013).

Bohn, Lauren E. (2011) 'Galal Amin: the people vs. the army', *The Cairo Review of Global Affairs*, 23 March, <http://www.aucegypt.edu/gapp/cairoreview/Pages/articleDetails.aspx?aid=32> (last accessed 5 August 2011).

Borkan, Brett (2011) 'TV, not internet, main source of information for Egyptians during Jan 25 protests, says poll', *Daily News Egypt*, 7 June, <http://www.thedailynewsegypt.com/people/tv-not-internet-main-source-of-information-for-e. . .> (last accessed 9 June 2011).

'Brotherhood seeks international support over elections' (2010) *Ahram Online*, 12 December, <http://english.ahram.org.eg/NewsContentPrint/1/0/1701/Egypt/0/Brothehood-seeks-intern. . .> (last accessed 16 July 2011).

Brown, Nathan J. (2011a) 'Egypt's Revolution struggles to take shape', *Carnegie Endowment for International Peace*, 17 March, <http://www.carnegieendowment.org/2011/03/17/egypt-s-revolution-strugges-to-take-shape/3kgr> (last accessed 20 March 2012).

Brown, Nathan J. (2011b) 'Can the colossus be salvaged? Egypt's state-owned press in a post-revolutionary environment', *Carnegie Endowment for International Peace*, 22 August, <http://www.carnegieendowment.org/2011/08/22/can-colossus-be-salvaged-egypt-s-state-owned-press-in-post-revolutionary-environ. . .> (last accessed 20 March 2012).

Chammah, Maurice (2012) 'Finding a voice: Egyptian state newspapers post uprising', *Carnegie Endowment for International Peace*, 4 April, <http://www.carnegieendowmwnt.org/sada/2012/04/04/finding-voice-egyptian-state-newspapers-post-uprising/a6ec> (last accessed 16 May 2012).

Chulov, Martin and Patrick Kingsley (2013) 'Mohamed Morsi's downfall determined by coffee shop rebels rather than army', *Guardian*, 5 July, <http://www.guardian.co.uk> (last accessed 7 July 2013).

Contenta, Sandro (2011) 'Could Egypt's rich deal decisive blow to Mubarak', *The Star.com*, 1 February, <http://www.thestar.com/printarticle/931165> (last accessed 20 July 2011).

Dahi, Omar S. (2011) 'Understanding the political economy of Arab revolts', *Middle East Report*, 41(2), no. 259, 2–6.

Davies, J. C. (1962) 'Toward a theory of revolution', *American Sociological Review*, 27, 5–19.

Detter, Dag and Steffen Hertog (2011) 'Public sector after revolution', *Jordan Times*, 16 May, <http://www.jordantimes.com/index.php?news=37344&searchFor-social-media> (last accessed 16 May 2011).

Dunne, Michele (2011) 'Revolution still "in progress" as protesters return to Tahrir', *Carnegie Endowment for International Peace*, 11 April, <http://www.carnegieendowment.org/2011/04/11/revolution-still-in-progess-as-protesters-return-to-tahrir/1wak> (last accessed 20 March 2012).

Dunne, Michele and Mara Revkin (2011) 'Rethinking internal security in Egypt',

Carnegie Endowment for International Peace, 16 March, <http://www.carnegieendow
ment.org/2011/03/16/rethinking-internal-security-in-egypt/2fry> (last accessed
20 March 2012).

'Egypt frees arrested opposition candidates' (2010) *Egyptian Gazette*, 13 November,
<http://213.158.162.45/~egyptian/index.php?action=news&id=12794&title=
Egyptfreesarr. . .> (last accessed 18 July 2011).

'Egypt "frees political prisoners"' (2011) *Aljazeera.net*. 8 February, <http://english.alja
zeera.net/news/middleeast/2011/02/201128153142101446.html> (last accessed
26 May 2011).

Egypt Independent (2013) 'Excerpts from General Abdel Fattah al-Sisi's speech', *Al
Masry Al Youm*, 24 July, <http://www.egyptindependent.com/print/1976936>
(last accessed 6 February 2014).

'Egypt President Mursi's first speech: Key quotes' (2012) *BBC News*, 25 June, <http://
www.bbc.co.uk/news/world-middle-east-18577334?print=true> (last accessed 29
June 2012).

'Egypt President-elect Mohamed Mursi hails Tahrir crowds' (2012) *BBC News*,
29 June, <http://www.bbc.co.uk/news/world-middle-east-18648399?print=
true> (last accessed 29 June 2012).

'Egypt sets minimum wage at $117' (2011) *Egyptian Gazette*, 1 June, <http://
213.158.162.45/~egyptian/index.php?action=news&id=18777&title=Egypt-sets-
mini. . .> (last accessed 13 June 2011).

'Egyptian legislative elections, 2011–2012' (2011) *FJP Press Release No. 24*, 17 December,
<http://fjponline.com/article.php?id=233> (last accessed 24 December
2011).

'Egyptian parliamentary election, 2010' (2011) *Wikipedia*. 2011, <http://en.wikipedia.
org/wiki/Egyptian_parliamentary_election_2010> (last accessed 2011).

'Egyptian parliamentary election, 2011–2012' (2012) *Wikipedia*, 13 August, <http://
en.wikipedia.org/wiki/Egyptian_parliamentary_election,_2011%E2%80%9320
12> (last accessed 9 September).

'Egyptians vote in run-off' (2010) *Egyptian Gazette*, 5 December, <http://213.158.162.
45/~egyptian/index.php?action=news&id=13526&title=Egyptiansvote. . .> (last
accessed 18 July 2011).

'Egypt's Brotherhood wins 47 per cent of parliament seats' (2012) *Al Masry Al Youm*, 21
January, < http://www.egyptindependent.com/print/612026> (last accessed 30
January 2012).

'Egypt's magnate Ezz hopes for fair trial' (2011) *Egyptian Gazette*, 8 March, <http://
213.158.162.45/~egyptian/index.php?action=news&id=15839&title=Egypt'smag
nat. . .> (last accessed 22 July 2011).

'Egypt's NDP complains of 52 candidates' (2010) *Egyptian Gazette*, 25 November,
<http://213.158.162.45/~egyptian/index.php?action=news&id=13184&title=
Egypt'sNDPc. . .> (last accessed 18 July 2011).

'Egypt's President-elect promises to put power in hands of the people' (2012) *CNN.com*.,
29 June, <http://edition.cnn.com/2012/06/29/world/africa/egypt-morsi/> (last
accessed 29 June 2012).

'Egypt's rich cannot escape from real world' (2008) *Gulf News*, 4 July, <http://gulfnews.

com/news/region/egypt/egypt-s-rich-cannot-escape-from-real-world-1.116. . .>
(last accessed 20 July 2011).

'Egypt's ruling military will not consider Mubarak amnesty, leaves investigation
to the judiciary' (2011) *Ahram Online*, 18 May, <http://english.ahram.org.eg/
NewsContentPrint/1/0/12377/Egypt/0/Egypts-ruling-military-. . .> (last accessed 18 May 2011).

'Egypt's ruling party heading for solid win' (2010) *Egyptian Gazette*, 29 November,
<http://213.158.162.45/~egyptian/index.php?action=news&id=13364&title=
Egypt'srulingp. . .> (last accessed 18 July 2011).

El-Dabh, Basil (2013) 'No one is going anywhere', *Daily News Egypt*, 24 July, <http://
www.dailynewsegypt.com> (last accessed 25 July 2013).

El-Din, Gamal Essam (2011) 'Mubarak awaits trial in Sharm El-Sheikh', *Al-Ahram
Weekly*, May, <http://www.weekly.ahram.org.ed/print/2011/1050/eg3.htm>
(last accessed 9 June 2011).

El Fadl, Khaled Abou (2013) 'Egypt: is political Islam dead?', *Aljazeera*, 8 July, <http://
www.aljazeera.com/indepth/opinion/2013/07/201378985916781.html>   (last
accessed 27 July 2013).

El-Ghobashy, Mona (Spring 2011) 'The praxis of the Egyptian Revolution', *Middle East
Report*. 41(1), no. 258, 2–13.

El-Hennawy, Noha (2011) 'Egypt's new Political Party Law fails to please everyone', *Al
Masry Al Youm*, 29 March, <http://www.almasryalyoum.com/en/print/379401>
(last accessed 14 June 2011).

El-Shobaki, Amr (2011) 'Subsidizing political parties', *Al Masry Al Youm*, 6 July,
<http://www.almasryalyoum.com/en/print/475056>   (last   accessed   6   July
2011).

Emam, Amr (2010a) 'Food, not politics, dominate polls', *Egyptian Gazette*, November,
<http://213.158.162.45/~egyptian/index.php?action=news&id=13259&title=
Food,notpoliti. . .> (last accessed 18 July 2011).

Emam, Amr (2010b) 'MP hopefuls vie for empty stomachs', *Egyptian Gazette*, 19
November, <http://213.158.162.45/~egyptian/index.php?action=news&id=129
76&title=MPhopefulsvi. . .> (last accessed 18 July 2011).

Emam, Amr (2010c) 'Agony and joy in election aftermath', *Egyptian Gazette*, 2 December,
<http://213.158.162.45/~egyptian/index.php?action=news&id=13432&title=
Agonyandjoy. . .> (last access 18 July 2011).

Emam, Amr and Ashraf Madbouli (2010) 'NDP prevails in troubled vote', *Egyptian
Gazette*,   7   December,   <http://213.158.162.45/~egyptian/index.php?action=
news&id=13577&title=NDPprevailsi. . .> (last accessed 18 July 2011).

Emam, Amr, Doaa Soliman, Ashraf Madbouli and Tamer Mohamed (2010) 'NDP set
to sweep Egyptian polls', *Egyptian Gazette*, 28 November, <http://213.158.162.45/
~egyptian/index.php?action=news&id=13340&title=NDPsettoswe. . .> (last accessed 18 July 2011).

Enein, Ahmed Aboul (July 2, 2012) 'President meets Ganzouri cabinet', *Daily News
Egypt*, 2 July, <http://thedailynewsegypt.com/2012/07/02/president-meets-gan
zouri-cabinet/> (last accessed 2 July 2012).

Eskandar, Wael (2012) 'Year of the SCAF: a timeline of mounting repression', *Jadaliyya*,

9 March, <http://www.jadaliyya.com/pages/index/3091/year-of-the-scaf_a-timeline-of-mounting-repression> (last accessed 15 May 2012).

'Ex-housing minister and Alaa Mubarak's father-in-law referred to criminal court' (2011) *Ahram Online*, 18 May, <http://english.ahram.org.eg/NewsContentPrint/1/0/12406/Egypt/0/Exhousing-minister-and-...> (last accessed 18 May 2011).

Fadel, Leila (2012) 'Egypt's youth movement loses luster', *Washington Post*, 13 January, <http://www.washingtonpost.com/world/middleeast/egypts-youth-movement-loses-luster/2012/01/10/gIQApyF2vPprint.html> (last accessed 21 March 2012).

Fadel, Mohammad (April 2011) 'Public corruption and the Egyptian Revolution of January 25: can emerging international anti-corruption norms assist Egypt recover misappropriated public funds?', *Harvard International Law Journal Online*, 52, 292–300.

Fayed, Shaimaa (2012) 'Egypt's Mursi takes symbolic oath to people', *Reuters*, 29 June, <http://www.reuters.com/assets/print?aid=USBRE85SOJP20120629> (last accessed 29 June 2012).

Fleishman, J. (2011) 'Young Egyptians mount unusual challenge to Mubarak', *Los Angeles Times*, <http://articles.latimes.com/2011/jan/27/world/la-fg-egypt-youth-20110128 (last accessed 6 February 2014).

Gabr, Mohamed (2012) 'Allies for democracy? Or not?', *Al Masry Al Youm*, 1 January, <http://www.almasryalyoum.com/en/print/579181> (last accessed 1 February 2012).

Ghannam, Angy (2011) 'Islamists in Egypt's tourist spots win surprise support', *BBC News*, 28 December, <http://www.bbc.co.uk/news/world-middle-east-16348229?print=true> (last accessed 2 January 2012).

Ghannam, Jeffrey (2011) 'Social media in the Arab World: leading up to the uprisings of 2011', *Center for International Media Assistance. National Endowment for Democracy*, 3 February.

Giglio, Mike (2011) 'Inside Egypt's Facebook revolt', *The Daily Beast*, 27 January, <http://www.thedailybeast.com/newsweek/2011/01/27/inside-egypt-s-facebook-revolt.print.html> (last accessed 24 March 2011).

Glanz, James and John Markoff (2011) 'Egypt Leaders found "off" switch for Internet', *New York Times*, 16 February.

Goldschmidt, A. Jr (2004) *Modern Egypt: The Formation of a Nation State*, 2nd edn, Boulder, CO and Oxford: Westview Press.

Grier, Peter (February 14, 2011) 'The Cairo effect', *Christian Science Monitor*, 24–31.

Hamzawy, Amr (June 2009) 'Rising social distress: the case of Morocco, Egypt, and Jordan', *International Economic Bulletin*, June, <http://carnegie-mec.org/publications/?fa=23290> (last accessed 18 April 2011).

Hendawi, Hamza (2012) 'Egypt's new president begins struggle for power', *Associated Press*, 30 June, <http://hosted.ap.org/dynamic/stories/M/ML_EGYPT?SITE=AP&SECTION=HOME&TEMPLATE=DEFAULT> (last accessed 2 July 2012).

Hendawi, Hamza (2013) 'Disputes between Morsi, military led to Egypt coup', *Associated Press*, 18 July, <http://hosted.ap.org/dynamic/stories/M/ML_PRESIDENT_VS_GENERAL?SITE=AP&SECTION=HOME&TEMPLA...> (last accessed 27 July 2013).

Howard, Philip N. (2011) 'The Arab Spring's cascading effects', 23 February, <http://www.miller-mccune.com/politics/the-cascading-effects-of-the-arab-spring-28575/> (last accessed 24 March 2011).

Human Rights Watch (2010) 'Egypt: pledge serious Human Rights reform', 16 February, <http://www.hrw.org/print/news/2010/02/16/egypt-pledge-serious-human-rights-reform> (last accessed 7 August 2011).

Human Rights Watch (2011) '"Eye-hunting" in Cairo: The military's assault on reporters', 2 December, <http://www.hrw.org/print/news/2011/12/02/eye-hunting-cairo-military-s-assault-reporters> (last accessed 17 March 2012).

Human Rights Watch (2012a) 'The road ahead: a Human Rights Agenda for Egypt's new Parliament', January.

Human Rights Watch (2012b) 'No joy in Egypt', 25 January, <http://www.hrw.org/print/news/2012/01/25/no-joy-egypt> (last accessed 17 March).

Human Rights Watch (2012c) 'Egypt: military impunity for violence against women', 7 April, <http://www.hrw.org/print/news/2012/04/07/egypt-military-impunity-violence-against-women> (last accessed 16 May 2012).

Human Rights Watch (2012d) 'Egypt: new law keeps military trials of civilians', 7 May, <http://www.hrw.org/print/news/2012/05/07/egypt-new-law-keeps-military-trials-civilians> (last accessed 16 May 2012).

Hussein, Abdel-Rahman (2012) 'Mohamed Morsi to pick woman and Christian as Egypt's vice-presidents', *Guardian*, 26 June, <http://www.guardian.co.uk/world/2012/jun/26/mohamed-morsi-christian-woman-egypt> (last accessed 27 June 2012).

Hussein, Abdel-Rahman and Julian Borger (2012) 'Muslim Brotherhood's Mohamed Morsi declared president of Egypt', *Guardian*, 24 June, http://www.guardian.co.uk/world/2012/jun/24/muslim-brotherhood-egypt-president-mohamed-morsi/print (last accessed 24 June 2012).

'Internet is easy prey for governments' (2011) *Cnn.com*, *2011*, <http://www.printthis.clickability.com/pt/cpt?expire=&title=Internet+is+easy+prey+for+gov. . .> (last accessed 5 February 2011).

'Islamists, secular party withdraw from poll' (2010) *Egyptian Gazette*, 1 December, <http://213.158.162.45/~egyptian/index.php?action=news&id=13417&title=Islamists,secul. . .> (last accessed 18 July 2011).

Kandeel, Amal A. (2012) 'Egypt at a crossroads', *Middle East Policy Council.* Journal Essay, <http://www.mepc.org/journal/middle-east-policy-archives/Egypt-crossroads?print> (last accessed 24 March 2012).

Kassem, M. (2004) *Egyptian politics: The Dynamics of Authoritarian Rule*, Boulder, CO, and London: Lynne Rienner.

Kavanaugh, Andrea, Seungwon Yang and Steven Sheetz (2011) 'Between a rock and a cellphone: social media use during mass protests in Iran, Tunisia and Egypt', *Computer Science Reports*, 7 July, TR-11-10 Virginia Tech. <http://eprints.cs.vt.edu/archive/00001149/> (last accessed 6 February 2014).

Kinsman, Jeremy (April 2011) 'Democracy rising: Tunisia and Egypt, when idealists got it right', *Policy Options*, April, 37–43.

Knell, Yolande (2012) 'Egypt president: Muslim Brotherhood's Mohammed Mursi',

BBC News, 24 June, http://www.bbc.co.uk/news/world-middle-east-18371427? print=true (last accessed 24 June 2012).

Kristof, Nicholas D. (2011) 'Democracy is messy', *New York Times Reprints*, 30 March <http://www.nytimes.com/2011/03/31/opinion/31kristof.html?_r=3&ref=opin ion&pagewante. . .> (last accessed 5 August 2011).

Levine, Mark (2012) 'Morsi's win is a victory for the revolution', *Al Jazeera*, 24 June, <http://www.aljazeera.com/indepth/opinion/2012/06/2012624183256269777- html> (last accessed 24 June 2012).

Lim, Merlyna (2012) 'Clicks, cabs, and coffee houses: social media and oppositional movements in Egypt, 2004–2011', *Journal of Communication*, 62, 231–48.

Liotta, P. H. and James F. Miskel (2010) 'The "Mega-eights": urban leviathans and international instability', 8 February, <https://outlookutpa.edu/exchange/ alianak/Inbox/Megacities%20%26%20International%20I. . .> (last accessed 7 March 2010).

Lynch, Marc (June 2011) 'After Egypt: the limits and promise of online challenges to the authoritarian Arab State', *Perspectives on Politics*, 9(2), 301–10.

Madbouli, Ashraf (2010) 'As campaigning starts, MP hopefuls woo voters', *Egyptian Gazette*, 15 November, <http://213.158.162.45/~egyptian/index.php?action= news&id=12847&title=Ascompaignin. . .> (last accessed 18 July 2011).

Madbouli, Ashraf (2011) '"Poor first" urged as Egypt's motto', *Egyptian Gazette*, 22 June, <http://213.158.162.45/~egyptian/index.php?action=news&id=19363&title= 'PoorFirst'urge. . .> (last accessed 22 July 2011).

Masoud, Tarek (2011) 'Liberty, democracy, and discord in Egypt', *Washington Quarterly*, 34(4), 117–129, autumn, <http://www.tandfonline.com/doi/abs/10.1080/ 0163660X.2011.610717> (last accessed 24 March 2012).

Massad, Joseph (2011) 'Under the cover of democracy . . .', *Aljazeera.net*. 8 June, <http:/ /english.aljazeera.net/indepth/opinion/2011/06/2011689456174295.html> (last accessed 16 June 2011).

'Meet the players: the National Democratic Party' (NDP)(2010) *Daily News Egypt*, 22 November,<http://www.thedailynewsegypt.com/egypt/meet-the-players-thenat ional-democratic-party-n. . .> (last accessed 1 June 2011).

Michael, Maggie (2008) 'Corruption plagues Egypt's bread', *Fox News*, 10 April, <http:/ /www.americancopticassembly.com/printart.php?main_id=1045> (last accessed 22 July 2011).

Michael, Maggie (2012a) 'Egypt president-elect vows to fight for authority', *Associated Press*, <http://www.boston.com/news/world/middleeast/articles/2012/06/29/ egypt_president_elect_to_head_to_tahrir_square/> (last accessed 29 June 2012).

Michael, Maggie (2012b) 'New Egypt president moves toward unity government', *Associated Press*, 26 June, <http://hosted.ap.org/dynamic/stories/M/ML_EGYPT? SITE=AP&SECTION=HOME&TEMPLATE=DEFAULT> (last accessed 27 June 2012).

Michael, Maggie and Sarah El-Deeb (2010) 'Egypt picks parliament after roundup of opposition', *Associated Press*, 28 November, <http://rr.com/news/topic/article/ rr/9000/27908374/Egypt_picks_parliament_after_roundu. . .> (last accessed 28 November 2010).

Mogahed, Dalia (2013) 'Deep runs the divide', *Carnegie Endowment for International Peace*, 25 July, <http://carnegieendowment.org/sada/2013/07/25/deep-runs-divide/ggen> (last accessed 27 July 2013).

Mohamed, Tamer (2010a) 'Legal battles over polls escalate', *Egyptian Gazette*, 25 November, <http://213.158.162.45/~egyptian/index.php?action=news&id=13179&title=Legalbattleso...> (last accessed 18 July 2011).

Mohamed, Tamer (2010b) '"Food bribes" for Cairo voters', *Egyptian Gazette*, 28 November, <http://213.158.162.45/~egyptian/index.php?action=news&id=13336&title='Foodbribes'f...> (last accessed 18 July 2011).

Mohamed, Tamer (2012) 'A rare chance: will they seize it', *Egyptian Gazette*, 2 July, <http://213.158.162.45/~egyptian/index.php?action=print_news&id=26568> (last accessed 2 July 2012).

Morsi Meter (2012) '50 days out of 100', 19 August <http://www.morsimeter.com/en> (last accessed 19 August 2012).

'Morsi's one-hundred day plan' (2012) *Carnegie Endowment for International Peace*, 29 June, <http://egyptelections.carnegeendowment.org/2012/06/26/morsi%e2%80%99s-one-hundred-day-plan> (last accessed 29 June 2012).

'Morsi's ouster in Egypt: a "bookend" for the Arab Spring' (2013) *NPR*, 22 July.

Muasher, Marwan (2011a) 'What's next for Egypt', *Carnegie Endowment for International Peace*, 14 February, <http://www.carnegieendowment.org/2011/02/14/what-s-next-for-egypt/3wmd> (last accessed 20 March 2012).

Muasher, Marwan (2011b) 'Arab Spring: eternal season of flux', *Carnegie Endowment for International Peace*, 28 June, <http://www.carnegieendowment.org/2011/06/28/arab-spring-eternal-season-of-flux/8khb> (last accessed 20 March 2012).

'Mubarak, wife questioned over wealth' (2011) *Jordan Times*, 13 May, <http://www.Jordantimes.com/index.php?news=37442&earchFor=politicalparties> (last accessed 13 May 2011).

Murphy, Dan (2012) 'For Egypt's new president, getting elected was the easy part', *Christian Science Monitor*, 27 June, <http://www.csmonitor.com/layout/set/print/content/view/print/533388> (last accessed 28 June 2012).

'Muslim Brotherhood's Morsi urges "unity" in first speech as Egypt's president-elect' (2012) *CNN.com*, 24 June, http://www.cnn.com/2012/06/24/world/africa/egypt-politics/index.html> (last accessed 23 June 2012).

Naguib, Rime (2011) 'A year in review: the SCAF rules in 93 letters', *Al Masry Al Youm*, 30 December, <http://www.almasryalyoum.com/en/print/575366> (last accessed 2 January 2012).

Nakhoul, Samia (June 29, 2012) 'Insight: in "Islamist" Egypt, generals still have final say', *Reuters*, 29 June, <http://www.reuters.com/assets/print?aid=USBRE85S0EH20120629> (last accessed 1 July 2012).

Nasrawi, Salah (2010) 'Egypt holds parliament runoffs amid fraud claims', *Associated Press*, 5 December, <http://rr.com/news/topic/article/rr/9000/28581498/Egypt_holds_parliament_runoffs_amid_...> (last accessed 5 December 2010).

Newton-Small, Jay and Abigail Hauslohner (July 9, 2012) 'How the military won the Egyptian election', *Time*, 180(2), 28–34.

'Official results: 16 opposition, 424 NDP, 65 "independents"' (2010) *Ahram Online*, 6 December, <http://english.ahram.org.eg/NewsContentPrint/1/0/1321/Egypt/0/Official-results---oppositi. . .> (last accessed 15 July 2011).

Olster, Marjorie and Tarek El-Tablawy (2011) 'In Egypt, fighting for a $50-a-month factory job', 16 July, <http://www.rr.com/news/topic/article/rr/9000/46394964/In_Egypt_fighting_for_a_50--mo. . .> (last accessed 16 July 2011).

'Opposition party to abandon seats won in vote' (2010) *Egyptian Gazette*, 2 December, <http://213.158.162.45/~egyptian/index.php?action=news&id=13446&title=Opposionpart. . .> (last accessed 18 July 2011).

'Opposition takes to the street' (2010) *Ahram Online*, 12 December, <http://english.ahram.org.eg/NewsContentPrint/1/0/1719/Egypt/0/Opposition-takes-to-the-st. . .> (last accessed 15 July 2011).

Osman, Magued (2013a) '"Rebellion" campaign', *Egyptian Center for Public Opinion Research ('Baseera')*, 29–30 May, <http://www.baseera.com.eg> (last accessed 1 June 2013).

Osman, Magued (2013b) 'The President's approval rating after 11 months in office', *Egyptian Center for Public Opinion Research ('Baseera')* 29–30 May, <http://www.baseera.com.eg> (last accessed 1 June 2013).

Ottaway, Marina and Amr Hamzawy (2011) 'Protest movements and political change in the Arab World', *Carnegie Endowment for International Peace*, 28 January.

'Party time' (2011) *Al Ahram Weekly*, 9 June, <http://weekly.ahram.org.eg/print/2011/1041/eg8.htm> (last accessed 9 June 2011).

Pew Research Center (2011a) *Global Attitudes Project*, 'Egyptians embrace revolt leaders, religious parties and military, as well', 25 April.

Pew Research Center (2011b) *Global Attitudes Project*, 'Arab Spring fails to improve US image', 17 May.

Pew Research Center (2012) *Global Attitudes Project*, 'One year later . . . Egyptians remain optimistic, embrace democracy and religion in political life', 8 May.

Pew Research Center (2013a) 'Country's economic situation: Egypt', *Global Indicators Database*, spring, <http://www.pewglobal.org/database/indicator/5/country/64/> (last accessed 10 August 2013).

Pew Research Center (2013b) 'Personal economic situation: Egypt', *Global Indicators Database*, spring, <http://www.pewglobal.org/database/indicator/14/country/64/> (last accessed 10 August 2013).

Pew Research Center (2013c) 'The world's Muslims: religion, politics and society', *Pew Forum on Religion and Public Life*, 30 April, <http://www.pewforum.org> (last accessed 1 June 2013).

Pew Research Center (2013d) 'Egyptians increasingly glum', *Global Attitudes Project*, 16 May.

'Polls open in Egyptian run-off vote' (2010) *Egyptian Gazette*, 5 December, <http://213.158.162.45/~egyptian/index.php?action=news&id=13511&title=Pollsopenin E. . .> (last accessed 18 July 2011).

'Pro-revolution coalition urges Morsi to fulfill his promises after wresting executive powers' (2012) *Ahram Online*, 13 August 2012, <http://english.ahram.org.eg/NewsContentPrint/1/0/50303/Egypt/0/Prorevolution-coalition-urges-Morsi-to-fulfill-his.aspx> (last accessed 17 August 2012).

Rashwan, Nada Hussein (2012) 'Morsi's coup against SCAF: the hows and whys', *Ahram Online*, 14 August, <http://english.ahram.org.eg/NewsContentPrint/1/0/50324/ Egypt/0/Morsis-coup-against-SCAF-The-hows-and-the-whys.aspx> (last accessed 17 August 2012).

Reuters (2013) 'Special report: how the Muslim Brotherhood lost Egypt', *Al Masry Al Youm*, 25 July, <http://www.egyptindependent.com/print/1979311> (last accessed 25 July 2013).

Rohac, Dalibor (2013) 'To save Egypt, fix the economy', *The Daily Caller*, 9 July, <http:// dailycaller.com/2013/07/09/to-save-egypt-fix-the-economy/?print=1> (last accessed 27 July 2013).

'Role and make-up of Parliament' (2010) *Egyptian Gazette*, 28 November, <http:// 213.158.162.45/~egyptian/index.php?action-news&id=13320&title= Roleandmake-...> (last accessed 18 July 2011).

'Ruling party "damaged" by opposition boycott' (2010) *Egyptian Gazette*, 3 December, <http://213.158.162.45/~egyptian/index.php?action=news&id=13470&title= Rulingparty'd...> (last accessed 18 July 2011).

Sadek, Ashraf (2010) 'LE 515 m spent on legislative vote – experts', (2010) *Egyptian Gazette*, 5 December, <http://213.158.162.45/~egyptian/index.php?action= news&id=13518&title=LE515mspent...> (last accessed July 2011).

Saldanha, Samantha (2011) 'Arab Spring: no roots for Democracy to flower', 12 December, <http://scholar.googleusercentent.com/scholar?q=cache:sJ3IuoHxU 9QJ:scholar.google.com/&hl=en&as_sdt=1,4&as_ylo=2011&as_...> (last accessed 24 March 2011).

Saleh, Yasmine and Tom Pfeiffer (2012) 'Egypt's new president faces burden of expectation', *Reuters*, 1 July, <http://www.reuters.com/assets/print?aid= USBRE85S0JP20120701> (last accessed 1 July 2012).

Sayed, Dina (2012) '"Morsi Meter" tries to keep Egypt's leader on toes', *Reuters*, 2 August, <http://www.reuters.com/assets/print?aid=USBRE8710Y420120802> (last accessed 7 August 2012).

Sayigh, Yezid (2011) 'The spectre of "protected democracy" in Egypt', *Carnegie Endowment for International Peace*, 15 December, <http://carnegieendowment.org/ 2011/12/15/specter-of-protected-democracy-in-egypt/8kfs> (last accessed 28 December 2011).

Sheedy, Caroline S. (2011) 'Social media for social change: a case study of social media use in the 2011 Egyptian Revolution', a Capstone Project for the Degree of Master of Arts in Public Communication, American University, 28 April.

Shenker, Jack (2013) 'Egypt's revolution continues as grassroots rage against fragmented elite', *Guardian*, 2 July, <http://www.guardian.co.uk> (last accessed 2 July 2013).

Shukrallah, Salma (2010) 'Opposition rallies against parliament', *Ahram Online*, 12 December, <http://english.ahram.org.eg/NewsContentPrint/1/0/1754/Egypt/ 0/Opposition-rallies-against...> (last accessed 15 July 2011).

Sid-Ahmed, Mohamed (2005) 'Elections 2005', *Al Ahram Weekly*, <http://weekly. ahram.org.eg/print/2005/770/op3.htm> (last accessed 9 June 2011).

'Social media, cellphone video fuel Arab protests' (2011) *The Independent*, 27 February, <http://www.independent.co.uk/life-style/gadgets-and-tech/social-media-cell-

phone-video-fuel-arab-protests-2227088.html?printServi. . .> (last accessed 24 March 2011).

Soliman, Doaa (2010) 'Voters bitter and fearful', *Egyptian Gazette*, 28 November, <http://213.158.162.45/~egyptian/index.php?action=news&id=13311&title= Votersbitteran. . .> (last accessed 18 July 2011).

Stacher, Joshua (2011a) 'Egypt without Mubarak', *MERIP: Middle East Research and Information Project*, 7 April, <http://www.merip.org/mero/mero040711?utm_ source=twitterfeed&utm_medium=twitter> (last accessed 24 March 2012).

Stacher, Joshua (2011b) 'Blame the SCAF for Egypt's problems', *Foreign Policy, 11 October*, http://mideast.foreignpolicy.com/posts/2011/10/11

Sullivan, D. J. and S. Abed-Kotob (1999) *Islam in Contemporary Egypt: Civil society vs. the State*. Boulder, CO and London: Lynne Rienner.

'Text of President Morsi's new Egypt Constitutional Declaration' (2012) *Ahram Online*, 12 August, <http://english.ahram.org.ed/NewsContentPrint/1/0/50248/Egypt/ 0/English-text-of-President-Morsis-new-Egypt-Constit.aspx> (last accessed 17 August 2012).

'The new media: between revolution and repression – Net solidarity takes on censorship. Arab springtime: is the web reaching new heights' (2011) 11 March, <http:// en.rsf.org/the-new-media-between-revolution-11-03-2011,39764.html> (last accessed 22 June 2011).

'The world revolution' (2011) *Tunisia News*, 29 January, http://translate.googleusercon tent.com/translate_c?hl=en&prev=/search%3Fq%3Dallintitle. . . (last accessed 26 June 2011).

'Tora prison: a notorious history of expansion and torture' (2011) *Al Masry Al Youm*, 18 April, <http://www.almasryalyoum.com/en/print/405002> (last accessed 7 August 2011).

Transparency International (2010) Corruption Perceptions Index 2010, http://www. transparency.org/policy_research/surveys_indices/cpi/2010/results (last accessed 6 February 2014).

'Turmoil in N. Africa: economy is key to protests' (2011) *Cnn.com*, 27 January, <http:// edition.cnn.com/2011/WORLD/africa/01/27/egypt.tunisia.compare/index.html ?hpt=C1> (last accessed 27 January 2011).

Ungerleider, Neal (2011) 'Massive Egyptian protests powered by YouTube, Twitter, Facebook, Twitpic [pics, video, updates]', 25 January, <http://www.fastcompany. com/node/1720692/print> (last accessed 24 February 2011).

Weiss, Margaret (2011) 'Continuing problems in Egypt's electoral process', *Washington Institute for Near East Policy*, 29 December, <http://www.washingtoninstitute.org/ print.php?template=C05&CID=3439> (last accessed 31 December 2011).

Werr, Patrick and Andrew Torchia (2013) 'Analysis: new Egypt government may promote welfare, not economic reform', *Reuters*, 17 July, <http://www.reuters. com/assets/print?aid=USBRE96G0IP20130717> (last accessed 27 July 2013).

Wing, Adrien K. and Hisham A. Kassim (2011) 'After the last Judgment: the future of the Egyptian Constitution', *Harvard International Law Journal Online*, 52, April, 302–10.

Worth, Robert F. (2011) 'Egypt's next crisis', *New York Times*, 27 May, <http://www.nytimes.com/2011/05/29/magazine/egypts-next-crisis.html?ref=egypt&page wan. . .> (last accessed 2 June 2011).

Zhuo, Xiaolin, Wellman, Barry and Yu, Justine (2011) 'Egypt: the first Internet revolt? ', *Peace Magazine*, July/September, 6–10.

Zogby Research Services (2013) 'After Tahrir: Egyptians assess their government, their institutions, and their future', June.

Chapter 4: Morocco

Abend, Lisa (2011) 'Protests in Morocco: just don't call it revolution', 20 February, <http://www.time.com/time/specials/packages/article/0,28804,2045328_2045 338_2052901,. . .> (last accessed 24 February 2011).

Agence Maghreb Arabe Presse (2011a) 'Fitch Ratings confirms sovereign Rating of Morocco with a "stable" outlook', 1 February,<http://www.map.ma/eng/sec tions/economy/fitch_ratings_confir/view> (last accessed 24 February 2011).

Agence Maghreb Arabe Presse (2011b) 'Morocco managed to balance Ideals of tradi- tion and Rule of Law with making safer society, UK paper says', 24 February, <http://www.map.ma/eng/sections/home/morocco_managed_to_b/view> (last accessed 24 February 2011)

Ali, Siham (2011) 'Moroccans salute King's speech', 10 March, <http://www.maghare bia.com/cocoon/awi/xhtmll/en_GB/features/awi/features/2011/03/10/. . .> (last accessed 18 March 2011)

Alianak, Sonia (2007) *Middle Eastern Leaders and Islam: A Precarious Equilibrium*, New York: Peter Lang.

Allen, Michael (2011) 'Islamist victory a "political electroshock" for Morocco's home- opathic democracy', *Morocco Board*, 28 November, <http://moroccoboard.com/ news/5504-islamist-victory-a-political-electroshock-for-morocc. . . > (last accessed 27 December 2011).

Amnesty International (2009) 'Morocco/Western Sahara: human rights in Kingdom of Morocco', <http://www.amnesty.org/en/region/morocco/report-2009> (last accessed 17 September 2010).

Amnesty International (2010a) 'Morocco must end harassment of Sahrawi activists', 9 April, <http://www.amnesty.org/en/news-and-updates/morocco-must-end-har rassment-sahrawi-acti. . . > (last accessed 17 September 2010).

Amnesty International (2010b) 'Document – Morocco: continuing abuses against individuals suspected of terrorism-related activities in Morocco', 16 June, <http:// www.amnesty.org/en/library/asset/MDE29/013/2010/en/1a0ad009-5ae6-4823- 9d86-. . .> (last accessed 17 September 2010).

'Authenticity and Modernity Party', (2010) 2 April, <http://en.wikipedia.org/wiki/ Authenticity_and_Modernity_Party> (last accessed 19 August 2010).

Baghough, Zouhair (2011a) 'Morocco Islamists: challenges ahead,' *Morocco Board*, 28 November, http://moroccoboard.com/viewpoint/124-zouhair-baghough-/5503- morocco-islamists-cha. . . (last accessed 27 December 2011).

Baghough, Zouhair (2011b) 'Morocco: Islamists' victory, post game analysis', *Morocco*

Board, 5 December, http://moroccoboard.com/viewpoint/124-zouhair-bag hough-/5511-morocco-islamists-vict. . . (last accessed 27 December 2011).

Belghiti, Moulay Ahmed (2013) 'Growth: the government meets its commitments', *L'economiste*, 3 July, <http://www.leconomiste.com/print/908479> (last accessed 8 July 2013).

Bencheikh, Suleiman (2013) 'Balance sheet. Constitution: two years for nothing', *Telquel*, 8 July, <http://www.telquel-online.com/content/bilan-constitution-deux-ans-pour-rien> (last accessed 8 July 2013).

'Benkirane: our government will be guided by competence, integrity and credibility' (2011) *Morocco World News*, 30 November, <http://moroccoworldnews.com/2011/11/benkirane-our-government-will-be-guided-by-co. . .> (last accessed 30 November 2011).

'Benkirane starts talks to form a new government' (2011) *Morocco World News*, 30 November, <http://moroccoworldnews.com/2011/11/benkirane-starts-talks-to-form-a-new-government. . .> (last accessed 30 November 2011).

Ben-Meir, Dr Yossef (2011) 'Morocco's Model: uniting democracy-building and sustainable development', 14 March, <http://www.eurasiareview.com/analysis/moroccos-model-uniting-democracy-building-and-. . .> (last accessed 18 March 2011).

Bennis, Adnane (2011) 'The PJD poised to emerge as bid winner of Morocco's legislative elections', *Morocco World News*, 26 November, <http://moroccoworldnews.com/2011/11/the-pjd-poised-to-emerge-as-big-winner-of-moro. . .> (last accessed 27 November 2011).

'Big Moroccan political party calls for reforms' (2011) *Africasia.com*, <http://www.afric asia.com/services/news_africa/article.php?ID=CNG.e4206a773b164839c1. . .> (last accessed 24 February 2011).

Bill, James and Robert Springborg (1990) *Politics in the Middle East*, Glenview, IL: Scott, Foresman/Little, Brown.

Boudarham, Mohammed (2013a) 'Public policy: the diagnosis of the Ombudsman', *Telquel*, 29 April, <http://www.telquel-online.com/Actualite/Maroc/Politiques-publiques-Le-diagnostic-du-Mediateur/568> (last accessed 9 July 2013).

Boudarham, Mohammed (2013b) 'Presse. Could do better', *Telquel*, 20 May, <http://www.telquel-online.com/Actualite/Maroc/Presse-Peut-miux-faire/570> (last accessed 9 July 2013).

Boudarham, Mohammed (2013c) 'Government. Chabat, Benkirane and King', *Telquel*, 22 May, <http://www.telquel-online.com/Actualite/Maroc/Gouvernement-Chabat-Benkirane-et-le-roi/571> (last accessed 9 July 2013).

Brouksy, Omar (2011) 'Moroccan king's reform pledges draw high praise', 10 March, <http://www.vancouversun.com/story_print.html?id=4417873&sponsor=> (last accessed 20 March 2011).

Byrne, Eileen (2002a) *The Middle East International*, 684, 27 September, 19–20.

Byrne, Eileen (2002b) 'Morocco: family values', *The Middle East International*, 685, 11 October, 18–19.

Byrne, Eileen (2002c) 'Morocco: technocrat in charge'. *The Middle East International*, 686, 25 October, 27–8.

Byrne, Eileen (2002d) 'Morocco: Jettou's choice', *The Middle East International*, 688, 22 November, 26–7.

Byrne, Eileen (2004) 'Morocco: turning the page', *The Middle East International*, 717, 23 January, 24–5.

Champion, Marc (2011) 'Morocco joins in, defying predictions', 21 February, <http://online.wsj.com/article/SB10001424052748704476604576157613018552154.html> (last accessed 24 February 2011).

Charai, Ahmed (2011) 'Moroccan democracy and the future of the Sahara', March, <http://www.fpri.org/enotes/201103.charai.morocco.html> (last accessed 18 March 2011).

Cherkaoui, Naoufel (2010) 'CCDH lauds Morocco's human rights reforms', 18 January, <https://www.zawya.com/Story.cfm/sidZAWYA20100119074444/CCDH%20lauds%20Mo. . .> (last accessed 18 September 2010).

Daadaoui, Mohamed (2011) *Moroccan Monarchy and the Islamist Challenge: Maintaining Makhzen Power*, New York: Palgrave Macmillan.

Denoeux, Guilain and Abdeslam Maghraoui (1998) 'King Hassan's strategy of political dualism', *Middle East Policy*, 5(4): 104–30.

Eddahbi, Ali Hassan (2013) 'Salafists. The mirage of freedom', *Telquel*, 25 April, <http://www.telquel-online.com/Actualite/Maroc/Salafistes-Le-mirage-de-la-liberte/566> (last accessed 9 July 2013).

'Elections in Morocco' (2009) 22 December, <http://en.wikipedia.org/wiki/Electioons_in_Morocco> (last accessed 18 August 2010).

'Elections in Morocco: voter turnout stood at around 45%, Interior Minister' (2011) *Morocco World News*, 25 November, <http://moroccoworldnews.com/2011/11/elections-in-morocco-voter-turnout-stood-at-arou. . .> (last accessed 30 November 2011).

El Yaakoubi, Aziz (2013) 'Junior partner says quits Morocco coalition, government fate unclear', *Reuters*, 10 July, <http://www.reuters.com/assets/print?aid=USBRE9690BD20130710> (last accessed 10 July 2013).

Ennaji, Moha (2004) 'The New Muslim Personal Status Law in Morocco: context, proponents, adversaries, and arguments', <http://www.yale.edu/macmillan/africadissent/moha.pdf> (last accessed 5 February 2014).

Ennaji, Moha (2010) 'Civil society transforming Morocco', 29 June, <http://www.commongroundnews.org/article.php?id=28059&lan=en&sid=1&sp=0> (last accessed 13 February 2010).

Erlanger, Steve (2011) 'Fears of chaos temper calls for change in Morocco', 20 February, <http://www.nytimes.com/2011/02/21/world/middleast/21morocco.html?_r=1&ref=morocco> (last accessed 24 February 2011).

Errazzouki, Samia (2013) 'Free speech sidelined in Morocco', *Index on Censorship*, 9 July, <http://www.indexoncensorship.org/2013/07/free-speech-sidelined-in-morocco> (last accessed 10 July 2013).

'Faith meet Morocco's new Islamist Prime Minister' (2011) *The Blaze*, 29 November, <http://www.theblaze.com/stories/meet-moroccos-new-islamist-prime-minister/> (last accessed 5 February 2014).

Financial Times (2011) 'Morocco's King tries to cool revolt', 24 February, <http://www.

ft.com/cms/s/0/55b93f5a-403a-11e0-9140-00144feabdc0.html> (last accessed 24 February 2011).

Goldstein, Eric (2009) 'Morocco: endangered model?' 16 November, <http://www.fpif.org/articles/morocco_endangered_model> (last accessed 24 February 2010).

Hazan, Pierre (2006) 'Morocco: betting on Truth and Reconciliation Commission', Special Report, United States Institute for Peace, July.

'HM the King addresses speech to the nation' (2011) 9 March, <http://www.map.ma/eng/sections/speeches/hm_the_king_addresse_6/view> (last accessed 18 March 2011).

'HM the King gives speech on ceremony of setting up Advisory Committee for the Revision of the Constitution' (2011) 10 March, <http://www.map.ma/eng/sections/speeches/hm_the_king_gives_sp_2/view> (last accessed 18 March 2011).

'"Hopes of genuine change" as Morocco holds elections' (2011) *BBC News*, 26 November, http://www.bbc.co.uk/news/world-africa-15905800 (last accessed 27 December 2011).

Human Rights Watch (2013) *'Just Sign Here': Unfair Trials Based on Confessions to the Police in Morocco*, <http://www.hrw.org/sites/default/files/reports/morocco0613web wcover.pdf> (last accessed 6 February 2014).

Iraqi, Fahd (2013a) 'Controversy, lack of debate', *Telquel*, 8 May, <http://www.telquel-online.com/content/la-polemique-faute-de-debat> (last accessed 8 July 2013).

Iraqi, Fahd (2013b) 'Crime against democracy', *Telquel*, 22 May, <http://www.telquel-online.com/Editorial/Crime-contre-la-democratie/571> (last accessed 8 July 2013).

Iraqi, Fahd (2013c) 'Divide and conquer', *Telquel*, 29 May, <http://www.telquel-online.com/Editorial/Diviser-pour-regner/572> (last accessed 8 July 2013).

Jarrah, Najm (2003, May 16) 'Jihadis strike', *The Middle East International*, 700, 10–11.

'Justice and Development Party (Morocco)' (2010) 21 July, <http://en.wikipedia.org/wiki/Justice_and_Development_Party_(Morocco)> (last accessed 19 August 2010).

Karam, Souhail (2011) 'Morocco election tests depth of king's reforms', *Reuters*, 24 November, http://www.reuters.com/assets/print?aid=USTRE7AN1D820111124 (last accessed 29 December 2011).

Kozlowski, Nina (2013) 'Visit. Erdogan in Morocco', *Telquel*, 3 June, <http://www.telquel-online.com/Actualite/Maroc/Visite-Erdogan-au-Maroc/573> (last accessed 9 July 2013).

Layachi, Azzedine (1998) *State, Society and Democracy in Morocco: The Limits of Associative Life*. Washington, DC: Center for Contemporary Arab Studies, Georgetown University.

Lopez, Alejandro (2011) 'Moroccan Government fears outbreak of mass protests', 3 February, <http://www.sws.org/articles/2011/feb2011/moro-f03.shtml> (last accessed 5 February 2011)

Maddy-Weitzman, Bruce (2012) 'Is Morocco immune to upheaval?', *Middle East Quarterly*, Winter, 87–93. <http://www.meforum.org/3114/morocco-upheaval> (last accessed 9 July 2013).

Maghraoui, Abdeslam (2003) 'Depoliticization in Morocco', in Larry Diamond *et al.* (eds), *Islam and Democracy in the Middle East*, Baltimore and London: Johns Hopkins University Press, 67–75.

Mednicoff, David (2002) 'Monarchical stability and political liberalization: connections between Jordan and Morocco', in George Joffe (ed.), *Jordan in Transition*, New York: Palgrave, 91–110.

Monjib, Maâti (2011) 'The "democratization" process in Morocco : progress, obstacles, and the impact of the Islamist–secularist divide', Washington/DC: Saban Center for Middle East Policy, 2011. Working Paper/Saban Center for Middle East Policy at the Brookings Institution, No. 5, <http://www.brookings.edu/~/media/Files/rc/papers/2011/08_morocco_monjib/08_morocco_monjib.pdf> (last accessed 6 February 2014).

'Moroccan government' (2010) 19 August, <http://www.moroccanamericantrade.com/morogov.cfm> (last accessed 19 August 2010)

'Moroccan parties call for political reform' (2011) 24 February, <http://www.gulftimes.com/site/topics/article.asp?cu_no=2&item_no=418301&version=1. . .> (last accessed 24 February 2011).

'Moroccans vote in first legislative elections under new constitution' (2011) *Morocco World News*, 25 November, <http://moroccoworldnews.com/2011/11/moroccans-vote-in-first-legislative-elections-und. . .> (last accessed 30 November 2011).

'Moroccans welcome King's reform promises' (2011) 10 March, <http://news.yahoo.com/s/afp/20110310/wl_africa_afp/moroccopoliticsunrest_2011031013> (last accessed 20 March 2011).

'Morocco: aftershock' (2003) *The Middle East International*, 702, 13 June, 19–20.

'Morocco country profile' (2011) 26 January, <http://news.bbc.co.uk/2/hi/middle_east/country_profiles/791867.stm> (last accessed 24 February 2011).

'Morocco counts votes in landmark polls' (2011) *Aljazeera.net*, 26 November, http://www.aljazeera.com/news/africa/2011/11/20111125143852639.html (last accessed 23 December 2011).

'Morocco creates Rights Council' (2011) 4 March, <http://www.vancouversun.com/story_print.html?id=4381586&sponsor> (last accessed 20 March 2011).

'Morocco: darkening skies' (2003) *The Middle East International*, 701, 30 May, 24–6.

'Morocco elections a foretaste for Egyptians' (2011) *Al-Ahram Weekly*, December, <http://weekly.ahram.org.eg/print/2011/1074/re4.htm> (last accessed 29 December 2011).

'Morocco: high ground' (2003) *The Middle East International*, 709, 26 September, 25–6.

'Morocco: history will keep its secrets' (2006) 28 June, <http://www.irinnews.org/Report.aspx?ReportId=59487> (last accessed 13 September 2010).

'Morocco holds first poll after King's reform drive' (2011) *Islam Online*, 25 November, http://www.islamonline.net/eng/article/1304971129578 (last accessed 2 January 2012).

'Morocco: thousands march for reform' (2011) 20 February, <http://www.hrw.org/en/news/2011/02/20/morocco-thousands-march-reform> (last accessed 24 February 2011).

'Morocco to vote on new constitution' (2011) 9 March, <http://news.yahoo.com/s/afp/20110309/wl_africa_afp/moroccopoliticsunrestking_2011030. . .> (last accessed 20 March 2011).

'Morocco will not be spared from unrest, royal family member says' (2011) 1 February,

<http://hken.ibtimes.com/articles/107129/20110131/morocco-tunisia-egypt. htm> (last accessed 5 February 2011).

'Moroccan general election, 2011' (2011) *Wikipedia*, 8 December, <http://en.wikipedia. org/wiki/Moroccan_parliamentary_election,_2011> (last accessed 28 December 2011).

Norton, Augustus (1995) *Civil Society in the Middle East*, Vol. 1. Leiden, New York and Cologne: E. J. Brill.

'Q&A: Morocco elects new parliament' (2011) *BBC News*, 17 November, http:// www.bbc.co.uk/news/world-middle-east-15738259?print=true (last accessed 27 December 2011).

Sabra, Matina (2004) 'Morocco's king takes a courageous step', <http://www.qantara. de/webcom/show_article.php/_c-476/_nr-77/i.html> (last accessed 25 August 2010).

'Subsidy reform dispute imperils Morocco's ruling coalition' (2013) *Voice of America*, July, <http://www.voanews.com/articleprintview/1664726.html> (last accessed 9 July 2013).

Sylomovics, Susan (2010) 'A Truth Commission for Morocco', <http://www. merip.org/mer/mer218/218_slymovics.html>   (last   accessed   8   October 2010).

Texte intégral du projet de nouvelle Constitution (2011) Morocco, <http://www.ambama roc.ca/Nouveau/Accueil/Document-Constitution.pdf> (last accessed 5 February 2014).

'Thousands demand change in Morocco' (2011) <http://www.google.com/hosted-news/afp/article/ALeqM5jySkTqssNzbeFrYpGkzMUpC2C...> (last accessed 24 February 2011).

Transparency International (2012) 'Corruption Perceptions Index 2012', <http:// www.transparency.org/policy_research/surveys_indices/cpi/2012/results>   (last accessed 10 August 2013).

Tuysuz, Gul (2011) 'In Morocco, protest efforts not taking hold', 2 March, <http:// www.vancouversun.com/story_print.html?id=4367444&sponsor=> (last accessed 20 March 2011).

US Department of State (2010) 'Background note: Morocco', 26 January, <http:// www.state.gov/r/pa/ei/bgn/5431.htm#econ> (last accessed 19 August 2010).

Villanti, Benjamin (2011) 'Democracy is a journey and a first step to set it in motion is voting'. *Morocco World News*, 24 November, <http://moroccoworldnews.com/ 2011/11/democracy-is-a-journey-and-the-first-step-to-set-it-in-motion-is-voting/ 16034> (last accessed 3 January 2012).

Waraich, Omar (2011) 'Inspired by Egypt, thousands protest on Moroccan streets', February,   <http://www.independent.co.uk/news/world/africa/inspired-by-egypt-thousands-protest-on-...> (last accessed 24 February 2011).

Wegner, Eva (2011) *Islamist Opposition in Authoritarian Regimes: The Party of Justice and Development in Morocco*, Syracuse, NY: Syracuse University Press.

Wolfe, Adam (2007) 'Morocco: democracy, Islam, monarchy', 11 September, <http:/ /www.speroforum.com/a/10936/Morocco-Democracy-islam-monarchy>   (last accessed 4 September 2010).

Chapter 5: Jordan

'2011 Jordanian protests' (2011) *Wikipedia*. Subsequently amended to 'Jordanian protests (2011–present)', 31 October, <http://en.wikipedia.org/wiki/Jordanian_protests_%282011%E2%80%93present%29> (last accessed 14 January 2014).

Abdullah, S. (2003a) 'Jordan: the status quo', *Middle East International*, 703, 27 June, 12–14.

Abdullah, S. (2003b) 'Jordan: closing rifts?', *Middle East International*, 713, 21 November, 20–1.

Abu-Rish, Ziad (2012) 'Getting past the brink: protests and possibilities of change in Jordan', *Jadaliyya*, 15 November, <http://www.jadaliyya.com/pages/index/8375/getting-past-the-brink-protests-and-the-possibilit> (last accessed 20 July 2013).

Abu-Rish, Ziad (2013) 'Romancing the throne: the *New York Times* and the endorsement of authoritarianism in Jordan', *Jadaliyya*, 3 February, <http://www.jadaliyya.com/pages/index/9949/romancing-the-throne_the-new-york-times-and-the-en> (last accessed 20 July 2013).

Alianak, Sonia (2007) *Middle Eastern Leaders and Islam: A Precarious Equilibrium*, New York: Peter Lang.

Al-Khalidi, Suleiman (2011a) 'Jordan panel to push reforms angers opposition', *Reuters*, 15 March, <http://www.reuters.com/assets/print?aid=USLDE72EOB120110315> (last accessed 26 May 2011).

Al-Khalidi, Suleiman (2011b) 'Jordanians protest against slow pace of reforms', *Reuters*, 18 March, <http://www.reuters.com/assets/print?aid=USLDE72HIU320110318> (last accessed 26 May 2011).

Al-Khalidi, Suleiman (2012a) 'Jordan king swears in new government to prepare for elections', *Reuters*, 11 October, <http://www.reuters.com/assets/print?aid=USBRE89A0W320121011> (last accessed 5 November 2012).

Al-Khalidi, Suleiman (2012b) 'Jordan sentences ex-spy chief to 13 years jail over graft', *Reuters*, 11 November, <http://www.reuters.com/assets/print?aid=USBRE8AA03520121111> (last accessed 15 November 2012).

Al-Sharif, Nabil (2011a) 'Not the end of dialogue', *Jordan Times*, 7 April, <http://www.jordantimes.com/index.php?news=32850&searchFor=socialmedia> (last accessed 7 April 2011).

Al-Sharif, Nabil (2011b) 'Jubilation and lamentation on World Press Freedom Day', *Jordan Times*, 16 May, <http://www.jordantimes.com/index.php?news=37072&searchFor=socialmedia> (last accessed 16 May 2011).

Al-Sharif, Osama (2011c) 'Jordan: trapped in a vicious circle', 5 July, <http://en.ammonnews.net/article.aspx?articleNO=12718> (last accessed 6 February 2014).

Barari, Hassan (2009) 'The rise of Muslim Brotherhood in strategic Jordan', *Ikhwanweb*, 12 December, <http://www.ikhwanweb.org/print.php?id=22355> (last accessed 6 February 2014).

BBC News (2011a) 25 February, <http://www.bbc.co.uk/news/world-middle-east-12582869> (last accessed 6 February 2014).

BBC News (2011b) 'Timeline: Jordan', 26 February, <http://newsvote.bbc.co.uk/

mpapps/pagetools/print/news.bbc.co.uk/2/hi/middle_east/countr. . .> (last accessed 28 February 2011).

'Country profile: Jordan' (2011) *BBC News*, 26 February, <http://newsvote.bbc.co.uk/mpapps/pagetools/print/news.bbc.co.uk/2/hi/middle_east/countr. . .> (last accessed 28 February 2011).

Dalgamouni, Rand (2011) 'Jordanian media at crossroads', *Jordan Times*, 16 May, <http://www.jordantimes.com/index.php?news=36980&searchFor=socialmedia> (last accessed 16 May 2011).

Davies, J. C. (1962) 'Toward a theory of revolution', *American Sociological Review*, 27, 5–19.

Dimou, Antonia (2011) 'Spring of reforms for the Hashemite Kingdom of Jordan', 12 June, <http://www.worldpress.org/Mideast/3757.cfm> (last accessed 5 July 2011).

'Elections in Jordan' (2010) *The Economist*, 4 November, <http://www.economist.com/node/17421579/print> (last accessed 1 June 2011).

'Encouraging development' (2011) *Jordan Times*, 2 June, <http://www.jordantimes.com/index.php?news=37842&searchFor-politicalparties> (last accessed 2 June 2011).

European Forum for Democracy and Solidarity (2013) 'Jordan: Parliamentary, 23 January 2013'.

'Former ministers implicated in housing "corruption" case' (2011) *Jordan Times*, 13 June, <http://www.jordantimes,com/?news=38426> (last accessed 13 June 2011).

Fox, David and Katrina Sammour (2012) 'Disquiet on the Jordanian front', *Carnegie Endowment for International Peace*, 27 September, <http://www.carnegieendowment.org/sada/2012/09/25/disquiet-on-jordanian-front/dx00> (last accessed 19 July 2013).

Freedom House (2012) 'Jordan', <http://www.freedomhouse.org/report/freedom-world/2012/jordan> (last accessed 5 November 2012).

Freij, Muath (2012) 'Popular movement members protest detentions', *Jordan Times*, 13 October, <http://www.jordantimes.com/print.html> (last accessed 5 November 2012).

'Full text of His Majesty King Abdullah's interview with *Le Nouvel Observateur*' (2013) *Jordan Times*, 12 January, <http://www.jordantimes.com/hard-work-ahead-to-ensure-that-arab-spring-brings-a-better-life----king> (last accessed 16 July 2013).

'Full text of His Majesty King Abdullah's speech on the occasion of Arab Revolt, Army Day and Coronation Day on Sunday' (2011) *Jordan Times*, 12 June, <http://www.jordantimes.com/index.php?news=38420&searchFor=kingreforms> (last accessed 16 June 2011).

'Full text of His Majesty King Abdullah's interview with London-based *Asharq Alawsat* . . .' (2013) *Jordan Times*, 26 June, <http://www.jordantimes.com/jordan-least-vulnerable-to-risk-of-sectarian-divisions----king> (last accessed 13 July 2013).

Gallup (2012) 'Mena residents put onus on government to help the poor', 27 November, <http://www.gallup.com/poll/158906/mena-residents-put-onus-government-help-poor.aspx?version=print> (last accessed 15 July 2013).

Gallup (2013) 'Fewer Jordanians than ever are "thriving"', 12 July, <http://www.gallup.com/poll/163481/fewer-jordanians-ever-thriving.aspx?version=print> (last accessed 15 July 2013).

Gavlak, Dale (2011) 'Jordan's King Abdullah vows to allow elected cabinets', *BBC News*, 12 June, <http://www.bbc.co.uk/news/word-middle-east-13744640?print=true> (last accessed 15 June 2011).

Gharaibeh, Ibrahim (2010) 'Implications of the Jordan parliament's dissolution', *Ikhwanweb*, 1 January, <http://www.ikhwanweb.org/print.php?id=22778> (last accessed 6 February 2014).

Ghazal, Mohammad (2011) 'King urges youth to help draw future roadmap', *Jordan Times*, 16 June, <http://www.jordantimes.com/index.php?news=38495&search For=kingreforms> (last accessed 16 June 2011).

Ghazal, Mohammad (2012) 'Hebron tribes vow full support for King's reforms', *Jordan Times*, 9 February, <http://jordantimes.com/print.html> (last accessed 20 February 2012).

Ghazal, Mohammad (2013) 'Rule of the law, justice will prevail – King', *Jordan Times*, 16 June, <http://www.jordantimes.com/Rule+of+the+law%2C+justice+will+pr evail+%E2%80%94+King-61550> (last accessed 13 July 2013).

'Government vows to protect peaceful demonstrators' (2011) *Jordan Times*, 7 April, <http://www.jordantimes.com/index.php?news=35950&searchFor-reformsking> (last accessed 7 April 2011).

Greenwood, S. (2003) 'Jordan, the al-Aqsa intifada and America's "war on terror"', *Middle East, Policy*, autumn, 10(3), 90–111.

Habib, Randa (2010) 'Loyalists sweep Jordan election', 10 November, <http://www.google. com/hostednews/afp/article/ALeqM5jSy0uULU30371.25kjdi9uHg6ahJw...> (last accessed 1 June 2011).

Habib, Randa (2011) 'Jordan tribes break taboo by targeting queen', 9 February, <http://www.google.com/hostednews/afp/article/ALeqM5hF2bnxbMFqWrES NtwFFzDuH...> (last accessed 27 October 2013).

Halaby, Jamal (2011) 'Jordan's king agrees to elected Cabinets', 13 June, <http://www. boston.com/news/world/middleeast/articles/2011/06/13/jordans_king_agrees_ t...> (last accessed 15 June 2011).

Hazaimeh, Hani (2011a) 'ACC investigates around 400 cases in three months', *Jordan Times*, 24 April, <http://www.jordantimes.com/index.php?news=36828&search For=socialmedia> (last accessed 16 May 2011).

Hazaimeh, Hani (2011b) 'Experts take stock of sector achievement and needs', *Jordan Times*, 29 April, <http://www.jordantimes.com/index.php?news=36981&serech For=socialmedia> (last accessed 16 May 2011).

Hazaimeh, Hani (2011c) 'Naour residents share concerns, needs with King', *Jordan Times*, 11 May, <http://www.jordantimes.com/index.php?news=37346&search For=politicalparties> (last accessed 11 May 2011).

Hazaimeh, Hani (2011d) 'Development of legislative environment included in new strategy', *Jordan Times*, 12 May, <http://www.jordantimes,com/index.php?news= 37403&searchFor=socialmedia> (last accessed 16 May 2011).

Hazaimeh, Hani (2011e) 'Two ministers resign on backdrop of Shahin case', *Jordan Times*, 2 June, <http://www.jordantimes.com/index.php?news=37904&search For=politicalparties> (last accessed 6 February 2014).

Hazaimeh, Hani (2012a) 'Majority of Jordanians support constitutional amendments

– Survey', *Jordan Times*, 14 February, <http://jordantimes.com/print.html> (last accessed 27 February 2012).

Hazaimeh, Hani (2012b) 'King's discussion paper sets clear post-elections roadmap – observers', *Jordan Times*, 31 December, <http://www.jordantimes.com/kings-discussion-paper-sets-clear-post-elections-roadmap----observers> (last accessed 16 July 2013).

'Human rights in Hashemite Kingdom of Jordan' (2009) *Jordan – Amnesty International Report 2010*, 18 November, <http://www.amnesty.org/en/region/jordan/report-2010> (last accessed 6 February 2014).

Human Rights Watch (2012) 'Jordan 2012 Human Rights Report', Country Reports on Human Rights Practices for 2012.

Human Rights Watch (2013) 'Continued prosecution of two Jordanian intellectuals cleared twice of wrongdoing', 6 May, <http://www.ifex.org/Jordan/2013/05/06/Jordan_end_free_speech/> (last accessed 19 July 2013).

Husseini, Rana (2011) 'Commentators acquitted on all charges', *Jordan Times*, 26 May, <http://www.jordantimes.com/index.php?news=37743&searchFor=politicalpar ties> (last accessed 26 May 2011).

International Foundation for Electoral Systems (2013) 'Elections in the Hashemite Kingdom of Jordan: January 23 Chamber of Deputies elections', 16 January, <http://www.IFES.org> (last accessed 6 February 2014).

'Islamic Action Front' (n.d.) *Answers.com*. <http://www.answers.com/topic/islamic-action-front> (last accessed 6 February 2014).

'Islamists: Jordan is not Egypt' (2011) *Jordan Times*, 1 February, <http://www.jordanti mes.com/index.php?news=34055&searchFor=hamzamansourking> (last accessed 5 July 2011)

'Jordan creates commission to examine reform' (2011) 14 March, <http://www.google.com/hostednews/afp/article/ALeqM5gUadiq4bBxmKnkqKydzarGsu. . .> (last accessed 3 July 2011).

'Jordan king names PM, security chief to push reform' (2011) 17 October, <http://www.france24.com/en/print/5257355?print=now> (last accessed 27 February 2012).

'Jordan loyalists sweep election' (2010) *Aljazeera.net*, 10 November, <http://english.aljazeera.net/news/middleeast/2010/11/2010111011597439770.html> (last accessed 1 June 2011).

Jordan Times (1997) Report, p. 3, 26 October.

'Jordan working to achieve comprehensive reform in all fields' (2011) *Jordan Times*, 16 May, <http://www.jordantimes.com/index.php?news=36869&searchFor=social media> (last accessed 16 May 2011).

'Jordanian general election, 2013' (2013) *Wikipedia*, 13 October, <http://en.wikipedia.org/wiki/Jordanian_parliamentary_election_2013> (last accessed 27 October 2013).

'Jordanian King unharmed in motorcade incident' (2011) 13 June, <http://www.voanews.com/english/news/middle-east/Jordanian-King-Unharmed-in-Motorc . . .> (last accessed 13 June 2011).

'Jordanians slam corruption, demand elected government' (2011) 10 June, <http://

www.google.com/hostednews/afp/article/ALeqM5j20J4MIU7QSnqRGBEhsVx
cedB. . .> (last accessed 15 June 2011).

'Jordan's new PM urged to rebuild trust with people' (2011) 18 October, <http://
www.france24.com/en/print/5257757?print=now> (last accessed 27 February
2012).

JT (2012) 'Cabinet endorses political parties draft law', *Jordan Times*, 1 February, <http://
jordantimes.com/print.html> (last accessed 27 February 2012).

JT (2013) 'Activists to protest against corruption on Friday', *Jordan Times*, 27 June,
<http://www.jordantimes.com/activists-to-protest-against-corruption-on-friday>
(last accessed 15 July 2013).

Kassay, A. (2002) 'The effects of external forces on Jordan's process of democratization',
in G. Joffe (ed.), *Jordan in Transition*, New York: Palgrave, 45–65.

'Key facts on elections and Jordan's political reform' (2013) Jordanian Embassy,
January, <http://www.jordanembassy.org.uk/forms/keyfacts.pdf> (last accessed
6 February 2014).

Kheetan, Thameen (2011a) 'Thousands rally to reaffirm national unity', *Jordan Times*,
27 March, <http://www.jordantimes.com/index.php?news=35853&searchFor=
reformsking> (last accessed 7 April 2011).

Kheetan, Thameen (2011b) 'Internal differences surface among March 24 members',
Jordan Times, 1 April, <http://www.jordantimes.com/index.php?news=36072
&searchFor=reformsking> (last accessed 7 April 2011).

Kheetan, Thameen (2011c) 'Pro-reform sit-in ends in violence', *Jordan Times*, 7 April,
<http://www.jordantimes.com/index.php?news=35865&searchFor=reformsking>
(last accessed 7 April 2011).

Kheetan, Thameen (2011d) 'Constitution review panel "has carte blanche"', *Jordan
Times*, 1 May, <http://www.jordantimes.com/index.php?news=37016&search
For=constitution> (last accessed 11 May 2011).

Kheetan, Thameen (2011e) 'Activists air grievances on Labour Day', *Jordan Times*, 2
May, <http://www.jordantimes.com/index.php?news=37047&searchFor=social
media> (last accessed 16 May 2011).

Kheetan, Thameen (2011f) 'Protests peter out as activists take wait-and-see approach',
Jordan Times, 11 May, <http://www.jordantimes.com/index.php?news=
37280&searchFor=constitution> (last accessed 11 May 2011).

Kheetan, Thameen (2011g) 'Protesters call for battling corruption, speeding up political
reform', *Jordan Times*, 26 May, <http://www.jordantimes.com/index.php?news=
37713&searchFor=politicalparties> (last accessed 26 May 2011).

Kheetan, Thameen (2011h) 'Several protests planned for Friday', *Jordan Times*, 2 June,
<http://www.jordantimes.com/index.php?news=38051&searchFor=politicalpar
ties> (last accessed 2 June 2011).

King Abdullah II of Jordan (2011) *Our Last Best Chance: The Pursuit of Peace in a Time of
Peril*, New York: Viking.

King Abdullah II of Jordan (2012a) 'Letter of designation to Abdullah Ensour', *Jordan
Times*, 10 October, <http://www.jordantimes.com/print.html> (last accessed 5
November 2012).

King Abdullah II of Jordan (2012b) 'Next parliament is the gate to comprehensive reform', *Jordan Times*, 23 October, <http://www.jordantimes.com/print.html> (last accessed 5 November 2012).

King Abdullah II of Jordan (2013) 'Towards democratic empowerment and "active citizenship"', *Jordan Times*, 1 June, <http://www.jordantimes.com/active-citizen sip-essential-condition-for-democratisation----king> (last accessed 13 July 2013).

'King decrees general pardon on Independence Day' (2011) *Jordan Times*, 26 May, <http://www.jordantimes.com/?news=37854> (last accessed 26 May 2011).

'King outlines vision for Jordan's future' (2011) *Jordan Times*, 16 June, <http://www.jordantimes.com/index.php?news=38425&searchFor=kingreforms> (last accessed 16 June 2011).

'King tasks panel to review the Constitution' (2011) *Jordan Times*, 11 May, <http://www.jordantimes.com/index.php?news=36893&searchFor=constitution> (last accessed 11 May 2011).

'King to address nation today' (2011) *Jordan Times*, 12 June, <http://www.jordantimes.com/index.php?news=38389&searchFor=kingreforms> (last accessed 16 June 2011).

Kuttab, Daoud (2013) 'Election season exposes flaws', *Jordan Times*, 2 January, <http://www.jordantimes.com/election-season-exposes-flaws> (last accessed 15 July 2013).

Luck, Taylor (2012) 'New government will not deter protesters from holding Friday rallies', *Jordan Times*, 11 October, <http://www.jordantimes.com/print.html> (last accessed 5 November 2012).

Luck, Taylor (2013), 'Islamists to sit out Jordanian election', *Washington Post*, 20 January, <http://www.washingtonpost.com/world/middle_east/Islamists-to-sit-out-Jordanian-election/2013/01/1> (last accessed 27 October 2013).

Lynch, Marc (2009) 'What will Jordan do without its lousy Parliament?', *Foreign Policy*, 24 November, <http://lynch.foreignpolicy.com/posts/2009/11/24/dismissed_jordanian_parliament> (last accessed 2 March 2010).

Malkawi, Khetam (2011a) 'Survey points to more government interference in media', *Jordan Times*, 3 May, <http://www.jordantimes.com/index.php?news=37088&searchFor=socialmedia> (last accessed 16 May 2011).

Malkawi, Khetam (2011b) 'Professional journalists can overcome obstacles in accessing information', *Jordan Times*, 16 May, <http://www.jordantimes.com/index.php?news=37125&searchFor=socialmedia> (last accessed 16 May 2011).

'MB in Jordan embarks on fresh protests' (2011) *Ikhwanweb*, 11 June, <http://www.ikhwanweb.com/article.php?id=28706> (last accessed 6 February 2014).

Moaddel, M. (2002) *Jordanian Exceptionalism: A Comparative Analysis of State–Religion Relationships in Egypt, Iran, Jordan and Syria*, New York: Palgrave.

Mustafa, Abdul Jalil (2008) 'Jordan dissolves 23 political parties', *Arab News*, 18 April, <http://archive.arabnews.com/services/print/print.asp?artid=109068&d=18&m=4&y=2008&...> (last accessed 5 March 2010).

Mustafa, Abdul Jalil (2009) 'Jordanians dissatisfied with Parliament's performance: Poll', *Arab News*, 29 May, <http://archive.arabnews.com/services/print/print.asp?artid=122993&d=29&m=5&y=2009&...> (last accessed 4 March 2010).

Neimat, Khaled (2011a) 'Proportional list likely new voting system', *Jordan Times*, 11

May,   <http://www.jordantimes.com/index.php?news=37014&searchFor=elec tion> (last accessed 11 May 2011).

Neimat, Khaled (2011b) 'Too much damage done to Islamic charity under government control', *Jordan Times*, 29 December, <http://jordantimes.ocm/print.html> (last accessed 27 February 2012).

Neimat, Khaled (2012a) 'Islamists demand government return control of charity society to Muslim Brotherhood', *Jordan Times*. 28 January, <http://jordantimes.ocm/ print.html> (last accessed 24 February 2012).

Neimat, Khaled (2012b) 'Political parties bill reflects government seriousness', *Jordan Times*, 1 February, <http://jordantimes.com/print.html> (last accessed 27 February 2012).

Neimat, Khaled (2012c) 'Government missed historic opportunity to make constitutional reform – IAF', *Jordan Times*, 14 February, <http://jordantimes.com/print. html> (last accessed 23 February 2012).

Neimat, Khaled (2012d) 'Majority supports constitutional amendment', *Jordan Times*, 14 February, <http://jordantimes.com/print.html> (last accessed 27 February 2012).

Neimat, Khaled (2012e) 'Parliament committed to civil society partnership', *Jordan Times*, 14 February, <http://jordantimes.ocm/print.html> (last accessed 24 February 2012).

Neimat, Khaled (2013) 'House blocs, associations reject fuel price hike', *Jordan Times*, 2 March, <http://www.jordantimes.com/house-blocs-associations-reject-fuel-price-hike> (last accessed 15 July 2013).

Nicholson, Robert W. (2013) 'Long live the Bedouin king', *Jerusalem Post*, 9 January, <http://www.jpost.com/LandedPages/PrintArticle.aspx?id=298986> (last accessed 18 July 2013).

Nicky, Adam (2012) 'Jordan gears up for parliamentary elections', *Jerusalem Post*, 29 December, <http://www.jpost.com/LandedPages/PrintArticle.aspx?id=297717> (last accessed 30 December 2012).

Nimah, Hasan Abu (2011) 'New Cabinet's chances of success', *Jordanpolitics.org*, 26 October, <http://www.jordanpolitics.org/en/index.php/articles-a-openions/1024-new-cabinets-chances-of-success-?tmpl=component&print=1...> (last accessed 28 February 2012).

Numan, Abeer (2011) 'Journalist released on bail "upon Monarch's directives"', *Jordan Times*, 2 June, <http://www.jordantimes.com/?news=38088> (last accessed 2 June 2011).

Obeidat, Omar (2011) 'Businesses can look to Jordan with confidence', *Jordan Times*, 26 May, <http://www.jordantimes.com/index.php?news=37693&searchFor= reforms> (last accessed 26 May 2011).

Obeidat, Omar (2013) 'Voters doubt elections will bring about change', *Jordan Times*, 13 January, <http://www.jordantimes.com/voters-doubt-elections-will-bring-about-change> (last accessed 16 July 2013).

Omari, Raed (2011a) 'Municipal polls in Sept. "tentatively"', *Jordan Times*, 11 May, <http://www.jordantimes.com / index.php ? news = 36748 & searchFor = participa tion> (last accessed 11 May 2011).

Omari, Raed (2011b) 'Reform plans progressing with no delay – Odwan', *Jordan Times*,

26 May, <http://www.jordantimes.com/index.php?news=37783&searchFor= politicalparties> (last accessed 26 May 2011).

Omari, Raed (2012a) 'Lower House endorses six constitutional amendments', *Jordan Times*, 14 February, <http://jordantimes.com/print.html> (last accessed 27 February 2012).

Omari, Raed (2012b) 'Jordanians doubtful over proposed changes in new parliament', *Al Arabiya*, 24 December, <http://english.alarabiya.net/articles/2012/12/24/ 256853.html> (last accessed 30 December 2012).

Ottaway, Marina and Marwan Muasher (2011) 'Arab monarchies chance for reform, yet unmet', *The Carnegie Endowment Papers. The Carnegie Endowment for International Peace*, December.

'Our priority today is political reform – King' (2011) *Jordan Times*, 27 October, <http:// archive.jordantimes.com/print.html> (last accessed 20 February 2012).

Petra (2013) 'PM launches new anti-corruption strategy', *Jordan Times*, 30 June, <http:// www.jordantimes.com/pm-lauches-new-anti-corruption-strategy> (last accessed 15 July 2013).

Pew Research (2012) 'The missing piece in Arab democracy', Global Attitudes Project, 12 July.

Pew Research Center (2013a) *Global Indicators Database*, Spring survey, <http://www. pewglobal.org/database/indicator/5/country/111>; <http://www.pewglobal. org/database/indicator/14/country/111> (last accessed 10 August 2013).

Pew Research Center (2013b) 'The world's Muslims: religion, politics and society', *Pew Forum on Religion and Public Life*, 30 April, <http://www.pewforum.org> (last accessed 6 February 2014).

'Pew Study: most Muslims want democracy, personal freedoms, and Islam in political life', (2012) *Ikhwanweb*, 12 July, <http://www.ikhwanweb.com/article.php?id= 30184> (last accessed 16 July 2012).

'Political reform to meet aspirations of Jordanian people – Monarch' (2011) *Jordan Times*, 18 May, <http://www.jordantimes.com/index.php?news=37355&search- For=kingreforms> (last accessed 18 May 2011).

Project on Middle East Democracy (2008) 'Country Backgrounder Series: Jordan', <http:// www.pomed.org/docs/Jordan_Backgrounder.pdf> (last accessed 6 February 2014).

'Protest camp set up in Jordan capital' (2011) *Aljazeera.net*, 24 March, <http://english. aljazeera.net/news/middleeast/2011/03/201132414304102344.html> (last accessed 6 April 2011).

'Recommendations made by the Royal Committee on Constitutional Review (2011)', 15 August, <http://www.jordanpolitics.org/en/index.php/political-documents/ 869-recommendations-made-by-the-royal-committee-on-constitutio. . .> (last accessed 28 February 2012).

Riedel, Bruce (2012) 'Jordan's Arab Spring', *Brookings Institution*, 15 November, <http:// www.brookings.edu/research/opinions/2012/11/15-jordan-arab-spring-riedel> (last accessed 19 July 2013).

'Royal court denies Jordan tribes targeting queen' (2011) *AFP*, 11 February, <http:// www.google.com/hostednews/afp/article/ALeqM5jL8otEgEqkoQ140habhpCV MM. . .> (last accessed 27 October 2013).

Sadi, Walid M. (2011) 'Seizing the opportunity', *Jordan Times*, 11 May, <http://www.jordantimes.com/index.php?news=37225&searchFor=consitution> (last accessed 11 May 2011).

Sandels, Alexandra (2011) 'JORDAN: Tribesmen slam Queen Rania, warn of revolt', *Los Angeles Times*, 7 February, <http://latimesblogs.latimes.com/babylonbeyond/2011/02/jordan-tribesman-slam-queen-ra. . .> (last accessed 27 October 2013).

Schwedler, Jillian (2003) 'More than a mob: the dynamics of political demonstrations in Jordan', *Middle East Research & Information Project*, 226, spring, 18–23.

Schwedler, Jillian (2012a) 'The politics of protest in Jordan', *Foreign Policy Research Institute*, 7 March, <http://www.fpri.org> (last accessed 9 March 2012).

Schwedler, Jillian (2012b) 'Al-Qaeda's gift to Jordan's King Abdullah', *Aljazeera*, 29 October, <http://www.aljazeera.com/indepth/opinion/2012/10/20121028132643365347.html> (last accessed 5 November 2012).

Shaikh, Salman (2012) 'Now the pressure's building on Jordan', *Brookings Institution*, spring, <http://www.brookings.edu/research/opinions/2012/03/15-jordan-shaikh> (last accessed 19 July 2013).

Sharp, Jeremy M. (2013) 'Jordan: background and US relations', *Congressional Research Service*, 7-5700, RL 33546.

Singh, R. (2002) 'Liberalization or democratization? The limits of political reform and civil society in Jordan', In G. Joffe (ed.), *Jordan in Transition*, New York: Palgrave, 66–90.

Susser, Asher (2011) 'Jordan 2011: uneasy lies the head', Crown Center for Middle East Studies, Brandeis University, June.

Susser, Asher (2013a) 'Can Abdullah take the strain?' *Jerusalem Post*, 22 January, <http://www.jpost.com/LandedPages/PrintArticle.aspx?id=300480> (last accessed 18 July 2013).

Susser, Asher (2013b) 'Jordan and the faltering fortunes of the Arab Spring', *Tel Aviv Notes*, 7(9), 9 May, 1–5, <http://www.dayan.org/tel-aviv-notes> (last accessed 6 February 2014).

Sweis, Rana F. (2011a) 'Uneasy balancing act in Jordan', *New York Times*, 13 April, <http://www.nytimes.com/2011/04/14/world/middleeast/14iht-m14-jordan.html?pagewante. . .> (last accessed 18 April 2011).

Sweis, Rana F. (2011b) 'Jordan tries to remake its political machinery', *New York Times*, 8 June, <http://www.nytimes.com/2011/06/09/world/middleeast/09iht-M09-JORDAN.html> (last accessed 5 July 2011).

'The Constitution of Jordan with all the amendments thereto' (2011) The House of Representatives of Jordan.

The Economist (2012) 'Jordan and its king: as beleaguered as ever', 13 October, <http://www.economist.com/node/21564595/print> (last accessed 29 December 2012).

'Thousands protest in Jordan' (2011) *Aljazeera.net*, 28 January, <http://english.aljazeera.net/news/middleeast/2011/01/2011128125157509196.html> (last accessed 6 February 2014).

Transparency International (2010) 'Corruption Perceptions Index 2010', <http://www.transparency.org/policy_research/surveys_indices/cpi/2010/results> (last accessed 6 February 2014).

Transparency International (2012) 'Corruption Perceptions Index 2012', <http://www.transparency.org/policy_research/surveys_indices/cpi/2012/results> (last accessed 6 February 2014).

US Department of State (2010) 'Background note: Jordan', January, <http://www.state.gov/r/pa/ei/bgn/3464.htm> (last accessed 2 March 2010)

Wiktorowicz, Q. (1999) 'The limits of democracy in the Middle East: the case of Jordan', *Middle East Journal*, autumn, 53(4), 606–20.

Wiktorowicz, Q. (2001) *The Management of Islamic Activism: Salafis, the Muslim Brotherhood, and State Power in Jordan*, Albany, NY: State University of New York Press.

Wiktorowicz, Q. (2002) 'Embedded authoritarianism: bureaucratic power and limits to non-governmental organizations in Jordan', in G. Joffe (ed.), *Jordan in Transition*, New York: Palgrave, 111–26.

Wilcke, Christoph (2011) 'Jordan: a measure of reform', *Human Rights Watch*, 8 March, <http://www.hrw.org/en/news/2011/03/08/jordan-measure-reform?print> (last accessed 15 June 2011).

World Bank (2012) *World Development Indicators*. The Development Data Group. <http://www.worldbank.org> (last accessed 24 December 2012).

Chapter 6: Conclusion

Alianak, Sonia L. (2012) 'Obamapower: the rhetoric, response, and reality', *Southwestern Journal of International Studies*, autumn, 5(1) 1–39.

Haas, Mark L. and David W. Lesch (eds) (2013) *The Arab Spring: Change and Resistance in the Middle East*, Boulder, CO: Westview Press.

Habeeb, William M. (2012) *The Middle East in Turmoil: Conflict, Revolution and Change*, Oxford: Greenwood.

Gelvin, James L. (2012) *The Arab Uprisings: What Everyone Needs to Know*, Oxford: Oxford University Press.

Gelvin, James L. (2013) 'Conclusion: the Arab World at the intersection of the national and transnational', in Mark L. Haas and David W. Lesch (eds), *The Arab Spring: Change and Resistance in the Middle East*, Boulder, CO: Westview Press, 238–55.

Goldstone, Jack A. (2001) 'Toward a fourth generation of revolutionary theory', *Annual Reviews of Political Science*, 4: 139–87.

Goldstone, Jack A. (2011) 'Understanding the revolutions of 2011: weakness and resilience in Middle Eastern autocracies', *Foreign Affairs*, May/June, 90(3), 8–16.

Lynch, Marc (2012) *The Arab Uprising: The Unfinished Revolutions of the New Middle East*, New York: Public Affairs.

Pew Research Center (2013) 'The world's Muslims: religion, politics and society', *Pew Forum on Religion and Public Life*, 30 April, <http://www.pewforum.org> (last accessed 2 May 2013).

Torchia, Andrew (2013) 'Corruption worsened in Arab countries since uprisings: Poll', *Reuters*, 9 July, <http://www.reuters.com/assets/print?aid=USBRE/96805U20130709> (last accessed 10 July 2013).

Index

Page numbers in *italics* refer to figures.